Autobiography in Black and Brown

Autobiography in Black & Brown

Ethnic Identity in Richard Wright and Richard Rodriguez

MICHAEL NIETO GARCIA

University of New Mexico Press • Albuquerque

© 2014 by the University of New Mexico Press
All rights reserved. Published 2014
Printed in the United States of America
First paperbound printing, 2016
Paperbound ISBN: 978-0-8263-5232-3
20 19 18 17 16   1 2 3 4 5

Library of Congress Cataloging-in-Publication Data
Garcia, Michael Nieto.
Autobiography in black and brown : ethnic identity in Richard Wright and Richard Rodriguez / Michael Nieto Garcia.
pages cm
Includes bibliographical references and index.
ISBN 978-0-8263-5527-0 (cloth : alk. paper) — ISBN 978-0-8263-5528-7 (electronic)
1. Wright, Richard, 1908–1960—Criticism and interpretation.
2. African Americans in literature. 3. Rodriguez, Richard, 1944–
—Criticism and interpretation. 4. Mexican Americans in literature.
5. Ethnicity in literature.
6. Autobiography in literature. I. Title.
PS3545.R815Z6635 2014
813'.52—dc23
2014002697

Book design by Catherine Leonardo
Cover illustration courtesy of Dreamstime.com
Composed in Minion Pro 10.25/13.5
Display type is Adobe Garamond Pro

Para mi padre, *in memoriam*—
storyteller, migrant worker . . . my first and greatest teacher

Contents

Preface ix

Acknowledgments xix

Introduction
A Tale of Two Richards: On Reference and Ethnic Identity in Autobiography   1

Chapter 1
Autobiographical Double Consciousness: The Ethnic Self as Representative Man in Richard Wright's Hybrid Autobiography   39

Chapter 2
The Black Existentialist and Collective Racial Experience: "Manning Up" the Ethnic Übermensch in Richard Wright's *Black Boy*   65

Chapter 3
The We in Me: The Communally Derived Ethnic Self in Richard Rodriguez's *Hunger of Memory*   93

Chapter 4
En el Nombre del Padre: The Immigrant Father as the Manikin of Autobiography, and Its Agon with the Print Culture Self in Richard Rodriguez's *Days of Obligation: An Argument with My Mexican Father*   113

Chapter 5
The Inauthentic Ethnic: Richard Rodriguez's *Brown*
and Resisting Essentialist Narratives of Ethnic Identity   *147*

Epilogue
The Hermeneutic Consequences of Writing While Ethnic   *165*

Notes   *173*

Works Cited   *189*

Index   *201*

Preface

Richard Wright was the grandson of slaves, Richard Rodriguez the son of immigrants. One black, the other brown, each author ostentatiously displays his race in the title of an autobiographical book: *Black Boy* and *Brown*, respectively. For these two autobiographers, despite their shared given name, dissimilarities multiply beyond birth and race—neither of which one can choose. One is affiliated with the radical Left, the other has long been associated with (rightly or wrongly) the reactionary Right. One rallied around the communist cause, the other celebrates ascendancy to a bourgeois life: "the achievement of desire" through education as a sure path to the middle class (*Hunger of Memory* 41). One is known as an activist agitator for social change, the other as a sometime defender of the status quo—the activist a conventional heterosexual, and the traditionalist a gay activist. One portrays hypermasculinized black male characters emasculated by a racist society; the other describes attempting to live up to the manly male image of the Mexican laborer by taking a summer construction job. Given the conspicuous differences between them, what, some might ask, could possibly be the grounds for comparison in any consideration of these two authors or their autobiographies?

Equally revealing is the mirror-image inversion of such comparison, of any attempt to place too narrow of a focus on their similarities; namely, how are we to explain the striking differences between these two Richards when they are both so similarly situated as marginalized minorities in American society? The answer to the latter question, I believe, is to be found in a single observation: that one was born early in the twentieth century, and that the other continues to write early into the twenty-first. When accounting for these differences in social context, many of the obvious dissimilarities between the two authors dissolve into common objectives on matters of race, class, gender, and the self in society. Diving beneath the surface arguments that reflect their respective sociohistorical eras, one finds two ethnic authors united in their preoccupation with issues of agency, class struggle, ethnic identity, the search for community, and the quest for social justice.

The surface differences are readily apparent when comparing the first of Rodriguez's autobiographical books with Wright's autobiography. Rodriguez's 1982 depiction of the literary ethnic self in *Hunger of Memory* contrasts sharply with that of Wright's *Black Boy*, which was first published in 1945. As I have suggested, however, much of the obvious outward disparity between the ethnic identities presented in those two texts is explained by the nearly four decades separating their publication. Within that time, the civil rights movement took place, abolishing the Jim Crow laws that terrorized Wright's generation and changing the tenor of race relations in America. Because Wright's psyche and identity were shaped by the social context of racial apartheid in Mississippi, and Rodriguez's by that of multiracial California, their texts appear on the surface as inversions of each other: *Black Boy* a social realist's engagé critique of racial injustice by depicting the self as racially representative and *Hunger of Memory* a prose stylist's agonized questioning of minority entitlement programs accompanied by the overt rejection of any claim to ethnic representativeness. Comparing the texts along these lines does not, however, establish them as irreconcilably different with respect to their more fundamental engagement with ethnic and identity issues. Rather, the two texts are chiastic to one another, transecting at the height of the civil rights era, their seemingly inverted stance on ethnic matters reflecting the vast differences between the societies in which each author wrote, and the concomitantly divergent ways in which each writer was situated in his society.

In addition to belonging to different literary and sociohistorical eras, Wright and Rodriguez tend to be classified under separate literary rubrics for another reason. Wright's work is critically and cognitively framed as African American literature (though Wright did not call himself an African American), whereas Rodriguez's work is categorized as Latino or even Chicano (though Rodriguez does not call himself a Chicano). The result is that the two texts are often read as if they were the literary artifacts of separate genres rather than as two exemplars of ethnic autobiography.

Ethnic framing, in other words, orients reader expectations like a genre does. And though readers may distinguish between distinct literary traditions such as the African American tradition and the Chicana/o, their reasons more often reflect the social location of ethnic minorities in society rather than recognizable literary conventions on the page. That is, the reader is taking the ethnicity of the author (rather than the content of the text alone) as a signifier of genre. Reflecting social relations in society, this extratextual reading practice unites texts by authors of disparate minority ethnicities under the common banner of—imagined or not, a literary genre or not—ethnic literature. This shared social and literary status calls for the comparative study of ethnic literature, and of the autobiographies of Wright and Rodriguez.

The thorny issue of whether to think of ethnic literature as a genre requires some unpacking here, beginning with a provisional disaggregation of genre as a set of narrative codes and conventions from its manifestation as a mutually exclusive cognitive paradigm for readers. Both Wright and Rodriguez resist the balkanization of their work as ethnic literature when ethnic literature is conceived of as separate from American literature.[1] Such segregation tends to have the effect of a separate-but-equal policy for literary texts, ethnic literature being defined in opposition to literature, and thus treated as inherently inferior. Mirroring the logic of ethnicity in society, the ethnicity of the author is often seen as determinative of the text's genre—overdetermining the semantic value of the author's ethnicity (or gender, race, and so forth) and impeding generic identification based on the character of a text's content rather than the color of the author's skin. Although the author's ethnicity has hermeneutic consequences for texts because it informs the reader's cognitive framing of that text (which is true not only of autobiographies but also of fictional works by ethnic authors), and though it constitutes a crucial axis of comparison, the limitations of conceiving of any text by an ethnic author as primarily ethnic are soon apparent. Wright, for instance, experimented with various narrative genres—poetry, essay, drama, fiction, nonfiction, journalism, and even haiku—and it would seem patently absurd to treat all these texts as a single genre: ethnic literature. Of course, not all genres are mutually exclusive, but one may be virtually so when generic framings exert a paradigm effect on readers such that seeing the text under the ethnic literature rubric eclipses awareness of other genre conventions.

Regardless of where we come down in this discussion, the vexing question of the extent to which we should think of texts by ethnic authors as a genre remains every bit as complicated as racial, ethnic, and gender stereotyping in society at large. The genre debate raises similar troubling questions about the value of presupposing that those of similar racial or ethnic background have had similar experiences and, perhaps even more important, about the extent to which personal experience is social or socialized. It is with keen awareness of these complexities, and of the ways in which genre classification can ghettoize texts and authors, that Wright presents himself as a black author even as he compares his work with that of Mencken and Dreiser, whereas Rodriguez seeks to put himself in the company of such literary luminaries by explicitly resisting the shelving of his book as ethnic literature (*Black Boy* 248–50; *Hunger* 7). Though resisting the de-privileging and segregation of their texts in relation to privileged non-ethnic texts, both authors are self-consciously aware of the ways in which readers will approach their works, and of the expectations that readers will likely bring to the text given the author's ethnicity. Together, Wright and Rodriguez join the tradition of ethnic authors attentive to reader expectations that perceive, and thus effectively render, any text by an ethnic author as like a genre—as at least partly following the logic of genre. Ethnic authors are thus always working within these genre-like conventions, even as they write against them.

Rodriguez aspires to write completely outside those genre-like conventions, deliberately transgressing, invading, and hoping to erase ethno-literary borders. With nostalgia, he recalls his boyhood public library, where "in those last years of a legally segregated America, there was no segregated shelf for Negro writers. Frederick Douglass was on the same casement with Alexis de Tocqueville, Benjamin Franklin. Today . . . our habit is willfully to confuse literature with sociology" (*Brown* 10). In abolishing ethnic literature as a genre, Rodriguez hopes to make texts by ethnic authors candidates for designation as universal literature—"the universality of dissimilarity," of "the particular" rather than the ethnically "typical" (*Brown* 12). Similar sentiments can be found in *Black Boy*, such as when noting the pains to which Wright goes to compare himself with H. L. Mencken: "[T]his man was fighting, fighting with words. He was using words as weapon," a characterization clearly associating Wright's own brand of socially engaged writing with that of the most conspicuous nonfiction writer of the age (*Black Boy* 248). Perhaps no less conspicuously, Wright also associates himself with scores of canonical literary figures by reciting a litany of their names as part of his reading regimen—Twain, Crane, Wells, Conrad, Flaubert, Tolstoy, and Dostoyevsky, to name just a few (*Black Boy* 248–49). His autobiography is the story of a particular black author in a specific racial context, but Wright wants the book to be read as universal. And though depicting himself as in many ways representative of the typical "black boy," the double narrative of his autobiography also aspires to Rodriguez's universality of the particular: *Black Boy* is a black existentialist's particular story, and not that of, say, his brother Leon, who grew up in the same household.

In terms of generic classification, it might even be argued that, in addition to the genre of autobiography, both *Black Boy* and *Hunger of Memory* are solidly situated within the religious literary tradition that includes spiritual autobiography and the conversion narrative. Thomas Cooley reminds us that the religious narrative is foundational to American letters, noting that "one-third of all autobiographies written in the country before 1850 were religious narratives, including spiritual autobiographies" (4). The tradition continues in various forms, such as through the "secularization, in fiction, of the Puritan spiritual autobiography" (169). When considering *Black Boy*'s debt to the slave narrative genre, it bears remembering that most slave narratives were themselves also religious narratives, as is clearly the case in one of the genre's urtexts, *Narrative of the Life of Frederick Douglass, an American Slave* (1845). In an illuminating essay, Wright scholar Robert Butler underscores the underexamined spiritual dynamic of *Black Boy*, arguing that the text "employs two integrally related stories: 1) An outward narrative documenting the injustices and brutalities of the deterministic social environment which trapped him in both the South and the North, and 2) an inward narrative which dramatizes his transcending that environment with his own spiritual energy and free will" ("Seeking Salvation" 47). In similarly identifying *Hunger of Memory* as a "conversion narrative," Raymund Paredes performs for Rodriguez's text an equally insightful archaeology of occluded literary and generic influences—literary influences that had been obscured by the paradigm of reading the text exclusively through the genre lens of ethnic literature, and further obscured by reading ethnic literature as if wholly separate and apart from other literary traditions (281).

In short, an overly rigid classification of ethnic literatures as belonging exclusively to only one literary tradition—black, brown, red, white, or yellow, to recite each ethnic tradition's racial proxies—can blind readers to significant literary influences and inheritances. As this book's title, *Autobiography in Black and Brown*, proposes, the literary traditions and the ethnic lives represented in autobiographical texts are by no means as sealed off from as each other as is suggested by the separately packaged five colors of the

American crayon box of race. When it comes to Wright and Rodriguez, those readers who take a "black or brown" perspective may miss significant shared literary and intellectual influences, such as the extent to which each author saw himself as writing within the Augustinian heritage of spiritual autobiography. To understand Wright, the reader must be familiar with a great body of works outside the African American literary tradition. The same is true of Rodriguez's work in relation to the framing of his books as ethnic literature. Indeed, it is hard to imagine a single work of ethnic literature that is better understood and appreciated inside the silo of a single literary tradition, ethnic or otherwise, than it would be if instead read through a comparative literature approach of some sort—one that cuts across genres and excessively rigid ethnic boundaries.

As these examples suggest, reader framing of texts written by ethnic authors as ethnic literature is real and cannot be ignored. At the same time, overlooking other salient dimensions of the complex, artistic, intertextual, and polysemous texts by ethnic authors is precisely one of the perils of one-dimensional ethnic framing. It is understandable that, not wanting readers to ignore these other dimensions, ethnic authors, along with literary critics, might question the generic classification of their texts as ethnic literature. We might raise similar concerns in regard to ghettoized genres such as science fiction and the detective novel. What is distinctive about ethnic literature as a genre, however, is that the classification is largely based in its reflection of social relations, whereas most other genres primarily reflect narrative conventions within a literary tradition. In terms of mimetic theory, ethnic literature imitates life, whereas conventional genres imitate art.[2]

In this insight are found the grounds for comparison across multiethnic literatures. Despite distinctive literary traditions, African American, Native American, Asian American, and U.S. Latino literatures and peoples share a similar social location in American society. And though readers distinguish between a text written by an African American and one by a Latino, they also conceive of both writers as ethnically othered in American society—a reflection of the commonality of their ethnic visibility in social reality. This is not to rule out other points of comparison between U.S. ethnic literatures or even global ethnic literatures, but to underscore a prominent, and often fetishized, feature of texts written by minority authors, especially when those texts are read as ethnic literature.

As a Book-of-the-Month Club selection, Wright's *Black Boy* was received enthusiastically by many readers who had not previously read anything by an African American author. These readers had no knowledge of the major tropes, themes, and literary conventions of what is now called the African American literary tradition. What they knew was that the author was black, and it was this knowledge that informed how readers approached the text as they first opened its pages. The hermeneutic consequences of such ethnic framing are profound, and raise a question that has far-reaching implications for literary criticism: given that the ways in which the author's ethnicity signifies in society is part of the interpretive lens through which the reader reads the text, to what extent does the visibility of the author's ethnicity therefore constitute part of the meaning of the text?

The example of strictly visual forms of visibility is one way reference to the ethnicity of the author constitutes part of the meaningfulness of the text to readers. Each of the editions of the four primary texts I use in this analysis features a cover photograph of the author: *Hunger of Memory* and *Brown* on the front, *Black Boy* and *Days of Obligation* on the back. This visual imprint of the author's ethnicity effectively embeds itself in the text. As suggested by the syllable *graph* in the word *photograph*, the author's visible (in this case visually so) ethnicity thus writes part of the text—that of the covering material. This iconic "spectacle of ethnicity," as Ellen McCracken argues, functions as one of the "textual deployments of ethnicity" instrumental to the commercial success of books by ethnic authors (169). To this analysis, I add that performative ethnicity of this sort also functions as one of the devices by which texts are ethnically framed and readers are subsequently (and mostly subconsciously) instructed on how to read.

The distinction between what is external to the narrative proper and formal shaping devices of narrative that are internal to the text is critical. Frederick Luis Aldama offers an example of such nuance in cataloging and discussing formal shaping devices in *A User's Guide to Postcolonial and Latino Borderland Fiction*. Among these devices are peritexts—including, among other things, the cover art, jacket blurbs, and typefaces—that Aldama insists "are not completely arbitrary: they establish initial reader contracts and cues that trigger in the reader's mind important scripts—comic or tragic, for instance—that we anticipate encountering once inside the story proper" (22). Aldama further notes that the implied author suggested by the narrative proper might be completely at odds with the peritext of the author photograph on the cover, and most authors do not get to pick their own covers (26). The astuteness of this observation is clear when reading a writer such as Rodriguez, who oscillates between performing ethnicity and rejecting its constraints. Moreover, in his definition of the term, Aldama argues that "the implied author is the image of the author constructed by the reader" (26). By extension, I argue that ethnic framing situates the text, authors focalize the narrative, and readers do the rest—their interpretation constituting part of the meaning of the text.

To demonstrate the hermeneutic consequences of ethnic framing, consider the following thought experiment: how would we read *Black Boy* differently, or even the fictional *Native Son*, for that matter, if we believed that the author of both of those texts had been H. L. Mencken? Readers would interpret the ethnically German writer's descriptions of the deprivations of Jim Crow much differently—given the assumed lack of epistemic privilege commensurate with the author's comparatively privileged point of view—than they would if believing he were African American. Such authorial deception desecrates the covenant—that autobiographers adhere to biological and historical facts—between readers and writers of autobiography. The fictitious author thought experiment (time and again perpetuated as a very real literary hoax), however, tests the limits of the epistemic gap between reliable knowledge of the actual author and assumed knowledge. By assumed knowledge is meant supposed contextual knowledge that is, in this case, really just part of the constructed narrative and thus fails to distinguish between biological author and narrative manifestations: from narrator (both reliable and unreliable) to authorial persona and what Wayne Booth dubbed the "implied author."

Equally interesting is the extent to which Mencken's German ethnicity no longer figures prominently for most readers of his work today, a consequence of the shifting nature of ethnicity and social relations. Likewise, texts by the ethnic referents of Wright and Rodriguez are approached quite differently than those of Russian émigré Vladimir Nabokov, even when the reader knows as little about African American and Latino literature and culture as about Russian literature and culture. Nabokov and Mencken are the counterexamples that prove the rule. Both are ethnic authors, but in both cases the relative absence of ethnic framing of their texts is a direct reflection of the low visibility in society of their respective ethnicities. That ethnic framing of Nabokov ranges from the negligible to effectively absent for most readers (but not the Russian émigré community) reveals the extent to which the textual and extratextual interaction between text, author, readers, and social reality is grounded in the referentiality of ethnic authors.

Through ethnic framing, even if only subconsciously, readers place "extratextual demands" on both fictional and nonfictional texts by ethnic authors, much the same as they do with autobiography (Loesberg, qtd. in Adams 9). We must consider the extent to which not only the valence of ethnicity as a signifier shifts (as does language itself) between the moment of writing and the various cultural moments in which the text is read by successive generations, but also that a particular Native American author might write self-consciously within the rich tradition of Native American literature whereas another might choose to reveal no awareness of that literary tradition. To suggest that the specter of the author's ethnicity haunts the text and plays a vital role in the interpretive acts of readers is not to claim that ethnicity is textually determinative. Nor is the awareness of ethnic referentiality inherent in an embodied realist approach intended—far from it—to encourage reductive readings of texts by ethnic authors. Though few literary critics today would deny the extent to which context comes to bear on our understanding of the text, ethnic literature (regardless of our literary approach) tests the limits of our shared sense of the permeability of texts, forcing us to reconsider the extent to which extratextual features such as the author's embodiedness do or do not factor in our interpretations.

Autobiography in Black and Brown argues that ethnic autobiography is a mirror that reflects the magnificent complexity of real ethnic identities. Such identities are indivisible from a visibly ethnic body yet simultaneously exist as a narrative self that is incorporeal, social, and fluid. Challenging both essentialist and wholly constructivist conceptions of ethnic identity, the literary selves of ethnic autobiography mirror the dual nature of identity by presenting a self that not only is narrated—the self on the page—but also reflects the reality of bodies inscribed with the markers of ethnicity in society. The autobiographies of Richard Wright and Richard Rodriguez exemplify the tensions and contradictions inherent in identities that are both narrated and embodied by depicting complex and often contradictory ethnic identities that call into question many of the prevailing notions of minority identity. In their presentation of the ethnic self, we see the rejection not only of essentialized notions of ethnic authenticity but also of any conception of an ethnic self that is not a communally derived self as well. The image reflected in their autobiographies also reminds us that consciousness is altered by our reading, and that the identities of modern ethnic selves may even be as dramatically shaped by print culture as by bodily experiences, such as how others see us.

Equally surprising and consequential are the questions that the mirror of autobiography raises for literary interpretation: to what extent do readers make the ethnicity of the author part of the meaning of the text when framing the text based on their knowledge of the author's ethnicity? Underscoring the insistence of this question is its relevance to what is perhaps the major theme of ethnic autobiography: the tension between the author's particular story of the ethnic self and the reader's expectation that the ethnic autobiographer be representative of the ethnic group (as that ethnicity is imagined in society)—an expectation that ethnic autobiographers in varying degrees reinforce, subvert, or try to reconcile with the narrative of their lives.

Playing to and against ethnic expectations is a predominant theme of *Autobiography in Black and Brown* and a pattern seen over and over again in the autobiographies of Richard Wright and Richard Rodriguez. Their texts offer models of complex ethnic identities wrought in the multidimensional tension between the inescapable embodiedness of ethnic subjects, the correspondence of ethnic markers with that embodied self, and the capacity for narratives of identity to revise existing ethnic scripts. As their autobiographical corpus illustrates, the literary ethnic self, the self of ethnic autobiography, is neither coextensive with the author in the flesh nor a complete construction with no external referent. Rather, the literary self takes form somewhere between the two, often-conflicting logics of *referentiality* (textual reference to an actual embodied self) and *revisability* (the fluidity of identity)—the specific manifestation of that self depending on the degree of authorial invention, the particular valence given by society to the symbols of ethnicity, and how readers interpret the textual self presented to them.

The divergences between the autobiographical narratives presented by these two ethnic authors confirm in unexpected ways the comparison between them—and both affirm a comparative ethnic literature approach and simultaneously erode the disciplinary walls erected between different ethnic literary traditions. What unites the texts of Wright and Rodriguez is the ethnic situatedness of their authors, whose embodiment as ethnic referents leads to the reenactment in their texts of the perpetual tension between the visibility of ethnicity that marks ethnic subjects in society and the revisability made possible through the perpetual revision of narratives of ethnic identity.

Acknowledgments

Over the many years it took to complete this book, I have benefited from the support and guidance of countless people and cannot hope to list them all here. Nevertheless, some deserve special mention for the feedback they gave or the inspiration they provided. Any such list would start with Shirley Samuels, Rick Bogel, Ken McClane, and Debra Castillo. Their guidance and encouragement have been invaluable, as have their perceptive comments on early versions of the manuscript. Also at Cornell, and likewise sharing a passion for ideas and the written language, are Ernesto Quiñonez and Helena María Viramontes. Mary Pat Brady inspired by scholarly example. Alas, the most difficult acknowledgments to make are to Joel Porte—a true Renaissance man, whose passing has not diminished the inspiration of his example—and Dan McCall, who has been equally inspirational. They will be missed. At the University of Nebraska, special thanks go to Ralph Grajeda, Dómino Pérez (now at the University of Texas–Austin), and Paul A. Olson, whose intellectual tutelage goes beyond measure. Along the way, I have also been inspired by numerous academic conversations with Mimi Yiu, Kimberly Manganelli-Snyder, Hyowon Kim, Alice Somerville, Hermán Carrillo, Wyatt Bonikowski, Ed Goode, Nadine Attewell, Akin Adesokan, Ogaga Ifowodo, Hilary Emmett, Jen Dunnaway, Andy Rehn, Sarah Heidt, Annette Portillo, Ariana Vigil, Belinda Rincón, Estella González, Anita Nicholson, and Danielle Heard.

Additional thanks to Frederick Luis Aldama, Steve Yao, Robert Butler, Jerry W. Ward Jr., Tony Day, Daniel Juan Gil, Neil Easterbrook, and Australia Tarver for many generous and perceptive comments as well as for thought-provoking conversations on ethnicity and identity. Colleagues at the National Association for Chicana and Chicano Studies (NACCS) and the inaugural U.S. Latina/o Literary Theory and Criticism Conference have provided for me and others not only a warm and supportive community but also an inspirational model of gracious and intellectually rigorous academic debate, with particular thanks to Ernesto J. Martínez, Manuel G. Gonzalez, Jaime H. Garcia, Ramón Saldívar, José David Saldívar, Dómino Pérez, Nohemy Solórzano-Thompson, Michael Hames-García, Ralph Rodriguez, David Luis-Brown, Rachel Ellis Neyra, Gene Melton II, Maria Lauret, Christopher Rivera, Aïda Valenzuela, and Richard T. Rodríguez. Y con gran agradecimiento a Mérida Rúa, Mari Castañeda, Alberto Sandoval-Sánchez, Sylvia Spitta, Ginetta Candelario, Stephanie Fetta, Carmen Whalen, Israel Reyes, Wilson Valentín-Escobar, Lourdes Gutiérrez Nájera, as well as the other founders and members of the New England Consortium of Latina/o Studies. Additional thanks to Ali Zaidi, Ana Y. Estevez, Pedro Ponce, Marina Llorente, Cecilia Martínez, Erik Melchor, Oscar D. Sarmiento, Liliana L. Trevizan, and others too numerous to name for creating a community of scholarship and Latinidad in the North Country.

While writing this book, I have benefited directly and indirectly from the following fellowships and academic support: the Sage, Provost's, and John S. Knight Institute for Writing in the Disciplines fellowships—all at Cornell; a Fulbright research fellowship to Indonesia; and a Mellon Postdoctoral Fellowship in Arts and Humanities at Hamilton College.

Earlier versions of some chapters were presented at conferences or previously appeared in print. A version of chapter 3 appeared as "The Communally Derived Ethnic Self in Richard Rodriguez's *Hunger of Memory*," in *a/b: Auto/Biography Studies* 28.1 (Summer 2013): 64–85. A version of chapter 5 appeared as "The Inauthentic Ethnic: Richard Rodriguez's *Brown* and Resisting Essentialist Narratives of Ethnic Identity," in *Prose Studies: History, Theory, Criticism* 34.2 (Aug. 2012): 129–50, the version appearing here reprinted with permission of Taylor & Francis Ltd, http://www.tandf.co.uk/journals. I am grateful for permission from the publishers to draw on them here. I am also grateful for the spirited and illuminating responses of Richard Wright scholars at the "100 Years of Richard Wright" conference, where a version of chapter 2 was presented in Salt Lake City on April 4, 2009.

Among those for whom I reserve my deepest gratitude and intellectual respect are my colleagues in the Department of Humanities and Social Sciences at Clarkson University, and in the Departments of English and

Comparative Literature at Hamilton College; the excellent librarians at Cornell, Texas Christian University, Hamilton, and Clarkson Universities; and my students at those institutions.

My deepest gratitude, also, to the editors and production team at the University of New Mexico Press, and especially to Elise McHugh, Beth Hadas, and James Ayers, as well as Helen Glenn Court, who expertly copyedited the entire manuscript. I would also like to thank the editors at those journals that published earlier versions of chapters, with special thanks to Emily Hipchen and Clare Simmons.

Richard Wright and Richard Rodriguez have inspired countless readers by their words. They also inspired me to write this book. Wright's written words continue to haunt me long after his death. Rodriguez's generous spirit has proven as inspirational as his writing, and his friendship—as all who know him well agree—is something cherished beyond what words can express.

For their friendship, as well as their intellectual incandescence, many thanks to Julieta Frank, David Newhouse, Marje Realuyo, Ali Subandoro, Kiran Gajwani, and Stephen Chong. And, where words fail, to Arti Wulandari.

And, last, to *la familia*—extended, far-flung, and too numerous to thank individually here, but loved and cherished for their diversity of beliefs, lifestyles, and personalities.

INTRODUCTION

A Tale of Two Richards

On Reference and Ethnic Identity in Autobiography

•◆•

In the chapters that follow, I introduce and discuss a literary comparison of the autobiographies of Richard Wright and Richard Rodriguez, hence the title *Autobiography in Black and Brown*. My central argument can be summed up in a single sentence: ethnic autobiography—by mirroring the dual nature of the self as both narrative and embodied, challenging our assumptions about literary interpretation and meaning, and transforming us into skeptical realists—can lead us to better understand identity, ethnicity, the social self, and how we read literary texts by ethnic authors.

This introduction presents some of the theoretical groundwork as well as the motivations for a comparative literary analysis juxtaposing the autobiographies of Richard Wright and Richard Rodriguez. Both authors underscore not an atomized or solipsistic ethnic self but the social aspect of selfhood in autobiographies: the triangulated social relations between self, ethnic group, and larger society. Conceptions of the ethnic self evolve with and within an ever-changing social context, such that Rodriguez chiastically inverts what might be summed up as Wright's pre–civil rights message, "I cannot be an individual because of my society," to contemporary variations on the theme that "It is society that allows me to be an individual."

Perhaps nothing better illustrates the extent to which personal consciousness is expanded by the thoughts of others than the impact of reading and writing on our lives. The consciousness of modern selves is so radically altered by print culture that no account of the ethnic self is complete without a consideration of the role of reading and writing in ethnic lives. We write and harbor scripts of ethnicity in the mind's eye, scripts that require ethnic autobiographers to negotiate their particular narrative of the ethnic self with the ethnic narratives anticipated by their readers. The high visibility of ethnicity, race, and gender in society leads readers of autobiography to expect correspondence—referentiality—between the literary self on the page and the ethnicity of the author as embodied self. However, such referentiality is neither direct nor absolute: the meaning of ethnicity's signifiers is always changing in social context, and the author's imagination plays a significant role in articulating the literary self. As a result, narratives of the ethnic self demonstrate the revisability of the ethnic self. This is clearly seen in ethnic autobiography. Rodriguez, for example, demonstrates the perpetual narrative revision of the self in having written multiple autobiographical books, each with a different emphasis, and each varying in its central metaphor for the self.

Chapter 1, "Autobiographical Double Consciousness: The Ethnic Self as Representative Man in Richard Wright's Hybrid Autobiography," is the first of two chapters on Wright's autobiography, *Black Boy (American Hunger)*, and explores the double narrative of depicting the self as distinctive and yet representative of the ethnic group. Wright saw writing his autobiography as an opportunity to testify—in the tradition of the *testimonio*—about racial oppression in the South. He could do so by depicting himself as a typical "black boy." *Native Son* had been read as racially representative, and Wright's autobiography would be too. Why not, then, take advantage of the expectations of representativeness that would be imposed on the text? Why not turn those expectations to an indictment of the Jim Crow South? He would map this representative self onto his own life, creating a hybrid text, part autobiography and part folk history. The double narrative would stand as a literary version of the "double consciousness" described by W. E. B. Du Bois. Unfortunately, Wright's experimentation with the genre, and the creative liberties that he had taken—such as apparently having made himself a composite character in his own autobiography—raised doubts about the text's authenticity. Even Du Bois doubted the authenticity of the narrative. The hybrid text, though, was true to Wright's commitment to emotional truth. To the extent that racial trauma is collectively shared, the only way that Wright could fully explain his thoughts, feelings, and experiences was to first tell readers about the racial experiences of others. Their experiences had such an impact on his life that he had to tell their story in order to tell readers about himself.

Chapter 2, "The Black Existentialist and Collective Racial Experience: 'Manning Up' the Ethnic Übermensch in Richard Wright's *Black Boy*," highlights often overlooked existentialist undertones in *Black Boy*, arguing that trying to reconcile the text's existentialism with its depiction of collective racial experience is no contradiction. Rather, Wright's existentialism is the foundation for his critique of racial discrimination. Wright's desire to be recognized as an existentialist self is rebuffed by the racial discourses imposed on his body, the devaluation of racial otherness in his society making full recognition as a person impossible for the black subject. However, whereas the extraliterary Wright is denied the voice to fully realize and articulate the self in this discriminatory social context, the literary self is free to critique the forces that oppress and exploit him as racial subject. Underlying and motivating Wright's self-portrayal—as representative of the unassimilated and marginalized other—is an internalized print culture paradigm of the universal, humanist self who has race imposed on him in a racialized society—a society in which full personhood is typically ascribed only to white, generally male, Americans. Print culture plays a double role in Wright's devastating critique of the prevailing racial discourses: as the source of classical liberal notions about the equality of all persons, and as a powerful medium through which ethnic authors can have a voice and counter oppressive social structures.

The next three chapters are devoted to Rodriguez's trio of autobiographical texts. Chapter 3, "The We in Me: The Communally Derived Ethnic Self in Richard Rodriguez's *Hunger of Memory*," questions what has to date been the prevailing view in Chicana/o studies, arguing against the common criticism that Rodriguez is excessively individualistic. That may be how we remember Rodriguez in *Hunger of Memory*, but a rereading of his text reveals just the opposite: that his notion of the self is firmly grounded in the search for community and a socially connected self. Why, then, have we misread Rodriguez as a solipsistic individualist for so long? We misread him, I argue, by trying to pigeonhole his thinking into existing categories of political identity and ideology that then lead us to read his texts through equally rigid and politicized interpretative lenses. Rodriguez challenges us with the presentation of an ethnic self that does not fit neatly into the dominant narratives of ethnic identity in activist and academic circles, or as framed by the binary of liberal and conservative political stances on ethnic issues.

Chapter 4, "En el Nombre del Padre: The Immigrant Father as the Manikin of Autobiography, and Its Agon with the Print Culture Self in Richard Rodriguez's *Days of Obligation: An Argument with My Mexican Father*," looks at Rodriguez from the fresh perspective offered by his second book to consider the role of print culture in shaping the consciousness, and thus the identity, of ethnic readers and authors. A related consideration is the role of literary genres in framing texts, shaping reader expectations, and both establishing and allowing for the constant revision of literary conventions. When calling their text an autobiography, ethnic authors ostensibly promise nothing more than a particular, one-life-only narrative of ethnicity. As a genre, however, ethnic autobiography both creates and reifies common conventions of ethnicity that readers come to expect from all ethnic authors. The mirror of ethnic autobiography thus reflects not only the image of the author, but also that of ethnic scripts and expectations in social reality.

Chapter 5, "The Inauthentic Ethnic: Richard Rodriguez's *Brown* and Resisting Essentialist Narratives of Ethnic Identity," explores Rodriguez's resistance to narratives of ethnic authenticity by reconsidering Rodriguez and how we read his texts in light of the radical message of cultural and racial miscegenation celebrated in his third autobiographical book, *Brown* (2002). Rodriguez's meditations on identity in *Brown* resonate with Gloria Anzaldúa's theorization of *mestizaje* and trouble the waters of any monolithic notion of ethnic identity. A close reading of Rodriguez's critique of ethnic authenticity illuminates his underlying philosophical worldview as well as why he takes—notoriously for his critics—some of the controversial stances he does. An analysis of both its eternal recurrence and the logic by which it operates helps us understand how and why lingering traces of ethnic authenticity and its essentialist logic can creep into conceptualizations of even such ostensibly anti-essentialist theorizations of identity as hybridity. Whether resistant or revisionist in spirit, rereading Rodriguez acknowledges the irredeemable complexity of identity—intersubjective, contradiction-laden, and brown.

A concluding chapter, "Epilogue: The Hermeneutic Consequences of Writing While Ethnic," suggests future lines of inquiry by exploring the hermeneutic consequences of ethnic visibility and the concomitant tendency to read non-autobiographical texts by ethnic authors autobiographically. Given that both phenomena are part of the interpretive framing of texts, what insights drawn from ethnic autobiography can be extrapolated—with many qualifications and much caution—to non-autobiographical genres and texts? Aware that even works of fiction are often read autobiographically whenever characters share the author's ethnicity, ethnic authors write both to and against the expectation. Overlapping reader expectations of this sort is the frequently very real presence of autobiographical elements in works of fiction, as many critics have commented on in Richard Wright's *Native Son*. What insights and concerns might be raised from pursuing similar questions in other texts, such as Helena María Viramontes's *Under the Feet of Jesus* and Junot Díaz's *The Brief Wondrous Life of Oscar Wao*, in which the protagonist is likewise associated with the author—perhaps for no other reason than that the two have the same ethnicity and gender? Important to such investigations would be a close look at the ethnic alter ego and the ways in which the author both associates herself with and distances herself from her fictionalized ethnic characters.

TWO RICHARDS

In a climactic scene of his autobiography, Richard Wright reveals the power of narrative when forging a note so that he can check out library books (*Black Boy* 247). In reading those books, Wright is able to imagine a world in which everyone is treated equally as a person, a world unimaginable in the Jim Crow South into which this grandson of slaves had been born. As for Frederick Douglass before him—in the iconic literacy scene of that most emblematic of all slave narratives—the key insight comes to Wright as an epiphany. Wright is reading H. L. Mencken when he realizes, "Yes, this man was fighting, fighting with words. He was using words as a weapon, using them as one would use a club" (248).

In this moment, the youthful Wright is inspired by the writer's courage. Wright will go on, as readers of his autobiography well know, to also become a writer who uses words as weapons, clubs in the struggle against social injustice. His intellectual and literary debt to Douglass is as clearly signaled as his debt to Mencken. Douglass uses deception to learn how to read, Wright does the same in forging the library note. Literacy, in both narratives, is the first step on the path to freedom. In scripting his narrative of the ethnic self, a *performative* self, Wright achieves agency not otherwise available to him. And in doing so, he can begin to break free of the *formative* narrative of racial scripts. Through written narrative he will also strive to do the same for others, using his writing to combat racial discrimination. As social realist writer, Wright comes to live by the adage that the pen is mightier than the sword. Years later, his epiphany about using words as weapons will crystallize into a second realization: that the autobiographical act itself—both on the page, and as played out on the public stage—is inherently subversive.

Wright's epiphany about narrative and ethnic identity is reenacted four decades later by a second Richard, Richard Rodriguez, who begins his autobiography with an unexplained allusion to the tradition of written culture that has so shaped his consciousness: "I have taken Caliban's advice. I have stolen their books. I will have some run of this isle" (*Hunger* 3). As the allusion to swarthy Caliban's possession and implied mastery of Prospero's magical books suggests, the consciousness of both ethnic subjects, Wright and Rodriguez, has been shaped by a shared print culture. Rodriguez's refusal to further explain the allusion—its Shakespearean provenance, the postcolonial themes of the play—underscores in black and white the potential universality of the written word: red, yellow, black, or brown, all of his readers share the imprint of Shakespeare's language and texts. A substantially different text, however, is inscribed on the ethnic body—that of visible difference.

The conceptual and linguistic convergence point of print culture, the narrative self, and the embodied self is the corpus. The word *corpus*, in its multiple senses, etymologically reflects the ontological union of the body (visibly ethnic) with the body of print culture (the literary corpus) through the human faculty of narrative. It is the union of this literary and extraliterary corpus that the autobiographies of Wright and Rodriguez revolve around, the complex nexus where the ethnic self negotiates identity in a social and textual context. Their shared obsession with exploring this site of convergence links their autobiographical texts at a fundamental level. Their tandem tracing of the theme across different social and historical contexts is, as this book argues, of tremendous import to modern ethnic lives.

Against the racial binaries and segregated literary traditions that challenge an intuitive comparison of these two authors are the much more salient commonalities of their exploration of race, identity, masculinity, print culture, narratives of ethnicity, and the relation between self and society. Most striking of these is their mutual interest in the tension between individual and community, their separate texts revealing a shift in emphasis that reflects the crossing chiasmus of ethnic subjects whose lives lie on opposite sides of the civil rights era.

Within the bounds of their respective societies, each author forges a measure of agency that contests and complicates constrictive scripts of race, gender, and ethnicity. This double gesture of narrating the self while negotiating ethnic and racial narratives that are mapped onto the body is one of the central subjects of *Autobiography in Black and Brown*. Broadly conceived, this is a book about narratives of the ethnic self. Specifically, it is a book about narratives of the ethnic self in the autobiographical works of two American authors and the ways in which each negotiates the complicated triangulation between self, ethnic group, and the larger society.

THE MIRROR OF AUTOBIOGRAPHY

In the pages that follow, I first introduce some of the theoretical concepts and terminology invoked in my approach to identity, ethnic autobiography, and the texts of Wright and Rodriguez. I go on to outline the epistemological assumptions of this book as well as the larger stakes involved in such a project: questions of agency, social justice, ethnic identity, narrative reality, and how we conceptualize the world. These larger stakes can be seen in stark relief through a brief comparison of postmodern accounts of identity with those from fields such as ethnic and feminist studies. After setting this context, I state the central premises of *Autobiography in Black and Brown* and then expand on key issues raised by the high-stakes debate between postmodernism and minority studies about reference and the nature of reality. The centrality of these core issues prompts laying out some important epistemological groundwork before proceeding to a discussion of ethnic autobiography as a genre. Finally, I closely compare the particular ethnic selves, Wright and Rodriguez, whose autobiographies are the focus of this book.

The account of identity and autobiography presented here uses the term *visibility* to indicate the ways in which the interpellation of ethnic subjects in the social matrix remains tethered to the body. This formulation is inspired by philosopher Linda Martín Alcoff's extensive theorization of *visible identities*, of which she writes synoptically: "The reality of identities often comes from the fact that they are visibly marked on the body itself, guiding if not determining the way we perceive and judge others and are perceived and judged by others" (5). I also introduce the terms *referentiality* and *revisability* to describe the two poles of identity—the one corporeally fixed, and the other narratively fluid. Referentiality acknowledges the embodiedness of the self while resisting essentialist positions; revisability acknowledges the narrative nature of identity, but without going so far as to claim that the self is therefore completely constructed.

A robust account of ethnic identity, I suggest, strives to focus these disparate frames of reference into a coherent image. Hence, the working subtitle of this book consisted of an image-inverting allusion to Richard Rorty's dismissal of reference as "the mirror of nature" (in his *Philosophy and the Mirror of Nature*), but with my version turning the catchphrase right side up, in titular and un-ironic usage, as "identity and the mirror of autobiography." Autobiography holds a mirror up to reality, but we would be mistaken to take the image in the mirror for its source—and even more so for taking the distortion of that image as proof that there is no source at all. Likewise, a realist account of identity eschews both essentialist notions of the ethnic self and complete constructivist interpretations of performativity. Also rejected are approaches that treat socially constructed aspects of identity as if they were inherited genetically, as often happens in narratives of ethnic authenticity and essentialist strains of culturalism and cultural nationalism. As Marcial González warns, "Cultural nationalism . . . [even as] . . . a response to Chicano racialization . . . creates a whole new set of contradictions—different in political substance, but just as problematic in effect" (113). It is at our own peril that we make a Cassandra out of González and other scholars with the foresight and hindsight to see the dangers in any swerve toward essentialism.

The turn back to realism is no easy task, however, given the self's dual nature: the perplexing ontology of consciousness, which cannot exist without the body, but which is also narrative in nature and has the uncanny ability to situate the self in social space following not the laws of physics but of discourse and social relations.[1] Despite this apparent dualism, we are right to reject notions such as the ghost in the machine, this or that mystical Geist, and other forms of Cartesian dualism, as well as their modern guises of a literal racial memory, collective mind, or the death of the author. More rigorous, convincing, and epistemologically useful, I argue, is a holistic, metaphysical realist account that acknowledges the ultimate oneness of nature and culture, at once respecting their different logics, or levels of reality, as well as their entanglement, an approach that, as Frederick Luis Aldama urges in *Postethnic Narrative Criticism*, "is careful not to confuse the transcription of the real world, where the criteria of truth and falsity apply, with the narrative mode governed by other criteria" (15). My focus on the narrative aspect of identity in this book is meant to underscore the spookiness of that entanglement, reminding us that narrative is part of the ontological nature not only of autobiography but also of personal identity.

Likewise observing that the link between narrative and personal identity extends beyond the page, distinguished scholar of autobiography Paul John Eakin writes, "I believe that our life stories are not merely *about* us but in an inescapable way and profound way *are* us, at least insofar as we are players in the narrative identity system that structures our current social arrangements" (*Living Autobiographically* x, emphasis in the original). Although this study focuses on literary selves—the ethnic self as depicted in autobiographical writing—we overlook the connection between written narrative and the larger world at our peril. In respect to the literary self of autobiography, personal identity is informed by the larger identity narratives in the society from which the text springs. The self on the page, in the simplest terms, is never far removed from the world it reflects.

THE EPISTEMIC VALUE OF ETHNIC AUTOBIOGRAPHY

The field of life writing poses many challenges to postmodernist accounts of self and world by raising questions about the status of the authorial referent (who is also the subject of autobiography), the embodiedness of the author (as opposed to the incorporeal "death of the author"), and the consequences of abolishing even the possibility of reference. The notion of the unified self may be a "useful fiction," as Raymond Martin and John Barresi note in *The Rise and Fall of Soul and Self*, but though "we are not unified by the soul or the self. We are unified by our bodies" (304). Ethnic autobiography, I submit, with its double focus on ethnicity and the referential task of autobiography, presents itself as an ideal genre not only for exploring issues of minority identity and social justice but also for testing and refining some of our epistemological assumptions. As Paul John Eakin notes, the "conceptual impasse that confronts theorists of autobiography in the age of postmodernism" is that between "the referentiality of the autobiographical text" and "the fictiveness of its subject" (*How Our Lives Become Stories* 3). The challenging questions about constructedness and referentiality that arise from the current impasse also suggest the possibility of refining our epistemological framework so as to offer a more sophisticated account of the interaction between social facts and the corporeality of human subjects. Furthermore, as Shari Benstock argues, "if the author is also marginalized (that is, if the writer is female, working class, black, Hispanic, lesbian)," their autobiography "serves as a kind of 'limit case'" (2). A coherent theory of ethnic autobiography must account for both the wholly linguistic ontology of the literary ethnic self (the self on the page) as well as the visibly ethnic status (social location) of the author. Such an investigation takes seriously the call by preeminent feminist scholars of life writing Sidonie Smith and Julia Watson that we view autobiographical texts by subaltern subjects "as sites for the re/production of knowledge" (22).

The epistemic value of ethnic autobiography redounds from the signifying practices by which the genre is read, cognitive acts by which the reader attempts to reconcile the textual self of narrative with their mental conception of the actual self of the author. The ethnicity of the author, for example, has hermeneutic consequences for the text in that the author as corporeal referent frames any reading of the text, even though most readers will never meet the author in the flesh. Ethnic autobiography thus dramatizes the interdependence between discursive self and embodied self, between narratives of identity and the bodies that particular narratives get mapped onto—and in so doing mirrors the paradox of ethnicity's visibility: that ethnicity can be visibly inscribed on the body even when its markers are nongenetic.[2] That is, the visibility of ethnicity is not necessarily in the flesh, just as the ethnicity of the author tends to be highly visible to readers even when the author is not in the room. In grappling with the twin poles of selfhood—its referentiality and its revisability, the inescapable embodiedness of the self and the fluidity of self narratives—and in exemplifying the indissoluble link between embodied self and narrative self, ethnic autobiography challenges us to refine our conceptualization of ethnic subjectivity and to begin to formulate a more complex understanding of identity.

The question of ethnicity's visibility raised here not only prompts greater appreciation for the variability and complexity of identity, but also suggests the possibility of developing an epistemological model that better accounts for the holism of biocultural reality—the inextricable entanglement of culture and nature as perceived and experienced by human subjects—than does either antirealism or naïve empiricism.[3] The two projects entail each other: a clearer understanding of the complexity of identity increases our understanding of the interaction between social reality and empirical reality, just as refining our epistemology illuminates our understanding of identity. This introduction sketches a realist epistemological model, but developing a refined and detailed model of the overlap between social reality and the rest of reality requires contributions from many fields and remains of central interest to interdisciplinary scholars. Indeed, such a project has no end, given the impossibility of achieving complete and perfect knowledge of any kind.

The works of ethnic autobiography I study here also raise important questions about agency, conceptions of community, the status of the ethnic subject, narratives of ethnic authenticity, the costs and benefits of assimilation, navigating between the twin poles of essentialism and absolute social constructivism, and balancing the expectation that minority writers be representative with autobiography's avowed focus on one life only (*Hunger* 7). For both Wright and Rodriguez, predominant themes include the inescapable contradictions of ethnic identity and the irresolvable tensions of ethnic lives. Of the many tensions endemic to ethnic identity and ethnic literature, perhaps the most central is that between the visibility of ethnic subjects and the revisability of narratives of ethnicity, a tension that is epitomized in the "referential art," as Eakin aptly describes the duality of ethnic autobiography (*Touching* 28). Again, although enticing and initially intuitive, a naïvely dualist notion of referentiality and revisability must be rejected in favor of a more interactionist model. The dualist conception imagines narrated or constructed aspects of identity as separate and apart from the embodied self, and in imagining narrative reality as irreconcilable with carnal reality must necessarily assume that reference is direct and unmediated. An interactionist model, by contrast, is interested in the ways in which the narrative self and the corporeal self interact, and in how narrative mediates our understanding of even something as inalienable from the self as our bodies. The narrative self and the embodied self coexist in tension rather than as separate entities. For ethnic authors, the revisable self of autobiography and self-identification coexist in tension with the visibility of their ethnicity in society. Indeed, negotiating the tension between the literary self and the ethnic expectations of their readers is a persistent theme for ethnic authors, such that the genre of ethnic autobiography in particular is an archetype for the dual nature of identity. We might envision this tension as a dance, or perhaps as something of less playfulness and much greater gravitas. The self on the page is not always the self the reader expects to see on the stage. The result is an agonistic embrace between the author's identity-forging enterprise of narrating subjective experience, and the seemingly incommensurable readerly expectation that the ethnic autobiographer's presentation of the self (and of ethnic identity) be representative of the ethnic group.

THE ABDUCTION OF THE EMBODIED SELF

The richer appreciation for the complexity of ethnic identities that a realist account calls for must move beyond the reigning theoretical approaches to identity in literary studies, yet recognize (and call upon) theory's significant contributions to the role of narrative in articulating the self. Surprisingly common essentialized descriptions of ethnic identity periodically ascendant in ethnic studies are also eschewed by a realist account. Though seeking to avoid identifiably problematic claims from either field, both literary theory and ethnic studies offer critical conceptual tools for the realist's toolbox. Indeed, part of the task of this book is to reconcile certain key insights of literary theory (such as the role of narrative in identity) with those of ethnic studies (such as the inescapable embodiedness of ethnic subjects). Before moving forward, a brief overview of what is at stake in the competing claims of these two fields warrants consideration. In the paragraphs that follow, I sketch some of the more problematic premises and conclusions of each field. Later, I offer a similarly brief sketch of a realist position that seeks to avoid such pitfalls, and to offer a more complex account of ethnic identity.

To those untouched by postmodernist epistemology, it might seem odd that the idea of the self as embodied should have to be defended. That the *I* reading this page has a body is self-evident. A body sitting in a chair and reading a book is ill disposed to doubt its existence, and the face one sees in the mirror each day confirms this sense of embodiment. The opposite conclusion—that the self has no corporeal basis—is so counterintuitive as to be hastily (perhaps too hastily) dismissed: if I have no body, then what is it I see (and what am I seeing it with) when I wave my hand in front of my face? Nevertheless, concepts such as the death of the author, the self as a purely a social construct (or an effect of discourse), and the social construction of reality have long been the coin of the realm in literary circles. Of course, one would be hard-pressed to name even a single literary theorist who genuinely claims that there is no biological basis to people whatsoever, just as one would be to name even one social constructivist who claims, as philosophical idealists of old did, that the very rocks and hills would disappear if the world were no longer peopled. But while playfully abstaining from literal pronouncements, the scale remains decidedly tipped toward antirealism in postmodern and poststructuralist accounts.[4] One logical consequence of strict adherence to the principle that there is nothing outside of the text is that people are also reduced to textual constructs. Even eschewing the strong version of the poststructuralist notion of the self and opting instead for a weak one leaves us with the conclusion that the discursive nature of the self renders insignificant the body on which those discourses are inscribed. In short, the cash value—to invoke the pragmatist parlance—of such a view is the abduction of the embodied self. In its place stands an impersonator, a postmodern doppelgänger whose ontology is purely linguistic—the author of the autobiographical text is deemed a ghost writer, literally so. This disembodied entity, the ghost-author, may haunt the text but is assumed to have no corporeal existence, neither in the text nor outside it.

The postmodern challenge to the intuitive notion of the embodied self takes various forms, including that of critical concepts such as discourse, subjectivity, born into, the given, always already, relations of power, and the self as linguistic or social construct. The usefulness of such concepts for deconstructing oppressive social structures is both potent and irrefutable. Additionally, the application of postmodern critiques breaks important ground in unmasking and interrogating the systemic and discursive structures to which bodies are subject and in which subjects are constituted. It is this usefulness, as emphasized by neopragmatists such as Richard Rorty, and the potential for radical critique, such as in the early work of Judith Butler, that makes postmodern theory, as an epistemological stance, so attractive to so many. Among its other virtues, a major contribution of Capital-T Theory has been to disabuse us of belief in an atomized, presocial self that is the legacy of classical liberal political philosophy and a cornerstone of neoliberal and conservative-libertarian attacks on progressive social programs. Unfortunately, a postmodernist epistemology presents us with severe epistemological consequences that seem unavoidable when postmodernism is taken to its logical conclusions: antirealism and an inability to rank some social values (such as social justice or mitigating inequality in society) higher than others. Even when asymptotically never quite touching the x-axis of unqualified antirealism, postmodernist positions locate us perilously close to absolute relativism and complete constructivism, long before which point the epistemic loss begins to exceed the epistemic value of the postmodern approach. At this point, postmodernism turns on itself, disallowing its legitimacy and disavowing the social justice aims for which it was engaged as a radical critique in the first place. Although spectacular at deconstructing oppressive social structures, postmodernism—in forsaking all reference to any kind of language- or discourse-independent reality—is incapable of dismantling those structures. Given these conclusions, many scholars have begun to wonder whether the cost of adopting a postmodern epistemology is too high (see, for example, Moya 12).

Ethnic studies, a field that takes particular interest in questions of social justice, has long been among the vanguard of those raising a skeptical challenge to the postmodernist turn. For ethnic subjects, marginalized by the visibility of their ethnicity—the markers of otherness inscribed on the body—the cost of ignoring the corporeal dimensions of their situatedness in society (enmeshed in the very discourses and relations of power that the postmodern critique has made us aware of) is the forfeiture of the means of agency by which marginalization can be resisted. If the ethnic subject is always-already determined as a purely linguistic or social construct, the mere effect of various discourses, then how can there be any possibility of meaningful resistance to the social forces by which subjects are marginalized? Would the adoption of such a worldview not both deny agency to marginalized subjects and empower the very forces that oppress them? The question has been turned over and over by ethnic and feminist scholars alike, and the unwelcome answer to such questions has prompted, in some circles, an essentialist turn that seeks to resist these nihilistic conclusions by raising from the grave previously deconstructed and dispatched notions of heredity and destiny as a means of resistance that opens up the possibility of social justice. Calling upon such dark powers offers a frightening prospect: in taking the expedient measure of invoking incarnations of strategic essentialism such as racial memory, ethnic authenticity, sexual determinism, and monolithic notions of collective identity, we might get what we wish for, successfully conjuring up revenants, as the title of John Su's "Ghosts of Essentialism" suggests, that do indeed rival even the specter of Theory.

SKEPTICAL REALISM

We may balk at the excesses of Theory, and shudder at past injustices committed under the essentialist banner, but no clear consensus on the way forward has emerged. Scholars in the humanities are prone to viewing realist approaches with suspicion as either—echoing a common view of the hard sciences—reductive or positivist. Writing primarily for a humanities audience, Satya Mohanty therefore proffers the term *postpositivist realist*, clearly signaling that by taking a realist position he decidedly does not mean to imply a positivist account of social reality (192). And though the theoretical foundations laid out by Mohanty in his *Literary Theory and the Claims of History* have been indispensable to my thinking as a realist—particularly in reference to the epistemic value of social identities, as well as texts and their contexts—neither Mohanty's postpositivist realist position nor any other variety of realism has yet to achieve the prominence still given to hyperbolically relativistic approaches in the humanities and social sciences. The source of this resistance to realism is self-evident in Mohanty's grammatically postpositive use of *positivist* after the prefix *post*. Given the ongoing history of disastrous applications of reductive approaches that, though successful in the hard sciences, lead to absurd and even destructive conclusions in the humanities and social sciences, it is no wonder that many humanists and social scientists are leery of any approach that suggests a return to empirical and quantitative reductionism. Moreover, many conclude that positivism is realism's default position. Mohanty's assurance that realism has now entered a post period to positivist and reductionist transgressions is a necessary if not sufficient inducement to skeptical humanist scholars well aware that neither physics nor mathematics can tell you much about *Othello* or any other literary text. Even given such assurances, however, scholars in the humanities remain hesitant to embrace the idea that any approach that trucks with truth claims made by the empirical sciences can tell us anything worth knowing about such nonempirical realities such as love, texts, narrative, identities, fictional characters, and all the things that really matter to us in life. Simply put, what can realism tell us about social reality?

Realism today goes by many names: metaphysical realism, philosophical realism, postpositivist realism, metaphysical naturalism (naturalism, for short), and skepticism. "Skepticism?" the reader might ask. "Isn't skepticism the opposite of realism?" What is more accurately called absolute skepticism is indeed an antirealist position, and an all-too-common theoretical position in postmodernist accounts. By contrast, moderate skepticism, in the sense of a skeptical attitude that brackets truth claims as always revisable, is a realist epistemological stance, given the impossibility of absolute certainty. The limitations of human knowledge warrant nothing short of such skepticism: an insistence that all truth claims are provisional and fallible. This is not to say that all truth claims are therefore equally relative, but rather that some are more justified than others on the basis of evidence, rational inquiry, and how well claims fit with our other beliefs and observations about how the world really is. Such a view does not see social reality as existing apart from the rest of existence, but rather takes a one-world approach that seeks to understand the overlays, intricacies, and interactions between social reality and all that would exist if there were no sentient life forms on planet Earth.

It is, in large part, the baffling complexity of the interaction between social reality and the rest of reality that turns humanist scholars into skeptics of realism. At the same time, these skeptical tendencies have sharpened our understanding of how science—the empirical methods by which we attempt to understand reality—actually works by providing correctives to positivist, absolutist, and reductionist assumptions. Realism, in short, is made more realistic by skeptical scrutiny. We might then, by way of acknowledging the indebtedness of realist inquiry to a skeptical stance, more accurately call realism *skeptical realism*. As a term, skeptical realism indicates the intertwining genealogy of rational inquiry between the two cultures—the skepticism of the humanities and the technoscience marvels of scientific realism. Skeptical realism combines an awareness of the mind-dependent logic of social facts with the realist belief in the mind-independent existence of the world. The skeptical realist thus rejects as implausible any view of the world that either denies the existence of the mind-independent world, or treats social reality as if operating by the same logic as that of the empirical world. Also rejected is the supernatural view that social facts exist separate and apart from the rest of reality. Social reality depends on mind-independent reality—it cannot exist without it. However, whenever it emerges, social reality is by no means apart from the rest of reality: ideas and beliefs, as Henry Adams observed, erect cathedrals. The effects of social reality on the world could not be more real. Social reality, that is, overlaps and interacts with the empirical world in ways and by logics we have yet to fully understand. The task of the skeptical realist is to sort out and better conceptualize those emergent qualities, intertwining logics, and complex interactions.

Indispensable to such a task is distinguishing less reliable from more reliable methods of epistemological inquiry, and determining in which contexts they apply, to reconcile the different ways of knowing—empirical, rational, mathematical, statistical, linguistic, political, textual, and hermeneutic ... as well as the power of the imagination to conceive and test theories, narrative worlds, thought experiments, and hypothetical models. The skeptical realist thus understands that we must distinguish normative from descriptive claims, that aesthetics takes precedence over the statistical analysis of literary texts (but not of Brownian motion)—and that as far as we can know anything at all, there is no getting outside interpretation. This is what a skeptical realist approach entails, and though it is less cumbersome to use the term *realism* than skeptical realism, it is useful to occasionally reinflate the shorthand term to the longer version so that readers in the humanities and social sciences do not mistakenly take a realist approach to mean positivism or a naïve realism that ignores the constructivist logic of social reality or the narrative logic of texts.

ETHNIC AUTOBIOGRAPHY

It is easy to see how a skeptical realist approach informs a consideration of ethnic autobiography. Texts have a narrative and semiotic logic that defies reductive empirical approaches. In giving print form to a narrative of personal identity that readers associate with the author and not any other person, the ethnic subjects who write those texts demonstrate the extent to which identity is, at least in part, narrated but also embodied. The social and narrative aspects of identity, which extend the self beyond the body and in relation to others, lead to what poststructuralists would call the indeterminacy of the ethnic subject. Because there is no getting outside the semiotic situatedness of our lives—our existence in social reality, how others read the text of our bodies, the narrative and performative presentation of the self, and the continuous revision of the signifier of ethnicity itself—discourse and interpretation play a role at every turn. Whether we read semiotic and discursive indeterminacy as a source of agency or as the denial of it is a matter of much debate in literary and ethnic studies. Life-writing scholar Leigh Gilmore underscores the critical potential of "an emphasis on the subject as an agent in discourse, where the subject itself is understood as necessarily discursive" (5). This is not to say, however, that the subject is disembodied. As Sidonie Smith adds, in her insightful contribution to the same volume, *Postmodernism and Autobiography*, "subjectivity is not, after all, an out-of-body experience. . . . current notions of the constitution of the subject anchor subjectivity very much in the body" ("Identity's Body" 266–67). No matter what our conception of the self, and no matter how socially diffuse and permeated individual consciousness might be, we must still conclude that personal identity, as discursive as it is, depends on the body. In simplest terms, you can have bodies (such as dead bodies and zombies) without selves, but you can never have a self without a body.

Perhaps nowhere is the complex interaction between social reality and the embodied self more emblematic than in the ethnic autobiographer's double bind. Although writing about the self, ethnic autobiographers are also fully aware that their texts will be read as representative of the ethnic group with which they are identified. The literary constraints that this expectation to be representative imposes and, more broadly, the attendant fixed "representational and rhetorical strategies" that it entails, are thoroughly critiqued by Kenneth Warren, who warns against the ossifying effects such expectations can have on ethnic literature (8). Further emphasizing the extent to which literary practices are informed by social context is Albert Stone's exhortation to "understand autobiography not simply as a literary convention but more broadly as a cultural activity" (*Autobiographical Occasions* 2).

The story of the self cannot, of course, be told without talking about the social relationships that define us, an insight about the relational nature of the self that Nancy Miller stresses in arguing that "Autobiography's story is about the web of entanglement in which we find ourselves" (544). At the same time, a communal testimonio can lose the particularity of the storyteller's life, experiences, and sense of personal identity. In the tradition of American letters, this tension between narrating the private self and the larger self is persistent and can be found in such foundational texts as Franklin's *Autobiography*, Emerson's "Self-Reliance," and Whitman's "Song of Myself." Jay Parini astutely observes of Franklin that his story "directly parallels the American story" despite focusing on Franklin's "progress and development" rather than his role in the birth of the nation (12). Emerson and Whitman continue the thread of relating the self to national identity and add to it a conception of the self as also a cosmic self, stressing our common humanity.

Ethnic autobiographers, however, encounter the private-self and larger-self duality in a different form: the self as synonym for a group identity, a type rather than a person. That is, rather than modeling a synecdochical relationship between self and society, group identity is conceived in this case as a stereotypical view of a subset of people perceived as different from mainstream society. G. Thomas Couser reminds us that autobiography "tends merely to reflect prevailing cultural assumptions rather than adequately to enact or express the relation between the individual, on the one hand, and social historical forces on the other," and so it should come as no surprise that readers frame their readings of texts based on what they know, or think they know, about the ethnicity of the author (24). Although external to the text, the writer's ethnicity signifies as if part of it. Thus extratextual features, such as the ethnicity of the author, are integral to the ways in which the text is meaningful to readers. Ethnic autobiographers, in short, find themselves having to balance the expectation that their account authentically represent their personal experiences and life with the countervailing one that their account will also be representative of the ethnic group.

Somewhat related is the status of the relationship between ethnic literatures and national literature. No consideration of U.S. ethnic literature is complete without an appreciation for the entanglement of American literatures. Ethnic literature is an integral part of American literature, and we might inadvertently distort the text when reading as if it were of a separate tradition. Undoubtedly, the question of precursors, influence, and genealogy varies from text to text, some clearly more indebted to one or the other historically marginalized literary traditions. We honor the text and the literary tradition in placing emphasis where it is due and attempting to "situate these . . . texts in appropriate literary traditions," as William Andrews describes it (6). More often than not, however, those traditions consist not of a pure or single literary lineage but of a continuous history of overlap and exchange with other literary traditions. "Political boundaries may seriously obscure our perception of cultural relationships," adds James Robert Payne (introduction xxix). That autobiographers still look to Augustine's *Confessions* as a literary model, and that Chicana/o authors often look to Latin American literary trends and precursors should likewise trouble the waters of any overdetermined notion of national literature.

Although national literature remains a vexing rubric, permeated with global borrowings and adaptations, the shared inhabitation of a geographic place and social space has tended to deepen the relationship between minority literatures and what has historically been conceived of as American literature, even when the minority tradition is writing and defining itself against monolithic notions of mainstream identity and literature. Wright models *Black Boy* on the African American slave narrative tradition, but he is also influenced by the autobiographical tradition inherited from Benjamin Franklin and Henry Adams. Following David Palumbo-Liu's description of ethnic literature as offering "a counterdiscourse [with] the ability to designate a shifting open space outside the hegemonic," Wright borrows from the Anglocentric tradition even as he critiques the Jim Crow laws and cultural practices deployed to maintain white superiority in the South (introduction 17). And just as Wright numbers Dreiser and Mencken among his literary influences, so Rodriguez is indebted to the "coruscating nonchalance" of African American writers such as James Baldwin (*Brown* 31).

In seeking to respect the pluralism of American literature, we must be careful not to conflate the different spheres of influence while striving for both greater inclusiveness and a better understanding of the ways in which these pluralistic literary traditions both reflect and shape the social reality they mirror. In addition, we must also consider the ever-changing social context in which texts are read. As Manuel Martín-Rodríguez argues in *Life in Search of Readers*, "historically, Chicano/a literature has been defined as much by its readers as by its texts and author," and so texts previously written and read as part of a distinctive tradition and for a specific audience may be read quite differently by future generations of readers (2). Through his scholarly detective "investigation of post-nationalist Chicana/o identities," Ralph Rodriguez confirms the truth of this insight, emphasizing the "proliferating and protean identity formations" in the "changing political and social environment" in which modern ethnic subjects find themselves (11–12). *Autobiography in Black and Brown* pays homage to both the dynamism of literary texts and the fluidity of ethnic identities, gazing Janus-faced into the past and the future to learn about present texts and identity formations, eagerly anticipating the evolving forms that future texts and increasingly complex and nuanced ethnic identities might take.

A final note is my occasional use of the term *literary*, a term that has endured recurrent bouts of supernatural interpretation. Two mystical senses of the word are germane to the current discussion. The first summons up literary debates about whether such a thing as literary language exists, and, if not, then under what justification or disciplinary auspices do we talk about something as apropos of literary study as, say, Cormac McCarthy's prose style and what distinguishes it from ordinary language or, to use the examples cited in Jonathan Culler's *Literary Theory*, a telephone directory or chemistry textbook (28–29). The second sense raises the specter of which texts come to be recognized as literary and who exactly makes these determinations. Both debates remind us that the word is by no means a self-evident designation. For the current discussion, what gets designated as literary has more to do with the various forces that arbitrate canons than with any inherent qualities in the text, a sociopolitical reality that is all too apt when discussing the literary status of ethnic literature. The four texts I offer here are all, for whatever combination of reasons, read as literary autobiographies—which, Jennifer Wallach notes, "intend to be works of art as well as chronicles of lives"—as opposed to, say, one of the many celebrity or political autobiographies, which are generally not read as "literature" (451).

More important, when referring to the literary self, I invoke the word *literary* in its most deflated sense to denote print narratives of the self—and more specifically, published autobiographies.

Two other terms merit some discussion here—namely, the brace of words juxtaposed in the expression *ethnic self*. As for the first of these, *ethnic*, although both Wright and Rodriguez are racialized in American society, I use the term *ethnic* in lieu of strictly racialized terms to emphasize the similarity of their social situatedness. Of particular interest to the present investigation are the ways in which ethnicity—though ostensibly predicated on nongenetic, cultural difference rather than social interpretations of biological (such as sex and race) difference—is not only visible in society but also always mapped onto individual bodies. Though the logic of alterity by which Wright and Rodriguez are framed as other varies in its particularity, each poignantly dramatizes the ways in which their ethnicity frames them, and by which—in the case of ethnicity, as opposed to that of, say, affiliation based on shared interests or views—group identities not only intersect with but also permeate personal identity, and do so on the body.

As for the term *self*, it both denotes and is synonymous with the *auto* in autobiography. In using the word *self*, and given my emphasis on recuperating the embodied subject, I want to be clear about what is not meant by invoking this term. Solipsism or any conception of the self that is not also a social self is rejected in this account.[5] The point is underscored in Alan Palmer's conceptualization of the "intermental mind" in *Fictional Minds*, which, though eschewing mystical formulations of collective consciousness, emphasizes "the *mind beyond the skin*" and "the social nature of thought" (11, emphasis in the original)—an account that he extends in *Social Minds in the Novel* by stressing that identity is always a "situated identity" (40). I could not agree more. And because minds are permeated by language, social reality, and relations of power, I also do not mean to suggest a naïve conflation of subjectivity with the physical self, as if there were any such thing as an atomized or presocial self. I do, however, assume that texts have embodied authors, and that each author has a personal identity.

In addition, I wish to stress in the account of the self that follows that because the self is always a social self, and because social location is constitutive of the self, that the *ethnic* in the ethnic self—the two words alloyed into a singular entity rather than standing as a conjugate pair—cannot be severed from any account or description of the self that we might put forth when talking about ethnic subjects. That is, because the self is always a social self, the structure of social relations constrains the extent to which the self can be universalized without distorting our conception of it. For as much as we all have a common humanity, overlooking the ways in which subjects are situated in relations of unequal power, as Mary Louise Pratt reminds us in her theorization of the "contact zone," can serve to legitimize instruments of oppression (4). And though the political abstraction of a universal self, or "all men," is useful and necessary for guaranteeing pluralistic representation in a democracy, it fails to adequately account for the formation of identity. Just as we have never to date successfully managed to imagine—pace completely constructivist readings of Judith Butler's notion of gender as a performance—the self as having no gender at all, so we fail, in social practice, to conceive of all persons as equally universal.[6] Any conception of the embodied self that we might put forth, then, must also take into account the ways in which subjects are constituted in social reality and perceived by others as visibly marked along lines such as race, gender, ethnicity, and social class.

In their autobiographies, ethnic authors deploy various strategies for resisting constrictive or exclusive narratives of ethnicity, and for reconciling the performance of identity with the embodiedness of the self. Tracing these tensions, reconciliations, and irreconcilable contradictions through close readings of the autobiographies of Wright and Rodriguez is a central theme of this book. Other persistent themes appear and reappear as leitmotifs: minority status, class consciousness, the search for community, and the social expectation that ethnic autobiographers be representative of the ethnic group.

THE GROUNDS FOR COMPARISON

Playing Against Type

In the chapters that follow, a common thread between Wright and Rodriguez—despite their different sociohistorical contexts—is the tension in their texts between writing both to and against expectations of ethnic representativeness. Wright plays to such expectations when, in the words of Timothy Dow Adams, depicting his life in *Black Boy* (1945) as that of "a typical black childhood" to expose the "history of hunger, deprivation, and constant racism" faced by "countless black Americans" (70). But Wright resists taking on the role of representative "black boy" in passages where he presents himself as an existentialist ethnic self. Rodriguez's first autobiographical text shows a similar interplay. Rodriguez plays to expectations by focusing on politicized ethnic issues in

Hunger of Memory (1982), even as he disavows his representativeness by adamantly proclaiming, "I write of one life only" (7).[7] In both cases, the authors reflect the contradictions of ethnic identity in their texts. In Rodriguez's case, critics have focused more on surface-level, internal contradictions in the text than on whatever identity coherence *Hunger of Memory* might exhibit as a realistic reflection of a complex and shifting ethnic subjectivity.

Wright and Rodriguez both resist the constraints of representativeness imposed on them as ethnic subjects, but Rodriguez's resistance goes far beyond narrative questions about how best to balance such expectations with the story of his own life. Rodriguez uses autobiography as a venue for weighing in on questions about ethnic identity itself. He defies expectations about his ethnicity by stressing the fluidity of identity. In penning multiple autobiographical books, each separated by a decade, Rodriguez exemplifies the extent to which identity is revisable. He embraces the performative aspect of identity, leading J. A. Marzán, in his essay "The Art of Being Richard Rodriguez," to observe that "he continues reinventing himself as if the undermining evidence in printed books did not exist" (59). In part through his persistent evasion of his ethnic situatedness, Rodriguez ends up demonstrating the limits of revisability. For, despite the disavowals and erasures, and despite his posturing as an individualist and an assimilationist, he ultimately cannot escape the ways in which he is marked by his ethnicity. In Marzán's words, "He [Rodriguez] will always be famous for being Hispanic and his career will be grounded on writing on that subject" (61).

Wright too is brought to account for ignoring the dark side of expectations about representativeness when, in trying to expose the perniciousness of racism by depicting black culture as having been debased by it, he incurred the wrath of middle-class blacks. Wright's critics knew that his portrayal would be taken as representative even if negative portrayals were used only as a social-realist literary tool to dramatize and manifest the perversity of Jim Crow racial logic. Despite these criticisms, both authors attempt to turn the tables on expectations by using representativeness as an instrument to develop the genre's capacity to "have a profound social and cultural impact" (Sayre x).

The question of collective identification extends beyond racial and ethnic identities for Wright and Rodriguez. Class figures as prominently as race, gender, and sexuality in the texts of both authors, each going beyond an ostensibly color-blind and culture-oblivious analysis of class and identity. Class and culture, they remind us, are inextricably linked. Any class-based identity—and any socioeconomic analysis—must also account for the complexity of culture and the varieties of culture in which we are enmeshed as subjects. Among other considerations, the exploration of ethnic identity and the search for community must also, as Richard T. Rodriguez argues in *Next of Kin*, seek to understand the "connections between masculinity, nationalism, and the family" (4). It must also consider, as Daniel Kim notes in *Writing Manhood in Black and Yellow*, "the interconnected rhetorics of race, writing, and manhood," for Kim's purposes, "by both African and Asian American authors" (3). To talk about ethnic identity and class, in other words, we must—and both Wright and Rodriguez do—also talk about these and other cultures, discourses, and interconnections.

Masculinity and Sexuality

In depicting the relationship between the emasculation of black males and the systemic impoverishment of the race, Wright makes explicit the connections between masculinity, nationalism, and familial exclusion. "I was a nonman," he writes, after sexually tinged racial harassment (fighting words intended to provoke him) backed by the threat of violence (in the context of lynching and castration) drives him away from learning a trade in the optics industry (*Black Boy* 194, 188). Rodriguez also explores these and related interconnections by delineating, for instance, the ways in which narratives of masculinity situate social location in conjunction with religious and sexual identity in perplexing and yet very real ways: "I was born Catholic. Is homosexuality, then, a conversion experience? No. I was born gay" (*Brown* 224). And so, though each author rebels against being cast as representative of any monolithic notion of collective identity—racial, sexual, gendered, religious, class-based, or otherwise—each also seeks a larger community to identify with because each of us is inseparable from the communities to which we belong, and the inescapably political act of living in the world is not possible apart from identifying and being identified with one or more collective identifications. The existential question that each ethnic author must grapple with, then, extends beyond "Who am I?" to "Who are my people . . . what families do I belong to?"[8]

Their common quest to expand conceptions of community and kinship beyond the constricted sphere of "minority nationalisms," narrowly conceived, leads each to "relinquish their dependency on exclusionary kinship relations," as we are urged to do by Richard T. Rodriguez (7). Wright symbolically and literally (under the enforcement of segregation and antimiscegenation laws) expands his kinship by marrying outside the race. Rodriguez slips the noose of cultural nationalism by rejecting what he sees as the small hoop of ethnic identity for a larger, more inclusive circle, that of the dominant culture and language. In the context of the culture wars, Rodriguez seems in *Hunger of Memory* to be opposing minority and mainstream cultures as if they are mutually exclusive and self-contained. Rereading the text today through the transracial, cosmopolitan vision of *Brown*, however, and in consideration of Rodriguez's advocacy on behalf of immigrants, suggests a radically postnationalist conception of identity and citizenship. If his readers, and perhaps Rodriguez himself, failed to conceptualize a more radical reading of Rodriguez's text at the time, it is perhaps because, as David Luis-Brown argues in making the case for what he calls hemispheric citizenship, "citizenship has traditionally been associated with legal and political rights promised within the space of a single nation-state" (21).

Even in the nationalist framing, however, other cultures and kinship ties have an impact. Despite framing language choice as an either-or question, *Hunger of Memory* also dedicates entire chapters to family, religion, masculinity, and education (depicted as a dramatically transformational and therefore alienating process). These dimensions of identity intertwine, of course, and cannot be considered in strict isolation. Although also invoking identity binaries, *Hunger of Memory* does not shy away from the complexities of identity. The "Complexion" chapter (4) depicts the young Rodriguez trying to live up to the manly, working-class image of the Mexican laborer (the *bracero*), weaving matters of race, class, and—even as it closets his sexuality—masculinity so tightly together that Rodriguez's silence about his homosexuality in *Hunger of Memory* would seem to support rather than undermine Ernesto Javier Martínez's paradigm-shifting thesis that "queer exodus is one of the keys to contextualizing Richard Rodriguez's conservatism about ethnic identity in his autobiography" (89). That is, as Martínez goes on to elaborate, Rodriguez rejects a Chicano identity in part "from his inability to foresee a queer identity successfully flourish in proximity to, and in relationship with, his ethnic home and community" (90). To the extent that this is so, Rodriguez's queer exodus mirrors his rejection of a Chicano nationalist identity that he sees as opposed to the English-language books and American education that have transformed him body and soul. This transformed self and the enhanced epistemic privilege that comes with it is—for both Wright and

Rodriguez—not just a matter of bridging ethnic, sexual, and other cultures, but also of class consciousness.

Class and the Race Question

Class consciousness leads Wright to join the Communist Party and to take up the banner of class struggle. In part 2, "The Horror and the Glory," of *Black Boy*, Wright describes his alienation from the party and his defiance of the party line. Not only does the Communist Party fail to adequately consider the role of race and gender in maintaining socioeconomic inequality but, even more deeply troubling for Wright, emerges as fundamentally intolerant of any kind of difference. In the struggle against inequality, the party has forgotten that the larger aim of greater equality and opportunity is to enrich human lives. The unity the party demands has taken a totalitarian turn toward "militant ignorance," demands for "proof of revolutionary loyalty," and the use of "tactics of terror, threat, invective, intimidation, suspicion" (332, 334, 362).

Wright's existentialist worldview—"But they had never been able to conquer their fear of the individual way in which I acted and lived, an individuality which life has seared into my blood and bones"—leads him to walk away from the collectivist demands of the party while continuing to fight, primarily through his art, for racial and socioeconomic justice, and for human freedom (*Black Boy* 363). The manner in which Wright portrays his departure from the party exposes the impossibility of absolute representativeness, the absurdity of treating people as fungible units.

Rodriguez is also in part rebelling against collectivist narratives of ethnic identity. However, in turning from cultural national demands, he ends up affirming similar ones from a different group: mainstream society. In this sense, his assimilationist arguments (about the importance of being recognized by the dominant society as culturally one of us to some significant degree) balance Wright's existentialist view with one that recognizes the demands of community. However, if read as a rejection of ethnic identities, Rodriguez's arguments seem individualist, particularly from the perspective of minority ethnic communities. These seeming paradoxes point, once again, to the inherent tension between expectations of representativeness and the staggering diversity of actual ethnic subjects.

Whereas Wright underscores his alienation, Rodriguez is motivated by the promise of social connection through a shared public culture and public language, and hence also through a shared print culture, which Benedict Anderson describes as integral to the formation of "imagined communities" (*Hunger* 19; Anderson 6, 13). In depicting the imagined selves—a phrase that, along with ethnic selves, served briefly as a working title for this book—out of which these imagined communities coalesce, *Hunger of Memory* stresses the potential agency of ethnic subjects. As counterpoint, *Black Boy*'s existentialist register is offset by a naturalistic and determinist depiction of the racial environment. Reflecting Rodriguez's emphasis on agency is his framing of racial and ethnic disadvantage as primarily a class issue, with the greatest stress on social class. Having been influenced by and deeply identifying with D. H. Lawrence's examination of the social and psychological shocks of class mobility (a shared personal experience that along with Lawrence's exploration of sexual identity make the twain kindred spirits), Rodriguez sees himself as choosing—perhaps unconsciously—to assimilate to middle-class life rather than to a particular ethnicity.

For Rodriguez, that is, greater equality, opportunity, and human flourishing hinge less on ethnic identity than on social class. Rodriguez's provocative arguments about assimilation, affirmative action, and bilingual education converge on a single point: full recognition as a person in society. And though some of Rodriguez's assumptions about how this is best accomplished often seem frustratingly at odds with the views and experiences of many in the Latino community, no one disagrees about the value of these larger aims. As Rodriguez sees it, recognition in society boils down to the intricacies of social class, but he seems at times to disavow the visibility of ethnicity as it is inscribed on ethnic bodies, and to suggest that cultural differences are to be understood only in a much larger sense of social class, and hence only incidentally ethnic, such as in the case of the working-class youth (the "scholarship boy") who goes to college and thrives by either assimilating or learning to pass in the dominant middle-class culture of colleges and careers (*Hunger* 48).

To rise above one's station in life, however, requires certain ambition, the motive force of which is captured in the metaphor of hunger. Of course, in the titular phrase "hunger of memory," hunger more directly suggests Rodriguez's nostalgia or desire for an irretrievable past. The theme of ambition is instead explored, in *Hunger of Memory*, through the paradigm of the scholarship boy who, until coming into his own, rises through the ranks through erudition and mimicry. A later chapter (2) is titled "The Achievement of Desire." Candid and constant in revealing his youthful ambition, Rodriguez develops the ambition theme even further in the "Poor Richard" chapter (4) of *Brown*. The metaphor, in short, is a major theme in Rodriguez's autobiographical oeuvre. The same is true for Wright. The working title of *Black Boy*—as delivered to his agent, and before expurgated and published by the Book-of-the-Month Club—had been *American Hunger*. Among the few details selected as emblematic of Wright's earliest childhood memories is the experience of gnawing hunger, including the poignant scene in which the starving child is told to go and catch a "kungry" if he wants to eat (15). His ambition to transcend his environment parallels Rodriguez's desire to transcend race. All told, the commonality and extensiveness of the hunger metaphor in their autobiographies is as striking as that of the religious dimension in their work, as well as their shared desire to achieve universality in their writing. As Wright and Rodriguez depict it, to hunger is human and the desire to rise above it is divine. Rather than denying their hungering ambition, each author displays it as the stamp of their humanity. Each has had to confront the injustice of social exclusion. Each serves as witness to the pervasive denial of class mobility on the basis of race. Each rebels against and defies the fixed linking of race to permanent lower-class status. The boundaries between collective ethnic group and private self overlap in this struggle, though for Wright and Rodriguez some distinction between the two must remain. Exposing and excoriating institutional racism, neither accepts the personal constraints it imposes on them or waits for the ideals of social justice to bring about racial equality overnight. In this, both writers seem to achieve some sort of synthesis between the pragmatic and compromising racial-uplift thesis of Booker T. Washington and the idealistic and uncompromising topmost-integration antithesis of W. E. B. Du Bois—both aspiring to the Talented Tenth and the top-down interventions imagined by Du Bois, though their upward-impelling hunger has more in common with the bottom-up drive and ambition of Booker T.

Perhaps most uniting Wright and Rodriguez is their preoccupation with class and the question of race in America. By exposing the cost of continuing to turn a blind eye to racial inequality, Wright hoped to shock America into full recognition of what was then routinely referred to as "the Negro problem." At the time of *Black Boy*'s writing, America was waging war overseas in the name of democracy while keeping its own army racially segregated and denying full rights to black Americans at home. This contradiction made the unrealized ideals of liberal democracy more painfully obvious than before: racism was undermining the liberalist ideals on which American government and culture was said to be founded. By indicting the subhuman treatment of people of color, Wright was arguing that the notions of person and black person should not be separate concepts.

A particularly relevant sociopolitical context in which ethnic identities and cultures were conceived of as necessarily separate from mainstream culture also framed the writing and reception, in the early 1980s, of Rodriguez's first and most well-known book, *Hunger of Memory*. Minority critics writing in response were quick to condemn him for an assimilationist stance. Rodriguez had been raised in a Spanish-speaking household in central California, and yet he was against bilingual education in schools. Learning the "public language" was necessary in order to have a "public identity," both of which, he argued, are prerequisites to class mobility. Although sharing Wright's preoccupation with questions of race, class, and social justice, Rodriguez presented a view of social integration that reflected a new era: rather than scaring America straight with the specter of a resentful underclass of Calibans subverting and overthrowing the system, his Caliban had joined the bourgeoisie.

The Caliban trope offers a literary triangulation between Wright and Rodriguez and a third ethnic writer of distinction: James Baldwin, a former protégé of Wright. In his introduction to *Notes of a Native Son*, Baldwin writes,

> From this point of view the Negro problem is nearly inaccessible. It is not only written about so widely; it is written about so badly. It is quite possible to say that the price a Negro pays for becoming articulate is to find himself, at length, with nothing to be articulate about. ("You taught me language," says Caliban to Prospero, "and my profit on't is I know how to curse.") (6)

In an intertextual allusion to both Shakespeare and Baldwin, whose essay style inspired him, Rodriguez also deploys, as the opening line of *Hunger of Memory*, the trope of the subaltern mastering the language and print culture of the dominant society, stressing the agency that this accords him as ethnic subject: "I have taken Caliban's advice. I have stolen their books. I will have some run of this isle" (3). There is irony in both Baldwin's and Rodriguez's presentation of the ethnic situation in these passages, each also revealing the other's opposing emphasis in their respective texts. Baldwin's concerns about having "nothing to be articulate about" are undone by his psychologically penetrating analysis, in scintillating prose, of race matters. Rodriguez's bravado about ethnic agency is undermined by his poignant description of and nostalgia for all that has been lost in the assimilation bargain.

This nostalgic vein features prominently in *Hunger of Memory* as Rodriguez laments his lost Spanish-language heritage, something that did not survive the long journey through English-language schools. In focusing on this personal loss, ethnic heritage and mainstream culture seem irreconcilable: you have to give up one to participate in the other. Rodriguez abandons this either-or dichotomy in a more recent book, *Brown* (2002), the title of which is a metaphor for the interpenetration of cultures. Brown is cultural impurity. It is the color you get when all the crayons melt together in the sun. One never completely loses one's ethnic heritage, and mainstream culture is not separate and distinct from ethnic cultures.

The theme of cultural miscegenation, and its paradoxes, is now Rodriguez's predominant theme—"I celebrate the browning of America," proclaims Rodriguez in a Whitmanesque voice (*Brown* xiii). His barbaric yawp seems antithetical to the conventional assimilationism that many readers associate with him: "I defy anyone who tries to unblend me" (xi). Thus the controversial endorsement of assimilation to mainstream culture in Rodriguez's first book is greatly qualified in his third book by nuancing the definition of mainstream culture so that it is conceived as a negotiation between countless smaller cultures rather than as a single uncontested and monolithic Anglo-Saxon Protestant one. Mainstream culture is assimilated to other cultures, just as other cultures are assimilated to it. American culture is replenished by minority and immigrant cultures as we all rub off on one another. People assimilate. We contaminate each other, making cultural purity a myth.

Self and Society

A central theme in the work of both Wright and Rodriguez is that of the individual in society. And although some of the most influential accounts of this theme ignore race, class, and gender, ethnic authors know that these important dimensions disproportionately affect ethnic lives. To explore the theme, Wright and Rodriguez teach us, is more accurately to explore what it means to be an individual in a society that fetishizes ethnic, racial, and gendered features, and in which wealthy individuals have options and opportunities unavailable to the poor. In the academic literature, Wright is frequently imagined as a collectivist who put social causes above individual interests, and Rodriguez is figured as a rank individualist whose rejection of ethnic nationalism reflects his solipsism. Wright was a longtime member of the Communist Party and dedicated himself to social change through protest literature. These attributes make Wright, in the minds of many, a committed collectivist. Against this popular conception, *Autobiography in Black and Brown* argues that Wright, although committed to social causes, was an ethnic existentialist. As we have seen, a classical liberal sense of the sanctity of the individual leads Wright to rebel against the collectivist demands of the Communist Party. This is not an isolated incident in *Black Boy*, which depicts in episode after episode the strong-willed Wright in conflict with and rebelling, like a Romantic hero, against the self-annihilating assault on various collective identities: family, church, racial identity politics, and the Communist Party. The protagonist of *Black Boy* in this picaresque narrative would seem to have more in common with the Rodriguez who is characterized as a rebel against group identification than with the image of the social realist writer who puts social causes above self.

Playing equally against type in his autobiographical texts is Rodriguez, who writes that the very notion of the individual is "communally derived" (*Brown* 200). Though resistant to the ways in which narratives of ethnicity can limit self-realization, Rodriguez is no solipsistic individualist. Like Wright, he explores the interdependence and inherent tensions between individuals and communities. This stress on interdependence offers a more complex understanding of selves and societies than defining the self in opposition to society or framing the relationship solely as the individual versus society. Even the most ardent individualist must concede that their primary notion of the self—the voice in their head—is expressed through the social medium of language, which we use to articulate the higher-order thinking that makes up most of conscious thought. In their common thematic exploration of the power of language, Wright and Rodriguez drive home this realization. For Rodriguez, society allows us to enlarge the self by allowing us to, paradoxically, connect with more people through a shared public language and the culture that is inseparable from it. As Rodriguez sees it, cultural narratives are more fluid, inclusive, and likely to intermingle than narratives of race, ethnicity, and gender are. Thus a shared language and culture allow individuals the widest circle of inclusion possible in which to conceptualize and express the self in relation to others.

Many see Rodriguez inhabiting a categorically different worldview in *Hunger of Memory* than that later revealed in *Brown*. This book argues that

Rodriguez's underlying thought has remained fundamentally consistent over the decades covered by the complete corpus of his autobiographical work. In the preface to *Brown*, Rodriguez describes each book as having a different emphasis, and as such offering different incarnations of himself and his views: "I believe it is possible to describe a single life thrice, if from three isolations: *Class. Ethnicity. Race*" (xiv, emphasis in the original). The changed emphasis alters the surface arguments in each subsequent book, but the core sentiments and philosophical underpinnings remain the same. The oracular pronouncements about cultural miscegenation in *Brown* tack in a different direction than the shared culture and language arguments of *Hunger of Memory*, but Rodriguez remains constant to his interdependence model of the self in society. Specifically, societies exist only as a community of diverse individuals, and people must be recognized as individuals if they are to flourish in society. Rodriguez sees this recognition of the full personhood of others as happening primarily through language (which entails a shared culture), and primarily in one-on-one human interactions. It is not against community that Rodriguez positions himself, but for community and for enlarging it, his earlier arguments for assimilation to mainstream culture in *Hunger of Memory* a means to that end.

Wright also makes central the theme of recognition as a person. For Wright, the problem is that others see only his race. Moreover, externally imposed racial narratives deny black individuals full personhood. *Black Boy* indicts racism by putting on display its crimes against the individual. To critique racism, Wright describes the effects of racism on black culture as well as its psychological effects on individuals. He also describes the effects of racism to tell readers about himself. No portrait of the self is complete without its being framed in a particular society. To tell his story, he must also tell us what it is like to be black in America.

Ralph Ellison, another rebellious protégé of Wright, once said in an interview that the search for identity is "*the* American theme" (*Collected Essays* 219, emphasis in the original). As a nation of immigrants, it could hardly be any other way. Early American authors began the exploration of identity while searching for a uniquely American voice—one that would be more representative of Americans and American society than of peoples and a culture an ocean away. This endeavor culminated around the 1850s, a time we now refer to as the American Renaissance. It was the age of Emerson, Fuller, Thoreau, Hawthorne, Melville, Poe, Whitman, and Dickinson. Discerning the first inklings of the Romanticist movement from an American point of view decades earlier, a young Emerson described it in his journals as "the age of the first person singular" (qtd. in Porte 20).

Future generations might look back on the contemporary literary epoch as the age of the ethnic self. In the late twentieth and early twenty-first century, ethnic literature has achieved new prominence. The last American to win the Nobel Prize for Literature (1993) was an African American, Toni Morrison, who is today widely viewed as the quintessential American author. In an increasingly diverse society, readers are hungry to learn something about the various ethnic cultures of their neighbors, and most readers prefer narrative accounts (either memoir or fiction) to sociological studies. It is no wonder then that so many ethnic authors have been met with both critical and popular acclaim from the American reading public in recent decades: Sandra Cisneros, Sherman Alexie, Jhumpa Lahiri, Junot Díaz, and other ethnic authors whose texts feature what is widely conceived of as an at least semiautobiographical narrator or ethnic protagonist.

Wright and Rodriguez take very different approaches—despite their shared emphasis on race and ethnicity—in narrating the self as a textual self. With the penetrating insight that is typical of their work, scholars of American autobiography James Olney and Timothy Dow Adams have each argued that the literary self depicted by Wright is meant to be representative of the typical "black boy's" experiences with racist oppression and social alienation.[9] Rodriguez's autobiographical essays, in contrast, go against the grain of expectations that he be ethnically representative: "Probably he [the bookstore clerk] will shelve it alongside specimens of that exotic new genre, 'ethnic literature.' Mistaken, the gullible reader will—in sympathy or in anger—take it that I intend to model my life as the typical Hispanic-American life. / But I write of one life only. My own" (*Hunger* 7).

The difference in referential aesthetic, to borrow Paul John Eakin's phrase, between the two authors reflects, in part, the distinctive ethnic and racial semiotics of the sociohistorical context that each writes to, and from (*Touching* 28–29). At first we are struck by the differences between the two narratives, but it soon becomes apparent that they are describing two sides of the same coin. Wright depicts African American lives destroyed by a racist society. Rodriguez depicts the larger society as a potential source of self-creation. Wright shows us how an out-group can be deemed nonpersons in a society. Rodriguez shows us the obverse side: that the recognition and effective self-realization of full personhood depends on social relations even when alterity no longer follows a strictly racial logic. In Wright's Jim Crow society, race was destiny, as was gender. In the post–civil rights and post–feminist movement era, Rodriguez suggests, the major schisms in the fabric of modern American society are less about race and gender and more about class and culture. Rather than race and gender as isolated variables that completely fix social identity, Rodriguez sees social class as the product of the complex interpenetration of multiple variables: race, class, gender, cultural awareness, linguistic proficiency, self-identification, and much, much more. Of course, the socially constructed discourses of race and gender continue to map signification onto individual bodies, a social fact he is well aware of, but for Rodriguez what happens in the overlapping spheres of class, culture, and language is far more relevant to individual lives today than how many X chromosomes one has or the color of one's skin.

Print Culture

Perhaps no other shared inheritance more unites Wright and Rodriguez than the extent to which each was shaped by his reading. As avid readers and professional writers, they each exemplify Walter Ong's thesis about the role of print culture in the formation of the modern psyche: "Many of the features we have taken for granted in thought and expression . . . have come into being because of the resources which the technology of writing makes available to human consciousness" (1). Extensive and wide-ranging childhood reading shaped the consciousness of both writers so deeply that each includes in his memoir at least one dramatic scene in which reading is presented as a life-changing epiphany.

It is their early childhood reading—promiscuous reading, reading without borders—that led both authors to later object to the segregation of literature into balkanized ethnic ghettoes. At the same time, each grapples with the realization that the mainstream print culture that they have been so heavily shaped by is often quite alien to their experience. "My reading had created a vast sense of distance between me and the world in which I lived," laments Wright. Rodriguez finds himself interpreting the experiences of his Mexican American life through the writings of British authors, as so many Americans do, such as Spenser, Shakespeare, Dickens, and Lawrence (253). Ultimately, however, both Wright and Rodriguez demonstrate that we cannot understand ethnic identity without also considering the role of mainstream print culture in forging ethnic consciousness. Conversely, their joint resolve that their texts not be viewed as ethnic literature conceived as apart from American literature—or considered less universal than nonethnic texts—affirms their shared understanding of mainstream print culture as the primary vehicle for relaying ethnic experience and culture to others.

Prose Style

Somewhat related to the question of literary influences is the matter of prose style. The difference in writing styles between Wright and Rodriguez is striking. Wright sculpted his prose for heightened emotional impact. In writing as he did, he hoped to motivate readers to social change. "Richard Wright has had but one story to tell," wrote his friend Horace Cayton. "That story is how it *feels* to be a Negro in the United States" (184, emphasis in the original). This is precisely the story offered in *Black Boy*, in which Wright describes the emotional and psychological reality of being black in order to tell us about himself. Wright's obsession with his "one story" partly determined his prose style. His was a passion-based aesthetics, an aesthetics Cayton described as writing on a "sea of emotion" (185).

Most writers do not write this way, however, and literary judgments of his prose have not always been kind to him. Baldwin and Ellison, for instance, rebelled against Wright's style of writing, and Baldwin disparaged Wright's most famous book, *Native Son*, as "Everybody's Protest Novel" (the title of what might well be Baldwin's most famous essay) by comparing it with *Uncle Tom's Cabin* (*Notes of a Native Son* 13–23). Baldwin's angle of attack is telling, in that it plays on the assumption that social protest literature, specifically that dealing with racial subject matter, is antithetical to literary merit. A one-dimensional focus on either the racial content or the social message of ethnic fiction, alas, can lead to egregious "underreading," as Sue Kim argues (94). Seconding this judgment, Sue-Im Lee singles out *Native Son* as "one of the best-known cases in which a work's stature in the canon of American literature is counterbalanced by questions about its artistic merit" (205). Despite invoking the false dichotomy between protest literature and literary writing, however, Baldwin's harsh judgment really boils down to the much more basic matter of a difference of aesthetic preferences. Whereas Wright compounded expressionistic affect and literary naturalism into emotionally charged message literature, Baldwin cultivated a lyrical writing style that eschewed naturalism and won the praise of critics as literary preferences shifted even further away from sentimentality of any kind. Similarly, Ellison's 1952 novel, *Invisible Man*, was hailed not only for its lyricism, but also for its subtlety and humor—traits less abundant in Wright's work. To many readers, Wright's style seems crude in comparison.

Many depreciate the literary value of Wright's prose, but I argue that it accomplishes exactly what its author intended: transporting readers into the psychological states of the text's ethnic protagonist, and rendering ethnic experience at the most visceral levels. As is clear from reading his essay "How 'Bigger' Was Born," Wright self-consciously strove to write this way. Few books hit a reader between the eyes like *Native Son* does, and the expressive power of *Black Boy* is testament to Wright's ability to conjure up intense emotional experience through his prose.

Rodriguez is also celebrated for the poignancy of his prose but, in contrast to Wright's reputation for crudely hewn raw emotions, Rodriguez is known as a prose stylist. Where Wright is criticized for his prose, Rodriguez is almost universally commended. Even those who most attack what they take to be the substance of his arguments praise Rodriguez's masterful writing style. Rodriguez self-consciously writes for readers with a "long education," a characterization that grows more pronounced in each subsequent collection of essays, if judging by the density of cultured allusions, unexplained references, and literary experimentation (*Hunger* 182). Known principally as an essayist, Rodriguez is often compared with James Baldwin, whose scintillating essays form the bedrock of his literary reputation. Like Baldwin's, Rodriguez's rhetorical skills are particularly formidable. Despite his contrarian posturing and rhetorical techniques, however, Rodriguez's stance on any particular topic or issue is not always clear. He is more often playful and reflective than direct and in earnest. In his essay "Faulkner and Desegregation," Baldwin is unequivocal in criticizing what he calls Faulkner's "middle of the road" stance on desegregation (*Nobody Knows My Name* 120). In contrast, even Rodriguez's most polemical essays remain open-ended and shot through with irony and paradox: "The loss implies the gain" (*Hunger* 27); "The scholarship boy is a very bad student" (67).

A Bridge of Words

Richard Wright ends his autobiography with a somber reflection on his alienation from a society that sees only his race: "I wanted to build a bridge of words between me and that world outside, that world which was so distant and elusive that it seemed unreal" (384). Tempering Wright's despair is a hopeful message about forging social connections with others through his writing, with the book in his reader's hands standing as a monument to the power of language, the narrative reality that it engenders, and of ethnic autobiography as a genre.

Through that bridge of words, Wright presents a narrative of the ethnic self while interrogating existing racial narratives. This double gesture is similarly strong in the autobiographical writing of Richard Rodriguez, and is one of the central subjects of *Autobiography in Black and Brown*. Specific to their prose style, each author has an aesthetic vision that operates in tandem with the social engagement of their texts. As we have seen, however, the stark contrast between their literary aesthetics—their autobiographical poetics—and the divergence of the sociohistorical context in which each was writing can obscure these fundamental commonalities.

Reading Wright is like watching a horror film, each reader gripped in the same stark emotions of terror and revulsion. Reading Rodriguez is more like gazing in a mirror, each reader seeing in the reflection either an affirmation or the abnegation of the emotions and sentiments that she or he brings to the text. Rodriguez's rhetorical choreography is intertwined with his challenging prose style, and the two taken together play a substantial role in the phenomena of polarized reader response to his texts. The playful prose and irreverent posturing of Rodriguez as a thinker and cultural commentator was familiar to rhetoric, composition, and literary scholars accustomed to ironic posturing and rhetorical capering in the writings of postmodern theorists such as Jacques Derrida and Michel Foucault. Chicano (not yet Chicana/o) scholars in the 1970s and 1980s, however, saw before them only the earnest image of a reactionary, dyed-in-the-wool conservative ideologue. This double image of Rodriguez's texts at least partly explains the perceived 2002 inversion, in *Brown*, of Rodriguez's former views. The liberal and progressive underpinnings of *Brown* came as a surprise to many of Rodriguez's former critics, raising questions about the extent to which Rodriguez had reversed his position on earlier views.

In chapter 3, which is devoted to *Hunger of Memory*, I argue that though Rodriguez opened the door to a reconsideration of his body of work—by qualifying, in *Brown*, that the mainstream culture that one assimilates to is an irredeemably brown, culturally miscegenated one—what changed was less the substrate philosophy of his thought and more the political and ideological interpretive lenses through which his text was read. This shift in hermeneutic approaches to Rodriguez's third text is a paradigm shift of Kuhnian proportions: we must now reread Rodriguez's earlier texts in the light of illuminating facets of the Rodriguez Weltanschauung unveiled in *Brown*.

What makes a clearer conception of Rodriguez's underlying thought such a fraught and challenging enterprise is also what makes his exploration of ethnic identity so appealing: his full embrace of the complexity and contradictions of identity—personal yet relational, private yet socially embedded, individual yet contingent on society. It is thus inevitable that paradoxes and ambiguities should emerge as a hallmark of Rodriguez's oeuvre. Likewise, though Rodriguez is often taken to task for invoking binary oppositions (such as private-public and individual-society in *Hunger of Memory*), it is Rodriguez who first complicates and undermines those same binaries: "The bilingualists insist that a student should be reminded of his difference from others in mass society, his heritage. . . . [but it is] in public [that] full individuality is achieved, paradoxically, by those who are able to consider themselves members of the crowd" (*Hunger* 27). The human capacity to hew a personal identity out of such contradictions is embodied in Rodriguez's metaphor of cultural miscegenation. Not only do no pure cultures with which one can exclusively identify exist, but the self is always a brown self: "Brown confuses. Brown forms at the borders of contradiction" (*Brown* xi). Ultimately, Rodriguez concludes that we cannot reconcile the contradictions of our lives: "The tension I have come to depend upon. That is what I mean by brown. The answer is I cannot reconcile" (*Brown* 224).

Though differing in their approaches, Wright and Rodriguez both seek to secure greater agency for ethnic subjects while holding up an interrelational and intersubjective model of ethnic self and community: Wright hoping to overcome his existential alienation by trying "to build a bridge of words between me and the world outside," and Rodriguez insisting that "individualism is a communally-derived value" (*Black Boy* 384; *Brown* 200). Despite a profound concern with optimizing personal agency, both authors also portray the ethnic self as embedded in social relationships—as a relational self. Each also grapples with the challenge of maintaining an equilibrium that balances readerly expectations of ethnic representativeness with an accurate reflection of their own lives. Richard Wright's attempt to do just that leads him to write a hybrid autobiography, and it is to that topic that we turn in the next chapter.

1

Autobiographical Double Consciousness
The Ethnic Self as Representative Man in Richard Wright's Hybrid Autobiography

Midway through *Black Boy*, Richard Wright recounts working as a porter in a clothing store and being asked by the boss's son, "Why don't you laugh and talk like the other niggers?" (182).[1] This question recapitulates, rather crassly, much of the criticism aimed at Wright on the release of *Black Boy*. Implicit behind the question is the assumption that Wright is—and should be—representative of the race.

His proxy employer finds Wright's response to the query unsatisfactory, and Wright is summarily dismissed. What follows is a series of very short-lived jobs. Wright is baffled; he cannot figure out what he is doing wrong. The answer comes from an old classmate, Griggs:

"Do you want to get killed?" he asked me.
 "Hell, no!"
 "Then, for God's sake, learn how to live in the South!"
 "What do you mean?" I demanded. "Let white people tell me that. Why should you?"
 "See?" he said triumphantly, pointing his finger at me. "There it is, now! It's in your face. You won't let people tell you things. You rush too much. I'm trying to help you and you won't let me." He paused and looked about; the streets were filled with white people. He spoke to me in a low, full tone. "Dick, look, you're black, black, *black*, see? Can't you understand that?"

> . . .
>
> "I'm teaching you how to get out of white people's way," he said.
>
> I looked at the people who had come out of the store; yes, they were *white*, but I had not noticed it. (*Black Boy* 183–84, emphasis in the original)

Wright's choosing to present the conversation in dialogue form, with the characters' spoken words all in the present tense, puts the reader in the moment. It is 1925 in Jackson, Mississippi. Wright has only recently graduated, as junior high school valedictorian at the age of sixteen, but his social schooling is incomplete until he learns that he can never completely evade the kinds of racial performance that others expect from him.

He must not, at risk of personal injury, comport as an individual. He is to perform a particular racial role, a role in which he must act as if accepting the fiction that he is less than human:

> What Griggs was saying was true, but it was simply utterly impossible for me to calculate, to scheme, to act, to plot all the time. I would remember to dissemble for short periods, then I would forget and act straight and human again, not with the desire to harm anybody, but merely forgetting the artificial status of race and class. It was the same with whites as with blacks; it was my way with everybody. (*Black Boy* 185)

Wright's choice of diction in this passage is revealing. To act as an individual and to treat others likewise is to act human. To act out a racial role, to dissemble, is implicitly subhuman.

What Wright wants his readers to know is that when racial narratives are too narrowly scripted, asking individuals to perform as members of a particular racial group is asking them to dissemble. He will discover this to be as true of himself growing up in the South as it is of himself writing books that will be read as representative of black culture and black experience. The trope of dissembling is so central that Timothy Dow Adams concludes that it is the medium by which Wright represents himself: "In *Black Boy*, Wright creates a version of himself whose metaphor for survival and for sustenance is falsehood" (83). Earlier critics read Wright's representation of himself and of black culture less figuratively. Exemplary of such criticism is the first sentence of W. E. B. Du Bois's review of *Black Boy* in the *New York Herald*

Tribune Weekly Book Review, which indicts Wright for dissembling: "This book tells a harsh and forbidding story and makes one wonder just exactly what its relation to truth is" (132).

Du Bois's barbed criticism, as with much of the initial reception of the autobiography by the black community, reflected a reaction against Wright's depiction of a collective body of black selves whose culture, identity, and consciousness had been warped by racism. *Black Boy*'s relation to truth is that it is a representation of reality, a particular interpretation of black experience in amalgamation with Wright's experiences. It is a representation self-consciously aware of its status as racially representative that at the same time seeks to represent a single life. Not only do readers read a black author's autobiography as racially representative, racial relations and the representational expectations imposed on black subjects are also so much a part of personal experience that they become integral to one's story. So, although ostensibly telling the story of one life only, Wright's personal autobiography also had to be, in part, a collective one. Rather than reject the onus of depicting the self as significantly representative of the minority group, Wright embraces it, capitalizing on expectations of racial representativeness as a tool for launching a trenchant racial critique.

The first of two on Wright's autobiography, this chapter explores the rationale for and implications of writing *Black Boy* as an autobiographical double narrative: telling the story of one's own life while figuring the self as representative of the ethnic group. Aware that his autobiography will be read as racially representative, Wright tries simultaneously to tell the story of his own exceptional life and to depict his protagonist as a representative black man, or "black boy." In doing so Wright pushes the boundaries of the genre and raises skepticism about the authenticity of the narrative. W. E. B. Du Bois, whose description of "double consciousness" is embodied by Wright, tagged *Black Boy* as "fiction or fictionalized biography." Many of the incidents described in the book did not happen to Wright, and yet the book had been marketed as autobiography. What Wright had actually written was a hybrid of personal autobiography and folk history, the term in the subtitle of his then most recent book, *12 Million Black Voices: A Folk History of the Negro in the United States* (1941). On one level, *Black Boy* could be described as a collective autobiography—though not collectively written—or a *testimonio*, bearing witness to racial conditions in the South. Wright's aesthetic commitment to emotional truth demands that his autobiography also be a partly collective one because the traumatic racial experiences of all those similarly situated in a racist society so affect his life that he has to tell his readers about the experiences of others to tell them about himself.

A DISMAL RECEPTION: NAVIGATING THE MINEFIELD BETWEEN REPRESENTATIONAL AND REPRESENTATIVE

As early as 1940, Wright's agent, Paul Reynolds, had suggested that he consider writing an autobiography.[2] Initially Wright balked. Still in his early thirties, he felt too young to write an autobiography. Reynolds, however, had been impressed with the power of Wright's 1937 essay, "The Ethics of Living Jim Crow, an Autobiographical Sketch."[3] Wright was the most renowned black writer in America. If he wrote an autobiography it would be sure to sell.

Wright's literary fame had only recently been secured with the publication of *Native Son* as a Book-of-the-Month Club selection in March 1940. By 1938, winning *Story* magazine's writing competition and subsequently securing the publication of *Uncle Tom's Children*, a collection of short stories set in Mississippi, had brought him some acclaim in literary circles. This, though, paled in comparison to the public reception of *Native Son*. Wright had packed everything he had into that novel, as if out of fear that he might not get a second chance to tell hard-hitting truths about American racial relations. Like the symbolic ringing alarm with which the novel opens, Wright wanted to wake white America up to the effects of racism on the black psyche. He wanted to show white readers that they were not safe from the rebellious violence that racism could engender.

Despite immediate calls for an autobiography following the runaway success of *Native Son*, *Black Boy* was not published until 1945. It, too, was a Book-of-the-Month Club selection, and an even bigger commercial success than *Native Son* had been. But the book also provoked considerable criticism. First was the problem of genre. W. E. B. Du Bois, as mentioned, had tagged *Black Boy* in his *Herald Tribune* review as "fiction or fictionalized biography" (132). The fictionalized feel stemmed in part from Wright's intention to produce a hybrid autobiography: part personal autobiography and part folk history, a collective testimonio against racial oppression. If the book was also the folk history of a culture, however, the portrayal of that culture was puzzlingly unsympathetic. Du Bois remarked scornfully that "the Negroes whom he paints have almost no redeeming qualities" (132).

That the Book-of-the-Month Club had adopted the book—requiring the excision of the entire second half of the book before they would do so—made it clear who the book was written for: mainstream American readers. But it wasn't clear who Wright was writing about. As negative criticism of the book revealed, his portrayal of other African Americans and the culture they shared was by no means recognizable to all American blacks. Yet mainstream readers were interested in the book largely because they saw Wright and his autobiography as representative. Reviewers such as R. L. Duffus, writing in the *New York Times Book Review*, felt it imperative to warn readers explicitly that "Mr. Wright does not, in fact, speak for all Southern Negroes" (134).

Wright had incurred the wrath of other blacks, particularly middle-class blacks, by painting a dismal picture of black culture. The magnitude of the offense was all the greater for his de facto appointment, following *Native Son*'s success, as a spokesperson for the race. Moreover, Wright was aware that his black characters would be considered racially representative. That he hoped to raise sympathy for the plight of blacks in America while portraying African American characters so unsympathetically in his autobiography seems, at first blush, an irreconcilable contradiction. In what follows, I address those and other contradictions inherent not only in *Black Boy* but also to ethnic autobiography as a genre. The criticisms leveled at *Black Boy* illuminate some of the narrative paradoxes facing other ethnic writers, among whom Richard Rodriguez is a prime example. Wright simply could not resolve the inherent contradictions of telling his story and simultaneously having that story read as representative of an entire race.[4] In a later chapter, I question the need to reconcile those contradictions. In this chapter, I emphasize just how successful Wright's narrative is given his political, aesthetic, and truth-telling objectives in writing it.

PORTRAIT OF THE ARTIST AS A HOMICIDAL MANIAC

What Wright hoped to do in *Black Boy* was the same thing that he had tried to do in *Native Son*. That is, he wanted to make a statement about race, in hopes of changing racial relations in America. Wright's first biographer, Constance Webb, argues that Wright's foremost literary objective was to address and agitate for a solution to "the Negro problem," and that he saw writing the story of his life primarily as a vehicle to such ends:

> And he would try to make a statement—could he do it? Using portions of his own childhood, stories told him by friends, things he had observed happening to others, he would write an 'autobiography'.... It would be autobiographical but it would be more than that; he would use himself as a symbol of all the brutality and cruelty wreaked upon the black man by the Southern environment. (205)

Substituting *Bigger* for *himself* in the last sentence also offers an accurate description of what Wright had done in *Native Son*. Moreover, *Native Son* is a narrative brimming with material drawn from Wright's life. Not all of his characters were representatives of an abstraction; they were sometimes based on people he had known or had knowledge of. Although writing in his essay "How 'Bigger' Was Born" that Bigger Thomas was a composite character, Wright had borrowed the name whole cloth from a bully he had worked with in a Jackson brickyard when he was fourteen (Rowley 29). As Wright began writing *Native Son*, another real-life Bigger, Robert Nixon, was arrested in Chicago for a murder committed during an attempted robbery. Wright followed the trial closely, asking his friend Margaret Walker to send him newspaper clippings. Elements of the Nixon case and the general racial hysteria surrounding it—the victim had been white—were worked into the novel, Wright fictionalizing some of the lurid accounts offered in the Chicago papers.

Although the name of the communist lawyer, Max, is a clear allusion to Karl Marx, and thus rather abstractly to the ideas of Marxism, Mary Dalton was, like Bigger, the name of a living person, an active member of the Communist Party who had once been put on trial for insurrection (Rowley 155).[5] Jan Erlone's name is an homage to Jan Wittenber, a white member of the John Reed Club, who stood alone—on which *Erlone* is a pun—among the Chicago communists as possessing any depth of humanity or understanding (Webb 403). Conversely, Max fairly represents the Communist Party as Wright had known it in Chicago and New York: sentimentalizing blacks as modern noble savages while blinded to the race problem by abstract theories limited to a strictly class-based explanation of injustice and inequality in society.

Other characters and historical events were also borrowed from real life, many of which lent the novel a greater sense of realism, as if a piece of true-crime reportage rather than fiction. Because not everyone would pick up on the allusions to real people and events, some of these risked coming off as gratuitous, written into the text as either an inside joke or out of a lack of imagination. Nevertheless, it could be argued that incorporating the Nixon case and naming a character Mary Dalton encouraged readers to make parallels between the characters and real people. It made the novel seem more like something that could really happen, an authentic depiction of the effects of racism and the psychological trauma and violence it could give rise to.

Even had Wright not so undisguisedly borrowed from real life, comparisons with his life were almost inevitable. Until the killing begins, the novel can easily be read as autobiographical. It is an association readers often make, conflating the narrator or central protagonist with the author. So strong are externally imposed identifications by race, gender, age, and geography—and so conditioned are readers to reading the text with the grain of the author's social identity—that authors who do not want to be confused with the narrator or main character in their fiction frequently find that the safest way to guard against this is to assign the narrator or character a different race or gender than the author's.

Rather than steering clear of such identifications, Wright invites them by hewing closely to the autobiographical even in his fiction. "All writing is a secret form of autobiography," Wright said, and all of his novels have a touch of the autobiographical to them, particularly regarding race and place (Rowley 410). His first published book, *Uncle Tom's Children*, is set in Mississippi, linking the young male characters (such as Big Boy, the central character of the leading story) to Wright by geography. Also semiautobiographical is Jake Jackson, who appears in *Lawd Today*—written before *Native Son* but published only posthumously in 1963—as a Chicago postal worker, a job that Wright once depended on, though he later turned down a much-coveted permanent position to move to New York in hopes of advancing his writing career. Cross Damon, the existentialist hero of *The Outsider*, is caught between the communists and the white police. When the novel appeared in 1953, his first novel in thirteen years, Wright had long since quit the Communist Party, though he was, ironically, still hounded by the Federal Bureau of Investigation (FBI) and other government organizations for his communist sympathies.[6] Bookending this partial list of autobiographical elements in Wright's fiction is *The Long Dream*, the last novel published in Wright's lifetime. The novel begins in Mississippi and ends with its main character, Fishbelly, fleeing an intolerably racist America for Paris, as Wright had done in 1946.

As for Bigger Thomas, Wright fueled association of himself with his violent character by playing the leading role in the 1951 film version of *Native Son*. Even without the film, however, the prerequisites for associating Bigger with Wright are already there: he is a black male from Chicago and the story is told from his point of view. To shake this association would have taken nothing short of Wright's being white or for readers to think that he was white.

Rather than distance himself from Bigger, as Dan McCall argues, Wright would try to put as much of himself—his darker sides, his own latent rage—into the character as he could: "[T]he creation of Bigger Thomas, for Richard Wright, was to get at the psychopath in himself, his twisted roots and frantic edges" (78). Although critical of reinforcing the stereotype of the "angry black man," James Baldwin would write in the essay "Many Thousands Gone" that "no American Negro exists who does not have his private Bigger Thomas living in his skull" (42). To Wright, the confession may have felt like an ironic commentary, given Baldwin's virulent attack on him—as the wounded Wright perceived it—in this and an earlier essay, "Everybody's Protest Novel," the first essay, as it turns out, that Baldwin wrote on arriving in Paris in 1949. Many critics, including Baldwin, saw Baldwin's scathing criticisms as acting out what Harold Bloom would surely describe as a proxy or figurative slaying of his literary father. In the essay, Baldwin criticized Wright for denying Bigger his humanity. That, however, is precisely the point of *Native Son*, a work of literary naturalism in which Bigger serves as an apt metaphor for the dehumanizing effects of a racist environment, its psychic toll, and the twofold violence—coercive repression, and aggressive rebellion against it—that it fosters.

Monstrous creation that he was, Bigger—having been imbued with more than a few autobiographical characteristics and associations—would forever be seen as, in some respects, Wright's alter ego. Indeed, it is also fairly safe to say that all of Wright's central male protagonists can be seen as alter egos on one level or another, but doing so only places more of a burden on critics to distinguish between the historical author and his fictionalized characters.

A HYBRID AUTOBIOGRAPHY

Coloring his fiction with autobiographical elements contributed to its potency, but fictionalizing an autobiography was a different thing altogether. *Black Boy* was to be presented as autobiographical whether Wright called it an autobiography or not, and readers expect works in the genre to adhere closely to historical and biographical facts. A certain amount of fictionalizing must necessarily go into shaping one's memories and experience into a compelling narrative, and it is understood that few authors are going tell the unvarnished truth if it makes them look bad—unless doing so for some larger dramatic purpose, or because sensational self-revelation sells books. From the reader's perspective, however, the limits of fictionalizing autobiography are much more rigid and clearly drawn than when an author incorporates elements of the self into his or her fiction. In previous work, Wright had always blurred the lines between autobiography and fiction, but now he would be doing so within the framework of a different genre—one dictated by the demands of nonfiction. Regardless of Wright's personal sense of how much he could experiment, readers would bring certain expectations to the text. Those expecting a comprehensive history of the author's life were to be disappointed. Not only did Wright withhold an adequate account of the development of, in James Joyce's words, "the artist as a young man," he also claimed to experience incidents he had not experienced directly.

Despite its being a gross violation of the autobiographical pact, Wright felt justified in doing this as long as the incidents happened, or could have happened, to another black man in Mississippi.[7] To him, blurring the lines between fact and fiction in his autobiography seemed reasonable if by doing so he could dramatize the reality of racial inequality and the psychological effects of a racist environment. In trying to transform this particular kind of folk history into the story of his life, however, Wright ended up writing scenes that frequently struck readers as implausible. Not only did the narrator's naïve reactions often seem extreme or largely unmotivated, the depiction of his family was also so unsympathetic that it defied belief rather than suspended disbelief. The protagonist's feigned innocence and ignorance further strained credulity.[8] Such moments gave some readers pause, but if the troubling description of a black culture deformed by prejudice seemed excessive, and the sketchy profile of a young black boy who would go on to become a great author seemed insufficient, the psychological depiction of the conditions under which blacks in the South lived was convincing enough. Moreover, because no existing biographies of Wright were available to separate the purely fictional from faithful retellings of his life, it was hard to pin him down on any particular misrepresentation: "Nothing that Richard Wright says is in itself unbelievable or impossible: it is the total picture that is not convincing" (Du Bois 133).

Du Bois's disparaging assessment of the book would almost certainly have been less critical had he, proleptically, had the benefit of Adams's insightful chapter on *Black Boy*. For, as Adams makes clear, *Black Boy* is bipartite not only in structure—divided between life in the South and life in the North—but also in narrative intent. In telling his story, Wright hoped also to turn reader expectations about the racial representativeness of the narrative's protagonist into a critique of racism. Turning the double bind of racial profiling into a double narrative, however, risks confusing readers about the referent of ethnic autobiography. Against these difficulties, what failed to convince Du Bois is ultimately convincing as reinterpreted by Adams. Namely, that Wright's narrative is realistic in that it strives to represent himself while simultaneously representing himself as a particular image of disenfranchised black youth:

> Olney's idea that the central figure be treated as a single person referred to as "black boy," a literary character representing the actual author both as child and as an adult—the famous writer imagining himself as representative of inarticulate black children—is finally convincing. That seems to be what Richard Wright meant to do, what he said he had done, and what he did. (Adams 74)

Critical to this analysis is James Olney's distinction between the protagonist, "black boy," and the book's author, Richard Wright.[9] Adams notes the difficulty Wright had in reconciling the two figures—and their dissimilar stories—as he wrote his autobiography:

> Although he meant the work to be a collective autobiography, a personalized record of countless black Americans growing up with a personal history of hunger, deprivation, and constant racism, he seems to have realized as he wrote that his own life was not a very characteristic one and that he was focusing as much on his particular problems as on a typical black childhood. (69–70)

Other ethnic writers—among whom Richard Rodriguez is a conspicuous example—resist characterizing themselves as representative. Wright aspires to do just the opposite: to speak on behalf of those for whom he is seen as representative.

THE SELF AS SOCIOLOGICAL DOCUMENT

The hybrid autobiography that *Black Boy* would become had its genesis in Wright's earlier texts, his two works of fiction and a lesser-known third book. This last was nonfiction. Rather than writing his autobiography when the idea was first suggested to him by his agent in 1940, Wright began work on *12 Million Black Voices*. His text would accompany documentary photographs taken by Farm Security Administration photographers during the Great Depression and selected by Edwin Rosskam. Wright's indictment of systemic racism in both the rural South and the urban North was so scathing that it prompted J. Edgar Hoover to send a sedition memo to the New York office of the FBI in 1942, ordering an investigation of Wright and his other books.[10] Wright would be under constant surveillance from one intelligence organization or another for the rest of his life (Rowley 275-76).

12 Million Black Voices is written in the first-person plural—"us black folk" (10). The book could very well be considered, as Adams has suggested, the other half of Wright's autobiography: "Although critics often point to Wright's first novel, *Native Son* (1940), as the other half of *Black Boy*, another model for this autobiographical work was his more recently completed *Twelve Million Black Voices*" (72). Moreover, Adams continues,

> Writing *Black Boy* in the spirit of folk history seemed a reasonable thing to do, and Wright apparently saw no hypocrisy in omitting personal details that did not contribute to what he was simultaneously thinking of as his own story and the story of millions of others. Wright's claim to be composing the autobiography of a generic black child is reinforced by the narrator's particular reaction to racism. (72)

In writing his autobiography, that is, Wright would merge the fictionalizing aesthetics of *Native Son* with the first-person-plural perspective of *12 Million Black Voices*.

Whatever Wright's larger aims in doing so, many of those who knew him personally did not see the value of fictionalizing aspects of his autobiography. "Some members of his family said he was telling lies, tall tales, and just making up stories," reported one of Wright's biographers (Walker 189).[11] Margaret Walker met with members of Wright's family in Natchez, Mississippi, and dutifully reported their thoughts about the historical accuracy of *Black Boy*.

Walker defends the fabrication of incidents in the autobiography, however, writing that

> although they may be embroidered and embellished and even exaggerated, they are *truth as Wright chooses to render truth.* This is not a book of purely factual and verifiable incidents. Wright has used the method of fiction, the same that he used in the stories of *Uncle Tom's Children*, the novel *Native Son*, and to a certain extent in the folk history *Twelve Million Black Voices*. *Black Boy* is an ingenious blending of fact and fiction, how much it contains of each we can never be sure. ... (190, emphasis in the original)

Walker's assessment is not at all controversial, though other claims and insinuations in her biography are. The consensus among Wright critics is fairly strong on this point: the autobiography is significantly fictionalized.

Not everyone agrees as to whether Wright's fictionalizing in the autobiography is defensible. Not everyone reads *Black Boy* as part folk history. The book's initial reception traced battle lines that continue to reflect reader responses to the text. Moved by the power of Wright's story, many critics suppressed their objections to scenes and depictions that strained credulity when reading the book as straight autobiography. If read as, in part, the social history of a specific place and time, then moments in *Black Boy* that just did not ring true might become pitch-perfect. The book's 1945 subtitle, "A Record of Childhood and Youth," gestured in this direction—eschewing titular claims that the book was an autobiography of one life only. *Black Boy* is Richard Wright's story, but the narrative of the ethnic self presented is that of an irreducibly social self.

◆

Thinking of *Black Boy* as a personal autobiography does not diminish its power as part folk history. In fact, much of its narrative power comes precisely from the ways in which the autobiography is able, using the first person, to indict the oppression of an entire race. Not only does the writing of *Black Boy* as partly collective autobiography serve this purpose, but doing so is indispensable to Wright's being able to tell his story.

One of the explicit messages of *Black Boy* is that many of the formative experiences that shape our thoughts and actions are not experienced first-hand. For Wright, the most salient way in which this principle played out was in his being a member of a racial group in a society divided hierarchically along racial lines. Some criticized Wright for an obsession with lynching—all but unheard of in Northern experience, and seemingly a thing of the past. Southerners, however, both white and black, knew that lynching a single black man was enough to strike terror into the hearts of all blacks. Although the effect of Wright's lynching scenes is too powerful to say that they are only metaphors, it can be said that they double as metaphors for the myriad ways in which individual identity bears the tincture of collective concerns. Rather than articulate this in abstract language, or soliloquizing in first-person narration, Wright tries to show the reader what racial terror was like:

> "You've heard, haven't you?" he asked.
> About what?"
> "My brother, Bob?"
> "No, what happened?"
> Ned began to weep softly.
> "They killed him," he managed to say.
> "The white folks?" I asked in a whisper, guessing.
> . . .
> What I had heard altered the look of the world, induced in me a temporary paralysis of will and impulse. The penalty of death awaited me if I made a false move and I wondered if it was worth-while to make any move at all. The things that influenced my conduct as a Negro did not have to happen to me directly; I needed but to hear of them to feel their full effects in the deepest layers of my consciousness. (*Black Boy* 171–72)

The first line of dialogue also serves to interrogate the reader: You've heard, have you not, of how narratives of race are enforced with violence? You know, do you not, that a part of the psyche is forged in the furnace of race relations?

To tell the reader about himself, Wright must first tell the reader about Bob. That he hardly knew Bob did not matter. What mattered was that Bob had been black, and he had been killed by whites for sleeping with a white woman. Such murders were a threat directed against all black men, and used by one social group to control another through fear and intimidation. Putting Bob's story in his own autobiography not only tells us about Richard Wright, and how such events affected "the deepest layers of [his] consciousness," but also bears witness to the injustices and psychological terror inflicted on an entire race.

Lionel Trilling, writing in the *Nation*, proposed that an African American autobiography in 1945 might have to speak for and about much more than just the autonomous self: "Perhaps a Negro's autobiography must always first appear under the aspect of sociology—a fact that is in itself a sociological component—and 'Black Boy' has its importance as a 'document,' a precise and no doubt largely typical account of Negro life in Mississippi" (Reilly 151). Trilling articulates the expectation that ethnic writers produce representative texts. He finds the typicality of the account believable. His appraisal also intimates that the task of being representative and documenting the Negro condition, its raison d'être, so overshadows other concerns that not much else of "importance"—aesthetic objectives and accomplishments, it is suggested, paling in importance to sociological ones—remains.

If *Black Boy* is part sociological document, its portrayal of "Negro life in Mississippi" is far from an admiring one:

(After I had outlived the shocks of childhood, after the habit of reflection had been born in me, I used to mull over the strange absence of real kindness in Negroes, how unstable was our tenderness, how lacking in genuine passion we were, how void of great hope, how timid our joy, how bare our traditions, how hollow our memories, how lacking we were in those tangible sentiments that bind man to man, and how shallow even our despair. After I had learned other ways of life I used to brood upon the unconscious irony of those who felt that Negroes led so passional an existence! I saw that what had been taken for our emotional strength was our negative confusions, our flights, our fears, our frenzy under pressure.

(Whenever I thought of the essential bleakness of black life in America, I knew that Negroes had never been allowed to catch the full spirit of Western civilization, that they lived somehow in it but not of it. And when I brooded upon the cultural barrenness of black life, I wondered if clean, positive tenderness, love, honor, loyalty, and the capacity to remember were native with man. I asked myself if these human qualities were not fostered, won, struggled and suffered for, preserved in ritual from one generation to another.) (37)

Wright's criticisms of black culture are unsparing. As if in apology for the harshness of the critique, these two paragraphs are set off by parentheses. Criticism is anticipated, and the passage—though rendered as a parenthetical aside—does not fail to provoke it. Baldwin seems to refer directly to this passage when lamenting in his essay "Many Thousands Gone" that "it is this climate, common to most Negro protest novels, which has led us all to believe that in Negro life there exists no tradition, no field of manners, no possibility of ritual or intercourse" (35–36).

At first, Wright's infamous parenthetical aside seems to appear incongruously: between his leaving the Memphis orphanage where his mother had left him while she was ill and his stopping over at his grandmother's house in Jackson, Mississippi. A second reading, however, suggests that the context in which the passage appears is significant to any interpretation of it: the earlier scene showcases Wright's displeasure over having been humiliated and forced to perform a social ritual out of conformity rather than as a genuine gesture, and suggests self-criticism of his own crude behavior in that environment. When leaving the orphanage, the young Wright is so excited that he forgets to shake hands and bid farewell to the other children: "My mother scolded me for my thoughtlessness and bade me say good-bye to them.... In shaking hands I was doing something that I was to do countless times in the years to come: acting in conformity with what others expected of me even though, by the very nature and form of my life, I did not and could not share their spirit" (*Black Boy* 37). Thus, from the perspective of those who would regard a proper farewell as basic civility, Wright's comments about "the strange absence of real kindness in Negroes" are also aimed at himself. Although he frames the two paragraphs as a criticism of mindless conformity, in mentioning his own thoughtlessness Wright is deflecting the harshness of his cultural criticism by casting himself as culpable.

That is not to say that he considers himself equally culpable. In scene after scene, the protagonist of *Black Boy* emerges as lone exception to the abject state of black culture as he depicts it, whereas the actions and attitudes of his peers seem only to confirm negative stereotypes of the race. Wright claims that he is the last to steal while at the Jackson hotel, doing so only reluctantly because the other boys call him a "dumb nigger" for abstaining (*Black Boy*

199). In any conflict with his family, Wright depicts himself as naïvely innocent. References to his early sexual experiences are expunged, though he indicts the promiscuous sexuality of others for causing the epidemic of gonorrhea afflicting his friends and neighbors. Wright's larger aim is to indict Jim Crow, but these cultural characterizations are also grist for the Jim Crow mill, which grinds them into fixed racial narratives.

Only in part 2 of the autobiography, when "black boy" has become an adult, will Wright make any mention of his sex life.[12] Wright was a known philanderer, and Margaret Walker reports being shocked by his "pungent epithets" when first becoming acquainted with him (72). Always—whether it involves gambling, cursing, family relationships, or sexual escapades—he sees himself as somehow a notch above the degenerate lifestyle he depicts.[13] Wright is with them, but not among them: "Curses and sex stories sounded round the clock and blue smoke choked the air. I would sit listening for hours, wondering how on earth they could laugh so freely, trying to grasp the miracle that gave their debased lives the semblance of a human existence" (*Black Boy* 197–98).

It is easy to see how it was the idea of *Black Boy* as sociological documentation, to borrow and adapt Trilling's term, that bothered Du Bois the most. In his review of the book, he rebukes Wright for sweeping generalizations about the character of "the whole Negro race!" (133). "Not only is there this misjudgment of black folk and the difficult repulsive characters among them that he is thrown with," Du Bois continues, "but the same thing takes place with white folk. There is not a single broad-minded, open-hearted white person in his book" (133). If ethnic literature were invariably ethnographic and sociological, then this particular piece of social documentation would be egregiously inaccurate and misrepresentative.

BLACK BOY AS PROTEST LITERATURE: USING LIES TO TELL THE TRUTH

Wright's focus on the dark side of human nature and the dysfunctional side of social relationships, Du Bois's indictment seemed to suggest, put him at cross-purposes with his overall goal of telling the truth about race. Wright's critique could hardly be effective if it was not honest in its depiction of the full spectrum of blacks, black culture, and race relationships. By eschewing inclusion of the positive aspects of black family and community, Wright was not only diminishing the realism of his account, but he was also undermining his credibility to speak for the oppressed "black boys" with which the title identified him. Middle-class blacks and those most concerned with projecting a positive image of the race as a whole felt particularly tarred by the broad brush with which Wright painted them.

Given the many demerits to telling his autobiography as he did, it seems a mystery that Wright would make the narrative choices he did. By partially turning an autobiography into a folk history, he risked ending up with both a bad folk history and a botched autobiography. Perhaps Wright never thought of it that way. More likely, he thought of it in terms of his previous writing experiences. Here was the same problem he had encountered when writing *Native Son*. If his account was too naturalistically deterministic, and Bigger too psychologically damaged, the book—though likely to have more of an emotional impact—and its author would be criticized for adding to the litany of negative stereotypes and images about Negroes. Wright's response, when faced with this dilemma, appears to be the same as before: he would risk alienating middle-class blacks and other critics to make his book more psychologically effective. He would "tell it slant" so as to hit unsuspecting readers even as they dodged the social truths they did not want to hear.

Here again, Adams's insights are illuminating. He argues that it is *Black Boy*'s generic ambiguity, along with its tone, that leaves some readers struck by its honesty, and others feeling that many scenes in the book simply do not ring true (69, 74–75). Adams concludes that "*Black Boy* should not be read as historical truth, which strives to report those incontrovertible facts that can be somehow corroborated, but as narrative truth" (82). Thus Adams eases reader concerns about the inauthenticity of numerous episodes in *Black Boy* by arguing that the narrative itself functions as a metaphor for lying. If the book makes us uneasy, we should be all the more uneasy when considering what kind of society it is that makes deception routine, and relationships between individuals of separate races a source of constant conflict. This is a world where one is never simply interacting one-on-one with another person, but within an apparatus of power and prejudice—the entire distorting matrix of racial relations in that society.

One of the more salient lessons of Jim Crow, as illustrated by Wright's autobiographical anecdotes, was the necessity of lying about one's true thoughts and feelings. Learning how to live in the South had taught him the value of dissembling, whereas telling truths about race and other taboo subjects tended to spark violent reactions. Giving the names of his assailants to his Northern boss, instead of lying and saying that no one was bothering him, could get him killed, as could asserting his full humanity in front of whites. As emblematic and moving as they were, it was almost unavoidable that the moments first described in Wright's essay "The Ethics of Living Jim Crow"—such as lying in a forged note to get books from the library—would come to form key episodes in *Black Boy*. Growing up in the Jim Crow South, where the art of dissembling was a survival strategy, well prepared Wright to become a liar by profession—a writer of fiction, a creator of what his grandmother had cursed as "Devil stuff" for which he would "burn in hell" (*Black Boy* 39–40). In his fiction, however, Wright dedicated himself to telling hard truths, the kind that could not be uttered in person. And whatever lies Wright told on the page, whether as fiction or nonfiction, were in service to the writer's truth-telling mandate.

Ralph Ellison would also eloquently express the art of lying on the page in order to tell deeper truths, writing of "the novel's capacity for telling the truth while actually telling a 'lie,' which is the Afro-American folk term for an improvised story" (introduction xxii). In a scene that echoes the falsehood metaphor that Adams identifies in *Black Boy*, the unnamed protagonist of *Invisible Man* is rebuked by the college president for a fateful lapse in the art of dissembling: "My God, boy! You're black and living in the South—did you forget how to lie?" (139).

As an author of protest fiction, and a student of propagandist techniques, Wright had no qualms with manipulating reality to tell important social truths. He seemed to think that any distortion of reality was acceptable as long as the reasons for doing so were right. Ralph Ellison, though, would critique and scrupulously avoid overly one-sided, patently manipulative, depictions of reality: "I was already having enough difficulty trying to avoid writing what might turn out to be nothing more than another novel of racial protest instead of the dramatic study in comparative humanity which I felt any worthwhile novel should be" (introduction xxviii). If you have to lie all the time, it helps to laugh a lot too, Ellison seemed to be saying, and demonstrating as well. When *Invisible Man*, ripe with a ludic sensibility, was published in 1952, it was heartily acclaimed as one of America's greatest novels. Wright's *The Outsider* was published soon after, but criticized with equal vigor for being overly intellectual and bleak, and its hero unrealistic.

Du Bois's questioning of *Black Boy*'s relation to truth, as illustrated by the contrast between Ellison's approach and Wright's, reveals the inherent difficulties of writing as a representative author. Both pronouns lay claim to the first person, but the gulf between *we* and *me* is wide. Minority authors who choose to be critical of the plural self in the *we* sense risk perpetuating negative stereotypes, particularly given that mainstream readers are reading their work as representative of the ethnic group. Because it affects them more directly, other members of the ethnic group are the first readers to notice literary depictions that rehearse anything short of group "uplift." So writers who wish to speak honestly of their personal experience and group interactions are caught in a double bind: either pretend that their writing will not be read as representative or perform a kind of literary minstrelsy that will please both minority and mainstream audiences. In the first case, the author fails to acknowledge the extent to which his or her ethnicity, race, gender, and the like inform the ways in which the text is meaningful to readers. Ignoring this in turn diminishes the writer's role as author and whatever effects the author hopes the text will have on readers. In the second case, the author is constrained by expectations about what kind of literary spectacle he or she is to perform. These kinds of limitations are particularly galling for authors trying to write fiction, where a premium is otherwise placed on imagination. The demand for narrative conflict, for example, can itself come into conflict with expectations that the text be both ethnically representative and racially uplifting.

Wright's particular dilemma in writing *Black Boy* involved all of these unresolved tensions. He wanted to write as a representative author, but also wanted to critique racism by displaying its dehumanizing effects. He was also trying to balance this with telling his personal story and keeping the book exciting enough to maintain reader interest. Wright had to decide which goals were primary whenever conflicting aims could not be reconciled. *Black Boy* would be a good story and a words-as-weapons truncheon for drubbing racism; a more balanced depiction of black culture and rigid adherence to the historical facts of his life would have to be subordinate to the first two aims.

The use of *Black Boy* as a weapon—one deployed to tell larger truths while eviscerating racism—led to what Leon Wright dubbed troubling "misrepresentations" in the text: "I do feel that my brother should not have found it necessary to make irresponsible statements involving members of the family to aid him in his cause" (qtd. in Rowley 325). Leon's account suggests that Wright not only appropriated the real-life stories of others as his own, but that in telling his own stories he misrepresented those of others. An infraction of the first type occurs in the scene in which his Uncle Hoskins teases the young Richard Wright, frightening the wits out of him by driving their horse and buggy right into the Mississippi River. Although a poignant incident that emotionally conveys the broken trust between family members, it did not happen to Wright, but to someone else. That someone was Ralph Ellison, who had told Wright of such an incident between him and his father (Webb 409).

Borrowing the incident and attributing it to himself does not seem to do much to advance Wright's concern with addressing "the Negro Question" in his autobiography, at least not in the way that Du Bois and other critics thought it should be addressed (*Black Boy* 346). The eidetic scene, however, is unforgettable, and Wright knew it. He would use it for its vividness and its emotive power. This particular scene evoked a visceral response from the reader: "[H]e loomed before me like a stranger, like a man I had never seen before, a man with whom I could never share a moment of intimate living. . . . I never trusted him after that. Whenever I saw his face the memory of my terror upon the river would come back, vivid and strong, and it stood as a barrier between us" (*Black Boy* 52–53).

The incident itself is, once again, presented dramatically, as a dialogue: "'We're going to the middle of the river so the horse can drink,' he said. . . . 'Naw!' I screamed. . . . 'Let me out!' I screamed" (*Black Boy* 51). By making another man's incident his own, Wright transforms an isolated childhood anecdote into a commentary on the disintegration of familial and intraracial trust. He thus avoids pontificating as a black Polonius, and instead makes deeply felt the irony that, rather than forging solidarity, racism under Jim Crow had created even greater distrust among blacks than between blacks and whites.[14] *Black Boy* is functioning as a sociological document, but not as a straightforward literal account. Rather, the documentation offered here is literary and dramatized, and any "misrepresentations" of others, and of black culture, are intended to document the ways in which racism dehumanizes.

EMOTIONAL TRUTH AS OVERRIDING AESTHETIC PRINCIPLE

"Richard Wright has but one story to tell," wrote Wright's friend and would-be biographer, Horace Cayton, in his review of *Black Boy*: "That story is how it *feels* to be a Negro in the United States" (184).[15] Cayton's statement reveals two insights. First, that, in writing about race, Wright was less concerned about distinctions between genres—fiction, nonfiction, poetry (including much of the haiku that he wrote late in his life)—than most readers and critics are. Second, not only did Wright have only one story, one main theme, but he had one way of telling it: through emotion. Cayton goes on to quote Wright as stating, "I try to float these facts on a sea of emotion" (184–85).

Cayton's summation of the emotional lens through which Wright accomplished his political aims further explains why Wright's characterizations of friends, family, and fellow blacks leave them with few, if any, redeeming qualities. Aside from the possible motive of trying to make himself look good at the expense of others (he reveals his own shortcomings, but those of others even more so), the explanation for such misrepresentations is simply that actual events and personalities were distorted so that Wright could make a larger, political point—more specifically, so that he could tell hard-hitting truths about race with as much emotional impact as possible.

Most of the violations of *vraisemblance* and historical fact in *Black Boy* can be accounted for by considering Wright's aesthetic and social objectives. Wright was not after verisimilitude, but emotional impact. His goal was not so much historical truth as emotional truth. Tim O'Brien famously made a similar distinction in differentiating happening-truth (historical fact) from story-truth (emotional impact) (171–72). In his fictionalized vignettes, O'Brien tries to render the emotional reality of war. Wright's texts do the same for racial experience, also blurring the line between fiction and the strictly autobiographical. O'Brien's modern literary sentiments, however, stand in contrast to Wright's social realist approach to art. Where they differ is on the question of how emotional truth is to be depicted, and to what ends. O'Brien backs away from making moral judgments: "A true war story is never moral. It does not instruct, nor encourage virtue, nor suggest models of proper human behavior" (65). This is a far cry from Wright's oft-cited vow to never again write a book that "bankers' daughters could read and weep over and feel good about" but instead to write one "so hard and deep that they would have to face it without the consolation of tears" ("How 'Bigger' Was Born" xxvii).

What Wright is arguing in these iconic lines—from an essay so illuminating that it has been appended to editions of *Native Son* ever since it appeared shortly after the novel's initial publication in 1940—is diametrically opposed to the objective stance espoused by O'Brien's narrator. Stories are moral, insists Wright. Furthermore, emotions and morality are inextricably linked: "The degree of morality in my writing depended upon the degree of felt life and truth I could put down upon the printed page" (xxx–xxxi). For Wright, not only does the emotional impact of the story serve a larger moral purpose, but morality in narrative, as is true of life, at least partly also depends on affect, sentiment, and "felt life." Granted, not all stories have a moral intent, and even fewer have a moral message, but those that Wright is interested in do. And many a story in which moral intent or authorial judgment is abstained from nevertheless revolve around the moral judgments of readers, which would seem to make war stories inescapably moral.

Writing for intended psychological effect on the reader casts Wright's prose into disfavor with contemporary literary tastes, which are scornful of sentimental writing as well as aesthetic theories that equate the universality of literature with the ungeneralizable specificity of the author's personal experience. R. G. Collingwood's conception of emotional expression in works of literature takes the latter view, arguing that "the object at which he [the artist] is aiming is not to produce a preconceived emotional effect on his audience but . . . to explore his own emotions: to discover emotions in himself of which he was unaware, and, by permitting the audience to witness the discovery, enable them to make a similar discovery about themselves" (318–19). Collingwood is dismissive of the idea that "the 'work of art' should produce its intended psychological effect," placing work of art in scare quotes to distinguish it from art proper, which he sees as individualizing emotions, and thus to categorize it instead as mere craftsmanship, which generalizes about emotional states (317–18). Likewise, Collingwood stresses that the artist does not arouse emotions but rather expresses them (314). Wright's goal as a writer is, without a doubt, to express emotions. However, Wright also, pace Collingwood, strives to arouse emotional states in his readers—Aristotelian and generalizable emotions such as pity, fear, and, ultimately, moral indignation. Wright wants the moral outrage that follows from linking emotions to questions of social justice to compel the reader to social change. The banker's daughters must be stirred to action, rather than simply have a good cry and quickly forget about the social injustice that the pathos of the text shines a spotlight on.

• ◆ •

Wright's emotion-charged aesthetics not only drives the narrative but also dictates his standards of narrative truth. His description of this aesthetics, as quoted by Cayton, sheds light on his approach to literary truth telling:

> I have always taken the writing of literature very seriously, and I've looked upon fiction and writing in general as a means of revealing the truth of life and experience rather than purely as a means of entertaining people. In other words, I feel that literature ought to be a sharp instrument to reveal something important about mankind, about living, about life whether among whites or blacks. That is why my work hews so close to facts, yet why I try to float these facts on a sea of emotion, to drive them home with some degree of artistic power, as much as is humanly possible, to the level of seriousness which characterizes science. I want people to enjoy my books but I also want them to be moved and conditioned by them. (184–85)

In Wright's ars poetica, "the truth of life and experience" is best conveyed on a "sea of emotion." To tell readers about himself, he also had to tell them about being black. It was not enough simply to tell them, though. He had to make them feel it on the deepest emotional and psychological levels of their being. Nelson Algren stressed the point: "[Wright] writes out of passion, out of his belly" (qtd. in Rowley 409). Dan McCall would turn the insight to an analysis of Wright's prose: "The power of the prose is explicable largely by its effect" (105). Where readings filtered through other aesthetic principles distort, Cayton's insight—"Richard Wright has but one story to tell. That story is how it *feels* to be a Negro in the United States"—snaps the reading of Wright's work sharply into focus (184).

These appraisals also explain incongruous lapses of realism and psychological realism in Wright's two gritty ubertexts, *Black Boy* and *Native Son*, books supposed by their author to be realistic, and all the more so as psychological realism. Wright's attempt to make us feel blackness leads him to err time and again in favor of the symbolic, hyperbolic, and downright implausible. *Black Boy*'s critique of racial inequality in general, and of Jim Crow society in particular, works by making the reader vicariously experience some of racism's more painful, degrading, poignant, and—perhaps most of all—emblematic moments.

Embedded in *Black Boy* is Wright's indirect notice to his readers, by which he subtly instructs his readers on the passion-driven aesthetics that is the text's narrative principle. In recounting the story about a black woman avenging her husband's lynching by shooting and killing four whites, Wright distinguishes between what may or may not be "factually true" and what is undoubtedly "emotionally true" (*Black Boy* 73). It is what he knows to be emotionally true that Wright seizes on as he recreates the story and his reaction to it. Not only does the story seem to be the germ of the idea for his short stories "Big Boy Leaves Home" and "Bright and Morning Star," it also seems to set the emotional pitch that those stories capture. The blaze of passion in these stories, and in Wright's other writing, reflects the way that books first presented themselves to him: "Ella's whispered story of deception and murder had been the first experience in my life that had elicited from me a total emotional response" (*Black Boy* 40). The story that Ella, a boarder at Granny's house, is reciting to Wright is *Bluebeard and His Seven Wives*, and his heightened emotional response makes it clear that such works of pure fantasy fired Wright's youthful imagination. Nevertheless, in his adult writing, Wright's equally firm commitment to an aesthetics of engagement would keep him at a permanent remove from escapist fiction.

Wright would conspicuously distance himself from both escapist and sentimental fiction when, as we saw earlier, famously vowing that *Native Son* would not be the kind of book that *Uncle Tom's Children* had been taken for: "a book which even bankers' daughters could read and weep and feel good about." (Ironically, as Wright composed *Native Son* he discussed it almost daily with an actual banker's daughter, Jane Newton. Jane, however—married to a politicized black man and cut off from her family—was probably not the type of person he had in mind when defining bankers' daughters as a class of readers.) Indeed, it could also be said of *Black Boy* that it was written unsentimentally, so that "no one would weep over it; that it would be so hard and deep that they would have to face it without the consolation of tears."

He wanted *Native Son* and *Black Boy* to hit hard, to shock their readers into recognition of the need for progress in race relations. In trying to go over the top, however, he was in danger of slipping into melodrama, and that risked rendering his naturalistic depictions unrealistic and unconvincing. Fueled by his passion, there wasn't much to decide on—he would take the risk.

Although protest literature has fallen into disfavor and critics continue to question his aesthetic judgment, Wright knew exactly what he was doing. Little in either *Native Son* or *Black Boy* was written without a specific effect in mind. Wright was aiming to manipulate his readers at the most visceral level, even if his emotional truths defied narrative realism:

> But in the writing of scene after scene I was guided by one criterion: to tell the truth as I saw it and felt it. That is, to objectify in words some insight derived from my living in the form of action, scene, and dialogue. If a scene seemed improbable to me, I'd not tear it up, but ask myself: "Does it reveal enough of what I feel to stand in spite of its unreality?" If I felt it did, it stood. If I felt it did not, I ripped it out. The degree of morality in my writing depended upon the degree of felt life and truth I could put down upon the printed page. ("How 'Bigger' Was Born" xxx–xxxi)

Based on these criteria, Wright felt justified in cramming an unrealistic number of people into Bigger's cell near the end of the novel. Jane Newton, with whom he discussed nearly every scene, demurred. It just wasn't credible that twelve people would be allowed into a murderer's prison cell (Rowley 156). Wright stuck by his original choice: "But I wanted those people in that cell to elicit a certain emotional response from Bigger. And so the scene stood. I felt that what I wanted that scene to say to the reader was *more important than its surface reality or plausibility*" ("How 'Bigger' Was "Born" xxxi, emphasis in the original).

Even today, when most consider protest literature to be inferior in literary terms (and, moreover, largely out of sync with reader sentiments), *Native Son* and *Black Boy* still hit first-time readers hard. As much as anything else, it is their shared emotional aesthetics that unites them, the similarity of Wright's aesthetic choices in the two works leaving *Black Boy* rife for comparison with *Native Son*. In each work, Wright's goal was to hit readers with emotional truths and to motivate them to action. Trilling, at least, felt that Wright had kept the vow he made when writing *Native Son:* "Mr. Wright's autobiography, so far as it is an account of misery and oppression, does not tempt its readers to such pleasures [moral escapism]. This is the mark of the dignity and integrity of the book" (152). *Black Boy* was emotionally powerful, a book written for effect, and the emotion-driven narrative was neither mawkish nor meretricious: "It is difficult to describe that power except, as I have tried to do, by speaking of its effect, by remarking that it does not lead us into easy and inexpensive emotions, although the emotions into which it does lead us are durable" (152).

Wright's narrative might be making a difference in the struggle for racial justice, but it did not resolve the problem of who was speaking for whom. In trying to convey the emotional truth of being a black man in the South, Wright's folk history of black culture presented a portrait of wretchedness. Despite his best intentions, Wright ultimately seemed to speak only for himself. He could not possibly speak in defense of others when distorting their stories so. Moreover, the book's version of truth is an emotional one, and not even *Black Boy*'s protagonist emerges with his image untarnished by the funhouse mirror of heightened emotions that the book holds up to social reality. Such were the contradictions and distortions of writing an autobiography that presented itself as representative. This is no book about black boys in America, the skeptical reader might conclude, but it is, beyond all doubt, a book about one "black boy" trying to be a person in the South.

As hybrid autobiography, *Black Boy* inherently embodies a number of contradictions that have long puzzled readers. An appreciation of Wright's aesthetics of visceral truth eases reader anxieties about the autobiography's apparent lack of correspondence to reality, reassuring the reader that the artist lies in order to tell deeper truths. The deeper truths in question are, in particular, those relating to the experience of race in America. The more representative of racial experience the narrative, including in its emotional dimensions, the more trenchant its critique of racism and injustice. The next chapter extends the analysis of Wright's social critique by turning to the existentialist character of the autobiography, its masculinist perspective, and the ways in which these deepen the critique rather than undermine it. It is, in part, the story of how Frankenstein's monster or, rather, his modern ethnic doppelgänger, is shaken from his lone rebellion and roused to collective action.

2

The Black Existentialist and Collective Racial Experience

"Manning Up" the Ethnic Übermensch in Richard Wright's *Black Boy*

◆

Richard Wright has long been read as a social realist writer, an engagé scribbler of "social protest fiction," as James Baldwin argued in "Everybody's Protest Novel," an oedipal, literary precursor–slaying essay that compared *Native Son* with the nineteenth-century sentimental novel *Uncle Tom's Cabin* (13).[1] This image of Wright contrasts starkly with existentialist themes in his work. In discussions of Wright's work, however, his reputation as a writer in the sociological vein often eclipses any sense of him as an existentialist writer. This is despite the fact that Wright not only self-consciously set out to produce existentialist works, such as "The Man Who Lived Underground" (1945) and *The Outsider* (1953), but also wrote an existentialist autobiography.

Classifying Wright's autobiography *Black Boy* this way would seem, at first glance, to suggest a glaring contradiction, for the book can also be read as a sequel to *Native Son*: a work of literary naturalism in which a corrupt society is critiqued by emphasizing the determinative role of the racialized protagonist's social environment. Where the earlier book tips the scales toward determinism, however, the sequel offers the hope of transcendence. That is, *Black Boy* inverts the ethno-terrorizing environmental determinism (a psyche-pervading assault by racializing, emasculating, and class-stratifying forces) of

Native Son by depicting the black protagonist triumphing over his environment rather than being corrupted or destroyed by it. In *Native Son*, Bigger's failed legal defense relies on stressing the determinative role of socioeconomic forces that made Bigger into what he is, Bigger so internalizing these discourses that he concludes: "But what I killed for, I *am!* It must've been pretty deep in me to make me kill!" (391–92, emphasis in the original). *Black Boy*, in contrast, offers a vision of escape from an oppressive social environment: "This was the culture from which I sprang. This was the terror from which I fled" (257).

As Wright's phrasing here suggests, however, *Black Boy* eschews the triumphalism that might be expected of a transcendence narrative—or what might more rightly be called an escape narrative, indicating the text's lineage in the slave narrative tradition. Despite the hero's successful escape from Southern racial prejudice, Wright goes on to encounter new forms of racial and socioeconomic marginalization in the North. And though Wright is freer in the North to revise, or existentially create, his identity rather than having it imposed upon him, he remains constrained by both race relations and the legacy of formative racial experiences: "I was persisting in reading my present environment in the light of my old one" (*Black Boy* 264). Although it inverts the deterministic ending of *Native Son*, *Black Boy* eschews any sense of absolute transcendence to instead hold in tension a shifting equilibrium between agency and the tyranny of racial discourse.

Wright must relate both realities, both polarities of the identity spectrum, in narrating the story of his life: that of identity self-determination as well as the extent to which identity is contingent on one's visibility in a particular discursive and social environment. This double gesture to both self and environment typifies Wright's wrestling with what Robert Butler insightfully describes as "the core of Wright's vision—how to achieve a human self while inhabiting a deterministic environment which systematically denies your status as a human being?" ("Seeking" 46). *Black Boy* may present itself as an existential act of self-creation—both as a literary text (the creation of the literary self on the page) and through the story it tells (an ethnic self escaping from, against all odds, a colonizing socioeconomic environment). It is, however, also a sociological record (subtitled "A Record of Childhood and Youth") that, as Charles Davis summarizes, "is based on the generalizing process that Richard is a black boy, any black boy experiencing childhood, adolescence, and early manhood in the South" (150; see also Adams 69–70). *Black Boy*, in other words, embodies the contradictions of a life that is simultaneously both existentially defined and racially situated—at once an act of identity revision as well as a testament to the force of identity ascription. In such ways, the text embodies the profundity and paradoxes of ethnic identity.[2]

Reading *Black Boy* as the narrative of an ethnic existentialist reframes what might otherwise be perceived as excessive individualism. Under the latter framing, one could easily conclude that Wright's philosophy of identity is best summed up in the maxim "I am an individualist, but my society imposes a collective identity on me." The gist of this maxim is a prominent theme in *Black Boy*, which dramatizes the constraints and limitations imposed on black subjects. It might be more accurate, however, to revise the maxim: "I am an existentialist, but my society denies the possibility of self-realization and full recognition as a person." Such a formulation both captures the identity limitations ("denies") imposed on actual ethnic selves and exemplifies the inherent ambiguity ("possibility") of ethnic identities. *Black Boy* holds the irresolvable tensions between the existential impulse and the social self in animated suspension. In this chapter, I argue that Wright's depiction is not only compatible with ethnic identity and collective action, but also the means for critiquing the social structures that oppress ethnic subjects as a group. His appropriation, revision, and performance of race and gender narratives allow him to negotiate his identity, which, as depicted in the autobiography, exemplifies the complexity of real ethnic identities.

In tracing the inherent tensions and contradictions of a complex ethnic identity as reflected in *Black Boy*, I underscore some of the apparent paradoxes in Wright's autobiography. I begin by briefly sketching existentialist aspects of *Black Boy*, including figuration of the autobiographical protagonist as a black Übermensch. In subsequent sections, I address the extent to which Wright's depiction of himself as a rebellious Romantic hero (or antihero) serves as an instrument for social critique. This leads to a discussion of resistance to the existentialist ethnic self from within the ethnic community, and the impetus behind it. Last, I acknowledge the role of print culture in instilling Wright with a liberal, humanist paradigm that motivates his critique of racial injustice.

Wright's "predisposition toward individualism, self-reliance, and nonconformity," as Jerry Ward suggests, may certainly be genuine. I argue, however, that in key scenes that operate as set pieces on the humanist theme, Wright rhetorically transforms his more complex sense of the self-in-society into a dimensionally one-sided narrative of individualism that he deploys to the paradoxically collectivist end of critiquing a social environment that oppresses racial subjects as a group (xvii–xviii). It is, however, a rhetorical strategy that inspires resistance from the ethnic community, not only because of the exigencies of strategic identities, but also because Wright's indictment of the racialized social environment extends to a critique of the shaping role of racial logic on black culture, which he depicts as precluding the possibility of participating in the same existentialist "white freedom," to borrow Richard Rodriguez's phrasing, enjoyed by Anglo Americans (*Brown* 142).

ETHNIC EXISTENTIALIST, BLACK ÜBERMENSCH

Black Boy's author was an existentialist before existentialism became fashionable in America. Wright biographer Constance Webb reports that on reading the French existentialists, Wright "pulled out *Black Boy*. 'Look,' he said, 'this is existentialist,' and read from his book" (279).[3] Fear, hunger, and alienation are major themes in *Black Boy*: "Man as an alone, anguished being in an unintelligible world which led him into areas of cold dread, fear, anxiety, and psychic pain was the everyday world of the American black man" (Webb 279). Hunger in *Black Boy* is both a gnawing physical ache and a metaphor for existential angst. The narrative arc in part 1 of the book traces a brutalizing existence of constant struggle against a hostile world, beginning with the author's birth into a Jim Crow South that does not recognize his existence as a full person, and ending with the self-defining act of successfully fleeing the environment that denies his humanity. In part 2, the black protagonist's alienation continues when confronting not just ongoing racial discrimination, but also ideological repression (*Black Boy* 369–75). As Wright depicts it, growing up as a racial other in a hostile world ruled by a perverse racial logic is the quintessential existentialist experience: absurd, alienating, and requiring subjects to create their own meaning—to "win some redeeming meaning for their having struggled and suffered here beneath the stars," as Wright phrased it in the 1945 ending to *Black Boy* (415).

Although some scholars have sought to find a clear line of intellectual influence that carries over from the French existentialists to Wright's early work, Sarah Relyea reminds us that the vector of influence also pointed in the opposite direction: "*Native Son* and *Black Boy* influenced the existentialist philosophy of Simone de Beauvoir and Jean-Paul Sartre, who shared Wright's emphasis on alienated consciousness" (187). Regardless of whatever exposure to French existentialism Wright had before writing *Black Boy*, he clearly describes having absorbed proto-existentialist views early on from both personal racial experiences and "[m]y reading," which Wright credits for sharpening his sense of alienation by "creating a vast sense of distance between me and the world in which I lived" (*Black Boy* 253).

Among the writers and thinkers Wright deems important enough to include in the litany of authors he was introduced to in reading Mencken are Dostoyevsky and Nietzsche, both considered, along with Kierkegaard, to be the fountainheads of twentieth-century existentialist thought (*Black Boy* 249). Wright's depiction of himself as becoming conscious of and then rejecting the slave morality—which he dubbed "the ethics of living Jim Crow"—of an unjust, hierarchical society certainly suggests a Nietzschean influence, and the title of Wright's short story "The Man Who Lived Underground" is a direct allusion to Dostoyevsky's novel *Notes from Underground*.[4]

Although he does not explicitly invoke Nietzsche's terminology, Wright's autobiographical depiction of his own morality-defying transcendence of the Jim Crow environment can easily be read as a dramatization of the Nietzschean Übermensch rising above the slave morality of a corrupt society: "I had seen how they acted, how they regarded black people, how they regarded me; and I no longer felt bound by the laws which white and black were supposed to obey in common. I was outside those laws" (*Black Boy* 200–201). In a later passage, Wright's self-as-existential-hero concludes, "I could submit and live the life of a genial slave, but that was impossible" (252). Although ambivalent about his decision, Wright ultimately decides that he is justified in stealing his way to freedom: "I was gambling: freedom or the chain gang" (205). He is also justified in earning transit money any way he can: "He was white, and I could never do to him what he and his kind had done to me. Therefore, I reasoned, stealing was not a violation of my ethics, but of his; I felt that things were rigged in his favor and any action I took to circumvent his scheme of life was justified" (203). As stand-in for the phrase "slave morality," Wright describes rejecting what he characterizes as the "peasant mentality" of lower-class black life, epitomized in the narrative by his sharecropper father and the spectrum of urban poor ranging from "black confidence men" to those of "naïve simplicity," this last represented by Bess and her mother, who live amidst the "pickpockets, prostitutes, and cutthroats" of Memphis's Beale Street (34–35, 208–14).

Among those alluding to existentialist and Nietzschean themes in *Black Boy* are some of the most distinguished scholars of Richard Wright and his work. In his insightful introduction to the 1998 printing of the restored text,

Jerry Ward imparts existential valence to the protagonist's transcendence of the self-negating social environment by invoking the existentially freighted word *becoming* to describe it: "It can be argued that as an artist Wright highlighted the negativity of accommodating and becoming in order to strengthen the act of transcending resistance that *Black Boy (American Hunger)* is" (xviii). Albert Stone further suggests not only an existentialist reading (of a "recreated" life), but an even more explicitly Nietzschean one when describing Wright's "young Mississippi self" as exhibiting a "triumph of will," a phrase that conjures Nietzsche's notion of the "will to power" ("After *Black Boy*" 171).

Complicating any overdrawn existentialist reading, however, is the status of the text, as reflected in Janice Thaddeus's argument that *Black Boy*, as originally published, is more triumphalist than the book that Wright had intended to publish. Six years before the publication of the 1991 Library of America restored edition of *Black Boy*, Thaddeus, in her essay "The Metamorphosis of Black Boy," made a call for the unification of the two separately published books (*Black Boy* in 1945 and *American Hunger* in 1977). The restored text reflects Wright's final intent before Book-of-the-Month Club intervention and is now considered the authoritative edition. However, it is still true, as Thaddeus argues, that the version of *Black Boy* read by readers for the greater part of the time that the book has been in print is the expurgated version—a truncated text that is more optimistic than Wright had originally envisioned. At the Book-of-the-Month Club's prodding, Wright had agreed to drop the second section ("The Horror and the Glory") of the 1944 manuscript, posthumously published as *American Hunger*, which had been the title for the complete autobiography when first set in page proofs. Under the auspices—if we can call it that—of Dorothy Canfield Fisher, Wright also revised the ending paragraphs of the book's first section ("Southern Night") for its publication as *Black Boy* in 1945. The final result, argues Thaddeus, is that "the rhetoric is more assured, the feeling more triumphant," changing the autobiography from an "open" one into a "defined" one (210, 199). "The writer of an open autobiography," Thaddeus explains, "differs from Douglass and others like him in that he is searching, not telling, so that like Boswell or Rousseau he offers questions instead of answers. . . . he refrains from shaping his life neatly in a teleological plot" (199). She concludes that through the influence and commercial power of the Book-of-the-Month Club, "*Black Boy* became a more definitive statement than its themes of hope and hunger could support" (213). In contrast, "When combined, both of these books emphasize the lack of conviction, the isolation, and finally the lack of order in Wright's world as he saw it" (214).

Wright's existentialism comes through in both the original and the restored versions of his autobiography. The restored text—what Wright had intended to publish—is the more existential of the two, its less deterministic framing more reflective of the radical free will and ultimately personal moral responsibility posited by existentialism. What is most compelling about Wright's rendering of the revised conclusion for the expurgated version is his choice to end the autobiography on a more triumphant note, a decision that reflects his existentialist optimism getting the upper hand even when depicting free will as impinged upon by social forces such as racial narratives. Wright, that is, offers a realistic conception of free will as limited and contingent on social context rather than presenting readers with abstract, absolute, and otherwise unrealistic notions of freedom. Taken together or separately, all three of these insightful readings by preeminent Wright scholars raise a vexing question. If Wright is such a self-creating existentialist and latent Nietzschean Übermensch, then why would he write an autobiography whose very title suggests not only that he is a typical "black boy" but also—in presenting any single individual as racially representative—that black identity is essentially fungible?

BLACK FRANKENSTEIN: THE REBELLIOUS ROMANTIC HERO AS INSTRUMENT OF SOCIAL CRITIQUE

As evident in signature scenes in his autobiography, Wright is committed to individual liberty and self-expression. Yet he also depicts himself as racially representative, and thus legitimizes collective identification. To explain this apparent contradiction through an existentialist framing, Wright is freely choosing to use himself, through his autobiographical narrative, as an instrument of racial critique. The trade-off of this two-part vision—the existential ethnic self who is also racially representative in some significant way—is that the more deterministic Wright's depiction of the racial environment, the less existentially free and agency empowered are the African American lives he depicts. The result is an unrelenting narrative tension between Wright's existentialism and his resolve to use his own life story as an instrument for criticizing racism. Not to be overlooked, however, is the extent to which this tension converges into lines of synthesis. Namely, narratives of racial determinism in *Black Boy* are specifically used to emphasize—and excoriate—perverse social restrictions on the personal agency of one group relative to another group in the same society. That is, by using deterministic depictions of social location to sharpen his critique of racial suppression, Wright is able to accomplish his ultimate goal of increasing existential freedom for ethnic subjects. One of his narrative tools for doing so—a literary device that maps onto self-conception as either a black existentialist or an ethnic Übermensch—is the trope of the rebellious Romantic hero.

In scene after scene, Wright depicts himself as rebelling against authority, a corrupt society, and the status quo. He opens the autobiography not with some idyllic or nostalgic memory from childhood, but with his four-year-old's awareness that "I would be punished if I did not obey," followed by his setting fire to the white curtains that he had been "forbidden to touch" (*Black Boy* 3). Although he "had not really intended to set the house afire," the scene leaves the impression that Wright was rebellious from an early age (5). In later scenes, he will rebel repeatedly against his family, pull a razor on his uncle, and challenge the authority of his school principal.

Wright's choice to write a hybrid autobiography makes it difficult, at times, to suss out which episodes in the autobiography are intended to heighten the racial critique and which reflect his individual disposition and sentiments. In some scenes, the racial critique is undermined by what the reader can judge about Wright's disposition. His attempts to weld the public and the private get even more complex in other episodes. Further complicating the already difficult task of uniting social protest with personal autobiography is Wright's strong-willed obstinacy. Several scenes exhibit his stubborn resistance to authority and to restrictive racial narratives.

One such scene is the showdown with the school principal over which version of his valedictorian speech Wright would deliver. The conflict is presented as predominantly over the racial content of Wright's speech, given that white Southerners will be in the audience. But it is clear that individual autonomy in the face of a racial authority figure is also at stake. The narrator's interpretation of the incident is editorialized by the author's selection and framing of details in the scene. In *Black Boy*, Wright triumphantly delivers his own speech, courageously risking the ire of any white folk in the audience who might be offended by his honesty. Omitted from this account, reports Michel Fabre, is that "in return Richard agreed to cut certain passages that might have antagonized the authorities" (54). Suppressing mention of this accentuates the triumph of the rebellious Romantic hero over the authority figure. Equally important, Wright frames this struggle in terms of a debate over racial narratives, over what can be said about race to a multiracial public.

The particular critique of racism that *Black Boy* makes is of the ways in which racism and racial narratives relegate black individuals to subhuman status. As with Frankenstein's monster, the rebellious acts of the protagonist function as a critique of the society that created him. Moreover, *Black Boy* constitutes a stalwart defense of the heroic, Romantic self, even as it speaks for an entire class of people. Written into *Black Boy* is a response to Du Bois's criticism that there are no broad-minded whites in the book. Such individuals are also dehumanized by racial narratives. Sympathetic whites found themselves powerless in the South. As in Wright's naturalistic novel, *Native Son*, the force of the social environment trumps the best intentions and efforts of individuals.

The spectacle of repressing individual autonomy as an instrument of racial exploitation and oppression is played out when Wright has his first chance to learn a real trade in Jackson, Mississippi. The owner of the small factory is a Northerner who "told me that he wanted to train a Negro boy in the optical trade; he wanted to help him, guide him" (*Black Boy* 187). He is unable, however, to protect Wright when two Southerners physically assault him to run him off the job. The attack had been presaged by the reminder that "This is a *white* man's work around here" (*Black Boy* 188, emphasis in the original). If Wright were to remain on the job, as the northern owner wishes, he could even be killed. In the southern milieu, the Northerner is forced to capitulate: "I'm from Illinois. Even for me, it's hard here. I can do just so much" (*Black Boy* 193).

Equally vivid in the scene is the justification for the attack, a verbal trap in which the protagonist is accused of failing to address a white man as "Mister" and then attacked for calling the white man a liar if he denies having done so: "'Now, be careful, nigger,' snarled Reynolds, baring his teeth. 'I heard you call 'im *Pease*. And if you say you didn't, you're calling me a liar, see?' He waved the steel bar threateningly" (*Black Boy* 189). As this scene demonstrates, and its exposure in the written text attests, some of the most important battles of the racial war are waged through language. Wright has language used against him, here, but it is through language, written language, that Wright himself is able to, in turn, interrogate racial discrimination.

The reader feels sympathy for the persecuted individual in such scenes. Presenting a single, embattled character, a Romantic hero, that readers can identify with—rather than making the case for civil rights more abstractly—sharpens the effectiveness of the appeal. The civil rights protest, however, is sometimes undermined by aspects of Wright's temperament: his alienation from others, his uncanny ability to irritate people around him, his distress at being "trapped by the community, the tribe" (*Black Boy* 153). The call to protect persecuted individuals is compelling, but loses some of its appeal if also seen as an endorsement of egoism, peevishness, and antisocial behavior.

Wright uses different strategies to discourage readers from associating his existentialist critique of society with negative character traits, traits that would be less than admirable in most social contexts. One is to address any shortcomings in his youthful personality directly. Although not always successful, these moments of honest self-revelation are framed so as to bolster the condemnation of societal wrongs Wright is critiquing in the book. On occasion, he frames such flaws as characteristic of the personal alienation that stems from inhabiting a degenerate culture. Reflecting on his untoward behavior and the constant conflict with family members, Wright wonders "what on earth was the matter with me, why it was I never seemed to do things as people expected them to be done." He elaborates, "Every word and gesture I made seemed to provoke hostility. I had never been able to talk to others, and I had to guess at their meanings and motives" (*Black Boy* 143). More than anything else, what is conveyed here—in the context in which it is said and in the larger context of the complete autobiography—is the protagonist's innocence. In scene after scene, Wright depicts himself as naïve about societal expectations. The reader thus experiences the point of view of the morally good and naturally innocent individual bewildered by an immoral and corrupting culture.

Through this presentation of the self, Wright's cantankerous temperament becomes a badge of honor worn by a rebellious spirit. In such moments, he is no longer naïvely innocent. Rather, he is Promethean in his defiance of a corrupt culture and the authority figures who try to preserve it. Demonstrating how far he is willing to go to defy various forms of authoritarianism and cultural conformity is Wright's admission to twice having threatened to cut family members to defend himself from a beating intended to make him conform. It is hard to say what is fictionalized and what of the protagonist's demeanor in such instances matches that of

Wright's actual self, but Wright's brother Leon felt that Richard's "account of events in his autobiography draws a quite honest self-portrait of his personality as I knew him" (qtd. in Rowley 325). What is remarkable about *Black Boy* is the ways in which what might otherwise be considered personality flaws are successfully enlisted as part of the criticism of the culture that Wright is vilifying in the narrative.

In *Richard Wright and Racial Discourse*, Yoshinobu Hakutani writes that "although *Black Boy* is strung with a series of episodes that illustrate forms of racial oppression, the center of attention lies in the hero's transcendence of racial oppression" (130). Hakutani's chapter on *Black Boy* emphasizes Wright's individualism, partly a product of Wright's innate temperament and what psychologists might call an internal locus of control:

> Becoming an aspiring rebel inevitably led to being a misfit. In Wright's life, however, it was his innate character that allowed this to happen. How self-assertive the young Wright was can be best shown in a comparison between him and his playmates. Although he identified himself with a mistreated group, there was a crucial difference between him and the other black children. (132)

To Hakutani's arguments about Wright's rebellious spirit and his exceptionalism, I add that *Black Boy* interrogates the notion that defying a collective identity must necessarily be pathological. Much depends on the context, and the context here is an overtly racist environment. The fictional Bigger Thomas's defiance of society (collective identity in the larger sense) in *Native Son* does indeed cross over into the pathological, but in *Black Boy* it is much more unambiguously the racist society that is pathologically deformed. The protagonist's defiance of society and of collective identities is the way to triumph in such an environment. Further, the reader's identification with the rebellious protagonist despite his antisocial behavior slides into a more trenchant critique of the pathological social context—the racist society—in which the rebel is defined as deviant. *Black Boy*, that is, undermines support for racist assumptions and practices by introducing mainstream America to a particular black man and then confronting them with that individual's full humanity.

Robert Butler also underscores existentialist themes grappled with by the rebellious antihero in *Native Son*, writing that "like Dostoyevsky's Raskolnikov, he [Bigger] is deeply shaken by the violence of his own criminal activity, and this feeling results in a reawakening of his conscience and a deepening of his consciousness" (*Black Hero* 114–15). Against a deterministic, literary naturalist reading of *Native Son*, Butler argues that "Bigger ... can create meaning in an otherwise absurd world by unlocking the doors to his consciousness, even while trapped in an outward prison. This deepening of consciousness enables Bigger to take responsibility for his actions" (115). It is, in other words, only in allowing Bigger to be a moral agent—free to choose—that he can be fully human.

Readers have long puzzled over the existentialist overtones of the condemned Bigger's concluding realization—"But what I killed for, I *am!*"—so troubling in its seeming justification of murder in the name of existential self-realization and self-creation (391–92, emphasis in the original). Rather than self-affirming, the idea seems only self-contradictory, as a philosophy that values self-realization and individual liberty must certainly be mutually exclusive with one that tolerates the annihilation of others. Yet the most seminal existentialist philosophers all dramatize existentialist characters as doing exactly that, annihilating others in order to define the self: Dostoyevsky has his Raskolnikov, Nietzsche his Übermensch, and Sartre his "hell is other people." Left open to debate is whether the point is to explore the inherent tension between self-interest and the interests of others (as selves themselves), or to conclude, unthinkably, that the existentialist is outside of all moral orders save those of his own making. Butler's reading of Bigger's transformation gives coherence to the existential dilemma: creating meaning in a meaningless world is not done in isolation. The existential self is a socially embedded self, not a solipsistic one, and thus the existential crisis is also about moral responsibility, the prerequisite for which is moral agency. (This theme has been debated since Adam—which is no hyperbole in the Judeo-Christian tradition—as the problem of free will.) This does not mean that you create your own morality and are beholden to no other, but it does mean that the full realization of our humanity requires being free to choose. How we choose, even for the Romantic rebel, reflects the depth of our humanity.

The question of our humanity, and the treating of others as fully human, is a thematic pulse coursing through the narrative of Wright's autobiography. It could be argued that Wright's sense of himself as equally human—despite racial narratives militating against this belief—is so great that he is able to transcend his racist environment and flourish as a human being. In crediting this transcendence wholly to Wright's innate character, however, we risk ignoring the role of print culture—the life-changing impact of reading widely and deeply—in forming that character. One might also argue that Wright's conflict with others, particularly members of his family, had nothing to do with race and everything to do with personality. But doing so would distort the truth of the situation in its own way. The more nuanced realization, which Wright emphasizes by relating almost all of the conflict in the book to race or the effects of racism, is that the formation of individual personalities is influenced by racial beliefs and narratives in society. Though certainly innate to some degree, the expression of Wright's rebellious temperament is inflected by and directed at racial relations in a particular social context. Not only did race relations have a profound effect on individual psyches, at the "deepest layers of . . . consciousness," but the range of personalities accepted as normal among whites was deemed pathological in blacks (*Black Boy* 172). The protagonist of *Black Boy* would not be so chastised for being indifferent, disrespectful, or individualistic if he were white. A white youth would not have to "learn how to live in the South" by altering his personality as drastically as was expected of the young, independent-minded Wright. Just the opposite: the rebel, particularly the young, male rebel, is a deeply rooted archetype in southern culture. The archetype, however, is a racialized one, and it is the segregation of the image and character type, and not the image itself, that Wright exposes and challenges by depicting his fictional characters and himself as a black rebel.

"MANNING UP" THE ETHNIC HERO THROUGH COLLECTIVE ACTION

The rebellious Romantic hero, if male and playing to type, must also exemplify virility, or the romanticized image of it. Masculinity is a major theme in Wright's work, and aptly so given the symbolic, socioeconomic, and all too often literal emasculation of black men in the Jim Crow South. The most poignant example is the castrating and lynching of black men as a terror tactic to monitor sexuality along racial lines and to more generally terrorize the entire minority community into submission to the status quo—namely, segregation, institutional racism, and entrenched inequality. Lynching is his prime example when Wright tells the reader that "the things that influenced my conduct as a Negro did not have to happen to me directly; I needed but to hear of them to feel their full effects in the deepest layers of my consciousness" (*Black Boy* 172). The formation of the ethnic self, in other words, is more than the simple two-dimensional plotting of the x-axis of individual temperament and its intersection with the y-axis of race relations. Narratives of masculinity and the social control of sexuality add their own tincture to the complexity of ethnic identities, and no exploration of racial identity, then, can be complete without a concomitant investigation of the dynamics of gender. Wright explores the entanglement of these discourses throughout his oeuvre, focusing in particular on male gender narratives and dynamics.

Cheryl Higashida gives particular attention to the race-gender nexus in "Aunt Sue's Children," arguing that "*Uncle Tom's Children* ultimately critiques the limitations of individualistic race rebellion, which is associated with black masculinism" (397). Stories or novellas appearing early in the collection depict the lone individual either fantasizing about taking on a white lynch mob or otherwise confronting the agents of racism in a deadly showdown or violent confrontation. In the final story of the original first edition, "Fire and Cloud," the black and white masses unite in nonviolent protest, however. The progression of the book, then, is from violence and reckless individualism to nonviolent, collective resistance—from would-be ethnic Übermensch to collectively empowered community. The interracial masses in the final story are led by the reverend of the black church, making the narrative arc of *Uncle Tom's Children* uncannily prescient in its anticipation of Martin Luther King and the civil rights movement. Here, narratives of gender and sexuality slip into an exploration of the interaction between individual identity and social narratives as the desperate and emasculated black male rebels in the stories are superseded by a hopeful and collectively empowered community of men and women. The lone ethnic subject is only able to "man up" through the collective "man" power of the ethnic community. Likewise in *Black Boy*, Wright does not, ultimately, depict rampant and excessive individualism as the answer to racism. Rather, the book is a call to mass action.

The feminist perspective is an indispensable part of the class solidarity called for in *Uncle Tom's Children*. "Bright and Morning Star," which was added to the collection in a second printing, features Wright's strongest female protagonist, Sue. As do Paul Gilroy and William Maxwell before her, Higashida reassesses old narratives about Wright's alleged misogyny, particularly, "grossly oversimplified views of his gender(ed) politics" (397). She concludes, "Beyond arguing that *Uncle Tom's Children* develops a protofeminist perspective on revolutionary struggle, I would also contend that this perspective provides an important corrective to limitations in certain strands of feminist analysis that rely on narrowly defined identity politics to uncritically rehearse narratives of Wright's misogyny" (419). Though critics may disagree over the nature of Wright's gendered politics, there can be no disagreement that his writing explores the connections between femininity, masculinity, sexuality, and class in depth. And he does so in excruciating emotional and psychological detail.

Although the role of sex and gender narratives in shaping racial discourse and ethnic identities is readily apparent in the Jim Crow racial context, understanding Wright's clashes with other blacks and with his own family is a more demanding task. The litany of scenes in which Wright clashes violently with family members is particularly conspicuous. In such scenes, Wright risks portraying himself as a truculent example of self-assertion gone awry. In selecting such scenes for inclusion, however, he also manages to depict the ferocity with which he must struggle to overcome the repeated denial of his humanity in the Jim Crow environment.

Wright's knife-wielding confrontation with his Aunt Addie is one of the more poignant scenes in the book:

"Hold out your hand!"
"You're not going to beat me! I didn't do it!"
"I'm going to beat you for lying!"
"Don't, don't hit me! If you hit me I'll fight you!"
For a moment she hesitated, then she struck at me with the switch and I dodged and stumbled into a corner. She was upon me, lashing me across the face. I leaped, screaming, and ran past her and jerked open the kitchen drawer; it spilled to the floor with a thunderous sound. I grabbed up a knife and held it ready for her.
"Now, I told you to stop!" I screamed.
"You put down that knife!"
"Leave me alone or I'll cut you!"
She stood debating. Then she made up her mind and came at me. I lunged at her with the knife and she grasped my hand and tried to twist the knife loose.... I bit her hand and we rolled, kicking, scratching, hitting, fighting as though we were strangers, deadly enemies, fighting for our lives.
"Leave me alone!" I screamed at the top of my voice.
"Give me that knife, you boy!"

"I'll kill you! I'll kill you if you don't leave me alone!" (*Black Boy* 108–9)

This is a scene in the most histrionic sense of the word. Note, for instance, how narration not in the form of dialogue serves as stage direction. It is also a scene in the second sense of histrionic as deliberately affected and over the top. By making a scene—both at the time of original incident, and through its dramatization for full eidetic and emotional impact—Wright is able to communicate more about his alienation, rebellion against authority, and struggle for self-determination than could be evinced from pages of existentialist narration.

The internecine struggle the scene depicts is fundamentally about power and unquestioned authority, a theme throughout the book. In a later scene, he will defend himself with razors when his Uncle Tom vows—intoning sententiously, "You need a lesson in how to live with people"—to whip him for impudence and sassiness (*Black Boy* 157–59). Both Aunt Addie and Uncle Tom have worked as teachers. Rather than hold them up as model middle-class blacks, however, Wright holds them in contempt for abusing their positions of authority. Their attempts to impose their will on a younger and more vulnerable individual leave them no higher in Wright's regard than his father, his Beale Street landlady, Mrs. Moss, and her daughter Bess, all of whom he is alienated from because of their "peasant mentality" (34–35, 214). In contrast, Wright ascribes to himself the higher consciousness of existential angst and classical liberalism, a "mind and consciousness . . . so violently altered" as to make him "forever strangers" with his kith and kin (34).

The narrative arc of *Uncle Tom's Children* from black rebel to collective action brings into focus the larger narrative and social goals of *Black Boy*. The protagonist of *Black Boy* is a rebellious individual, but the author has also depicted him as representative of the race, doing so in service to the loftier objective of galvanizing public opinion against racism and inequality. The rebellion of Wright's protagonist against the black community and family members serves the narrative and rhetorical function of criticizing authoritarianism in all of its forms. Ultimately, it is power and its abuse that engender and preserve social inequality. Wright's rebellion against intolerance and authoritarianism of all kinds is therefore also directed at black authority figures and hegemonic collective identities (including racial ones)—and not just at the white defenders of Jim Crow and racial inequality. Against intolerance, authoritarianism, and "crazy witch hunts," Wright pits an existentialist, masculine-qua-universal vision of "free thought,—which no man could escape if he read at all ... that made a man feel, whether he realized it or not, that he had to work and redeem himself through his own acts" (*Black Boy* 368–70). What at first glance seems an unexplained paradox (the existentialist individual calling for social justice through collective movements) in Wright's work is no contradiction: he is a skeptic of collective identity but a believer in the power of collective action.

ELLISON AND THE PRE-INDIVIDUALIST BLACK COMMUNITY

Perhaps the critic who saw most clearly what Wright was doing in *Black Boy* was Ralph Ellison. Years after Wright's death, Ellison would defend "fictional techniques" used in the autobiography to "drive home to Americans. . . . the cost, that is, of growing up in a society which operated on one side of its mind by the principle of equality while qualifying that principle severely according to the dictates of racism" (*Collected Essays* 672). Ellison's childhood experiences in Oklahoma had been a world apart from Wright's, but he was close enough in age to see where Wright was coming from. Their racial experiences merged when the two men were both living in New York City at the same time, experiencing identical forms of subtle and overt racism as adults. For three years, until the completion of *Native Son*, Wright and Ellison were in regular—sometimes daily—contact. Ellison writes that he "read most of *Native Son* as it came off the typewriter" (670). He would serve as best man at Wright's first marriage to the dancer Dhimah Meidman. Ellison's reading of *Black Boy* in his essay "Richard Wright's Blues" was therefore not only a perspicuous and incisive reading of the text by a fellow author, but also an argument about Wright's writing by someone who had known Wright intimately.[5]

Trained as a musician before Wright encouraged him to start writing, Ellison argues that "the specific folk-art form which helped shaped the writer's attitude toward his [Wright's] life and which embodied the impulse that contributes much to the quality and tone of his autobiography was the Negro blues" (*Collected Essays* 129). "The blues is an impulse to keep the painful details and episodes of a brutal experience alive in one's aching consciousness, to finger its jagged grain," Ellison elaborates, "and to transcend it, not by the consolation of philosophy but by squeezing from it a near-tragic, near-comic lyricism. As a form, the blues is an autobiographical chronicle of personal catastrophe expressed lyrically" (129). Thus it is misguided to criticize *Black Boy* for its negative depictions of people and its dreary outlook on life. That is precisely what the blues does—it focuses on the pain. One could say in general of the blues that those "whom [it] paints have almost no redeeming qualities," as Du Bois had charged. Thinking of *Black Boy* as Richard Wright's blues allows readers to conceive of it as an artistic representation rather than as an egregious misrepresentation of black culture.

Even more revelatory are Ellison's insights about the individual in that community: "The pre-individualistic black community discourages individuality out of self-defense. Having learned from experience that the whole group is punished for the actions of the single member, it has worked out efficient techniques of behavior control" (*Collected Essays* 140). Wright's individuality gets him in trouble not just with whites but also the African American community. The struggle to be an individual is most pronounced in conflict with members of his family who try, as Ellison describes, to squelch his aspirations out of custom and self-defense.

Rather than speaking for the collective, *Black Boy* is, in such moments, an account of rebelling against it. The assault on his personal autonomy leads the young protagonist, out of desperation, to defend himself with razor blades when his Uncle Tom promises to beat him for being impolite, threatening, as Wright sees it, "to teach me to grin, hang my head, and mumble apologetically when I was spoken to" (*Black Boy* 158). The characterization suggests that Uncle Tom's name is apt, for he embodies the attributes of his namesake. At the same time, the allusive intent of the phrasing is so clear that the reader begins to wonder whether the uncle in question was really named Tom. In a later Uncle Tom scene, Wright is himself libelously accused of being an Uncle Tom by the theater troupe he is working with in Chicago. Although on opposite sides of the accusation in these two scenes, Wright depicts himself in both instances as the victim of race-motivated censorship and appeasement. Uncle Tom's code of conduct requires Wright to modify his tone, to stand out less as an individual, to do what authority figures tell him to do. As an adult, Wright will look back and see the instilling of a submissive subculture as a by-product of Jim Crow ethics, the black community inculcating its members with the proper deferential attitude to keep anyone from "causing trouble" with the white folk. Because punishment for violations of Jim Crow ethics is often collective, the pressure to conform also comes from within the race. Both collective punishment and collective conformity are an affront to Wright's sensibilities, leading him to make a leitmotif of his stubborn resistance to attempts to make him conform to the community's standards of the proper demeanor for a boy growing up black in the South.

The tension between the self and the collective in *Black Boy* reflects and informs the narrative tension of trying to tell both a personal autobiography and a collective one. On one level, Wright seems no different from any other rebel trying to assert himself as an individual against the community's reluctance to let him do so. As we have seen, however, there is more to it than that. The identity and behavioral conformity demanded of *Black Boy*'s protagonist by the ethnic community mimics, and often dovetails with, the racial oppression descending from mainstream society—which is most acute in the Jim Crow South. The collective will that Wright depicts himself rebelling against is not the liberating communal resistance imagined by advocates of identity politics. Rather, it is merely another instrument of repression deployed against ethnic subjects. As such, Wright must denounce it.

Ultimately, *Black Boy* is as much a defense of the ethnic self as it is a critique of discrimination against racial groups. What is more, these two narrative and rhetorical strands intertwine, reinforcing each other. The author writes as an existential act of self-creation, but also weaves the threads of this liberal self and its higher consciousness into a series of knots, a flail liberally applied as the scourge of racial injustice. The protagonist of *Black Boy* hungers to be recognized as a person, a desire that is fundamental not only to self-expression but also to universal human rights. Hunger is one of the master tropes of the autobiography, Wright's existential hunger striking a harmonic resonance with the perennial physical hunger of his black boy self. It is a hunger that will bring him into conflict with the middle-class black community even as he agitates for black freedom.

PRINT CULTURE AND THE LIBERAL, HUMANIST ETHNIC SELF

The rebellious ethnic self that *Black Boy* presents to us is a force majeure, an unrelenting force of nature in his rebellion against the dominant racial narratives of his day. But where, the reader of *Black Boy* must wonder, does a black youth raised in the Jim Crow South come into such notions? How does it ever occur to such a man to question the status quo, to think outside the racial narratives he has been born into? As we have seen, certainly something is to be said for temperament, for always having been a rebellious spirit. How, then, does Wright arrive at the particular notions of the existentially and politically free subject that he comes to defend? He dramatizes the answer to our questions in the library scene (in which he forges a note so that he can check out books), as well as through the aside interjected in the free thought passage, of which, he asserts, "no man could escape if he read at all" (*Black Boy* 370). Such notions, that is, come from the impress of print culture, which indelibly stamps a liberal, humanist paradigm on Wright's psyche. In the simplest terms, Wright's passionate defense of the ethnic subject as a liberal, humanist self has its genesis in his passion for reading.

In struggling to assert his individuality, Wright is above all laying claim to his full humanity. The desire to be recognized as human (once again, figured in masculine-qua-universal terms: to be a man is to be fully human), and Wright's anxiety about not being regarded as such by others, is voiced more than once in *Black Boy*: "I was a non-man, something that knew vaguely that it was human but felt that it was not" (194). The protagonist comes to realize that the culture of fear, mistrust, and deception that Jim Crow breeds is negative and dehumanizing. A black man's personal integrity, and otherwise acting righteous (both of which ascribe moral agency), is a threat to the racial hierarchy because it undermines the pretexts for regarding others as less than human:

> So, pretending to conform to the laws of the whites, grinning, bowing, they let their fingers stick to what they could touch. And the whites seemed to like it.
> But I, who stole nothing, who wanted to look them straight in the face, who wanted to talk and act like a man, inspired fear in them. The southern whites would rather have had Negroes who stole, work for them than Negroes who knew, however dimly, the worth of their own humanity. Hence, whites placed a premium upon black deceit; they encouraged irresponsibility; and their rewards were bestowed upon us blacks in the degree that we could make them feel safe and superior. (*Black Boy* 200)

Faced with this state of affairs, Wright proclaims, "I no longer felt bound by laws which white and black were supposed to obey in common. I was outside those laws; the white people had told me so" (*Black Boy* 201).

Proclaiming moral exceptionalism, here, is a double gesture. Just as *Black Boy* is part social critique and part autobiography, so Wright in these passages is staking a claim based on the de facto social reality of racially separate moral spheres while insisting on his individuality. He is appealing to group solidarity, joining other blacks who have come to similar conclusions about the illegitimacy of legal and moral claims imposed by a racially ordered society on minority subjects. Wright's isolation, however, constitutes an even more prominent strand of the narrative:

> Again and again I vowed that someday I would end this hunger of mine, this apartness, this eternal difference; and I did not suspect that I would never get intimately into their lives, that I was doomed to live with them but not of them, that I had my own strange and separate road, a road which in later years would make them wonder how I had come to tread it. (*Black Boy* 126)

In this passage, Wright stresses his apartness from other blacks. On one level, it is his minority group affiliation that justifies his claim to being outside the laws of the dominant society. On another, it is liberal democracy's promise of individual equality and its ostensible guarantee under the law that motivates his illegal and extralegal activities. Wright eschews the Übermensch's solipsistic, moral exceptionalism in favor of the ideal of legal and ethical equality. He violates the letter of the law to realize the spirit of the law. He justifies his personal actions by framing them in terms of race warfare, but still recognizes the power of the dominant society to punish him if caught. The risks are high no matter how he explains or justifies his thievery. Moreover, despite feeling that his exclusion justifies his stealing, Wright never loses sight of his larger goal of self-realization as a person through significant participation in society: "I did not like to feel tension and fear. I wanted something else, to be human, to be caught up in something meaningful. But I must first get a job" (*Black Boy* 211).

The job, too, will be part of his ticket north. The life of a criminal is too marginalizing, itself a reflexive and conventional trap of sorts, and too suffused with "tension and fear" to be other than a means to an end: "Late one night I resolved to make that week the last. The gun in the neighbor's house came to my mind, and the cans of fruit preserve in the storehouse of the college. If I stole them and sold them, I would have enough to tide me over in Memphis until I could get a job, work, save, and go north" (*Black Boy* 206). Throughout *Black Boy*, Wright sees himself as different from the rest of his family, and here he sees himself as different from his confederates in crime.

His involvement in the movie house scam of double selling tickets is a calculated move to escape just such dehumanizing conditions, a desperate bid to get himself one step closer north: "I was gambling: freedom or the chain gang" (205).

Of course, many others were escaping to the North, where they too would gain back a measure of the human dignity denied them in the South. What is distinctive about the protagonist of *Black Boy* is that he discovers his humanity before he goes north. The escape north is made with the full consciousness of striving to get to a place where he can express that humanity. Written in the style of literary naturalism as a searing indictment of a soul-corrupting environment, *Black Boy* makes it difficult for the reader to imagine where that consciousness could have come from. The moments that explain just that are the most uplifting ones, constituting much of the appeal to the Book-of-the-Month Club crowd that was so instrumental to the book's initial success.

Fortunately, a model already existed for merging an inspirational story of racial uplift with an unremitting critique of the society the protagonist was freeing himself from: the slave narrative. In that literary tradition, Wright's forging of the note so that he could check out library books pays homage to Frederick Douglass's account of trading food for reading lessons and later forging his pass in the *Narrative of the Life of Frederick Douglass, an American Slave* (1845). Wright's own forged "pass" reads, "*Dear Madam: Will you please let this nigger boy*—I used the word 'nigger' to make the librarian feel that I could not possibly be the author of the note—*have some books by H. L. Mencken?* I forged the white man's name" (*Black Boy* 247, emphasis in the original).

Wright's original ending to part 1 of the autobiography punctuates the slave narrative feel of the text: "This was the culture from which I sprang. This was the terror from which I fled" (*Black Boy* 257). When the Book-of-the-Month Club agreed to adopt the book only if the subsequent Chicago portion of the narrative was cut, Wright extended the ending of the truncated manuscript from the original ending. In the six additional pages, he stressed the serendipitous yet indispensable role of reading in awakening his consciousness and securing his freedom:

> It had been my accidental reading of fiction and literary criticism that had evoked in me vague glimpses of life's possibilities. . . . it was out of these novels and stories and articles, out of the emotional impact of

imaginative constructions of heroic or tragic deeds, that I felt touching my face a tinge of warmth from an unseen light; and in my leaving I was groping toward that invisible light. (*Black Boy* 413)

Through his reading—which presented him with the liberal, print culture paradigms of equality, natural rights, and people as ends in themselves—Wright was able to imagine a world in which everyone is treated as fully human. "It had been only through books—at best, no more than vicarious cultural transfusions—that I had managed to keep myself alive in a negatively vital way" (*Black Boy* 413).[6] Others in his world, however, "handicapped by illiteracy," did not participate in these cultural transfusions and seemed unable to imagine the possibility of such a world (136). Wright's reading changed his thinking, and in the oppressive environment in which he lived this served only to alienate him from those around him. This message was clear also in the emended ending to the autobiography: "My reading had created a vast sense of distance between me and the world in which I lived and tried to make a living" (253).

Although it sharpened his sense of isolation in an unjust world, his reading also enabled Wright to imagine what was otherwise unimaginable in the Jim Crow South into which he, a grandson of slaves, had been born. As depicted by Douglass before him—in that iconic literacy scene of the most emblematic of all slave narratives—the key insight about the emancipatory power of literacy comes to Wright as an epiphany. In forging his pass to escape the South, Douglass found that literacy not only figuratively but also literally opened the gates to freedom. In Wright's pre–civil rights era "slave narrative," the literacy scene reaches its climax while he is reading the book given to him by the Memphis librarian, Mencken's *A Book of Prefaces*:

> Yes, this man was fighting, fighting with words. He was using words as a weapon, using them as one would use a club. . . . I concluded the book with the conviction that I had somehow overlooked something terribly important in life. I had once tried to write, had once reveled in feeling, had let my crude imagination roam, but the impulse to dream had been slowly beaten out of me by experience. Now it surged up again and I hungered for books, new ways of looking and seeing. It was not a matter of believing or disbelieving what I read, but of feeling something new, of being affected by something that made the look of the world different. (*Black Boy* 248–49)

In this pivotal scene, the biological hunger of his early years is surpassed now by Wright's intellectual and existential hunger. "Fighting with words" and writing with "feeling" will become his métier, the hallmarks of his distinctive voice and writing style. Reading had cut him off from others in the Jim Crow South, but his writing would soon connect him to an entire world of readers.

FROM *BLACK BOY* TO *BROWN* MAN: COMPARATIVE ETHNICITY AND CROSSING THE CIVIL RIGHTS DIVIDE

Reading Wright's autobiography we get a particularly good picture of the brutal environment that forged him into a writer of protest literature. We do not, however, necessarily get a satisfactory answer to the impertinent question from the eminent sociologist Robert Park on first meeting Wright in 1941: "How in the hell did you happen?" (qtd. in Rowley 250). *Black Boy* tells us all about the environmental obstacles militating against Wright and other young southern blacks, but only hints at the combination of interiority and external experiences that could have set Wright on a path to international fame so far removed from the dismal fate of his peers.

Compounding the confusion is Wright's decision, conscious that he will be read as a racially representative writer, to use an imaginative telling of the self as an instrument to indict racism and its effects. Although his biological self is constrained by his society, he is free to imagine a literary self that will challenge those constraints. As we have seen, one of Wright's techniques for challenging racial constraints is to indict racism by showing its corrosive effects on black culture. Because mainstream readers read Wright as a representative author, many of them saw any negative portrayal of blacks or black culture as problematic. To these readers, it made no more sense that Wright should risk reinforcing negative stereotypes than it did that he should deliberately downplay positive aspects of both black culture and the educational and economic advantages of family members as a way to sharpen the racial critique.

Black Boy's defense of the ethnic self sharpens and extends the book's critique of racism and of the society that engenders it. In placing the protagonist's alienation in the spotlight, the autobiography also gives us some insight into the sensibilities that led Wright to gravitate toward books and into the internal experiences that followed from his readings. This part of his account is confirmed by his brother, Leon: "I recall that he read continuously and seemed to live almost exclusively in a world of books and ideas" (qtd. in Rowley 325). Despite taking factual liberties typical of the genre, the autobiography both poignantly and accurately depicts an ethnic self shaped by print culture, and provides an emotionally true record of the environment in which the ethnic self is forged.

One of the lessons of *Black Boy* is that one has to tell readers about one's society to tell them about oneself. Wright's society, however, represses more than it expands any notion of higher consciousness and meaningful connections with others. His autobiography communicates to the world the visceral experience of any such denial of our full humanity. Moving north was a first step, but it was through his writing that Wright was finally able to articulate the hope of a communally connected ethnic self.

• ⬥ •

Among the persistent contradictions of ethnic identity is the cultural expectation that ethnic subjects assimilate by relinquishing their ethnic heritage even though mainstream society will continue to perceive them as representative of the ethnic group (which is seen as culturally other). In the Jim Crow South of Wright's childhood, the racial subject is likewise expected to conform to the dominant society's social expectations but will never be fully acknowledged as belonging to that society. The ethnic subject is thus, to adapt W. E. B. Du Bois's metaphor in *The Souls of Black Folk*, both "within and without the Veil" at the same time (xxiii–xxiv). The image that comes to mind is of a theater curtain or scrim dropped squarely on the head of the actor rather than behind the actor, as scripted. Half the body remains awkwardly on display for the audience, with the other half fronting (even if facing away from) the backstage cast and crew. This is not to say that inhabiting a dual identity is necessarily a wretched condition, though this is sometimes the case. Quite the contrary. Ethnic subjects today embrace their miscegenated racial and cultural identities, their double consciousness—even while struggling with the challenges of a complex identity.[7]

This change in ethnic consciousness reflects the changes in society between that of Wright's day and the post–civil rights era of today. The old cultural and identity tensions remain, however, though our conceptualization of the triangulation between self, society, and ethnic heritage has evolved. I use ethnic heritage in the largest sense, to include ethnic community, minority cultures of all sorts, and anything that can be lumped together under the rubric of the visibility of ethnicity. Visibility refers to the ways in which ethnicity is scripted on the body in various ways, including not only racial and gender signifiers, but also linguistic, onomastic, and other such markers.

In set-theory terms, ethnicity is a more inclusive category than race. Insofar as racial discourse depends on the visibility of the racial subject's race to others—the Venn diagramming would show—all racial subjects are also ethnic subjects (even though not everyone who shares an ethnicity also shares a race). This is the case because the visibility of the racial subject subjects them to at least one shared ethnic experience: the frequent expectation from others that the person shares a cultural identity with others of the same race or ethnicity. The ethnic Chinese baby adopted and raised by Anglo Americans grows up apart from an ethnic Chinese culture, but will also have racialized experiences that forge some sort of ethnic consciousness—an awareness that her visibility in American society in some collectively imagined way unites her with those who are visible in similar ways and thus subjected to similar expectations about a shared cultural identity.[8]

This is not to confuse race with ethnicity, conflating them beyond distinction. But it is to stress that racial experience always has a cultural aspect to it, and thus is always in some sense ethnic. One might also note the ways in which ethnic identity and the concomitant cultural expectations of others exceeds racial narratives—the visibility of ethnicity signifying above and beyond racial signifiers. African Americans who travel to Africa will tell you that the local Ghanaians, for example, can spot them at a soccer field's length away, marking them as American simply by the way that they walk and dress. If all racial subjects are also ethnic subjects, then there must certainly be times when using the term *ethnic subjects* to refer to those who are also racial subjects is not only justified but also epistemically useful. The same is also true of related terms such as *ethnicity* and *race*, the justification for such substitution hinging on whether, in the case at hand, the use of one term rather than the other elucidates more than it distorts, a distinction that varies also with the precise wording of the syllogism by which we are operating.

It is in striving to honor and acknowledge the full complexity of racial and ethnic identities—the indissoluble amalgam that the two together form, alloying also with gender, class, and other aspects of identity—that I approach

Wright's autobiography. That approach, comparative and yet attuned to the complexity and specificity of each particular ethnic self, also applies to the subject of the following chapters, the autobiographies of Richard Rodriguez. The first of those is the story of a brown man and his hunger for a communally connected ethnic self.

3

The We in Me

The Communally Derived Ethnic Self in Richard Rodriguez's *Hunger of Memory*

A scene in the British Museum marks the culmination of Rodriguez's formal education, his arc as a scholarship boy. Here, Rodriguez dramatizes "The Achievement of Desire," the title of the scene's chapter. Despite all his scholarly accomplishments, and having attended a host of prestigious schools—Stanford, Columbia, and Berkeley—it is not triumph that he describes experiencing in this moment, but the overwhelming desire "to be less alone" (*Hunger* 71). The "silence" of the museum reading room is its most salient feature, and writing his dissertation now seems "an act of social withdrawal" (70). In a subsequent chapter, Rodriguez revisits the scene, underscoring the angst of his solitude: "But then came the crisis: the domed silence" (160). Though a dedicated reader, he describes being bothered by "the isolation reading required . . . the loneliness" (60). In these poignant passages, Rodriguez reveals his intense desire for social connection, a desire that casts Rodriguez's assimilationist arguments in a new light and simultaneously cuts against the grain of any conception of Rodriguez as an individualist who is antithetical to the very idea of community.

To date, that is how Richard Rodriguez has been read, as an individualist whose *Hunger of Memory* (1982) is a manifesto for ethnicity-erasing assimilation. This first of three chapters on Rodriguez seeks to complicate the Rodriguez-as-individualist reading of *Hunger of Memory*, as well as to question the possibility of a world in which ethnicity no longer matters. The view of Rodriguez as an individualist has a tradition dating back to the earliest criticism of *Hunger of Memory*, its most salient aspect being the direct line drawn between assimilationist arguments in the book and individualism. Among Chicana/o scholars, some of the most prominent cultural and literary critics in the field have called attention to this connection. In his landmark study, *Chicano Narrative: The Dialectics of Difference*, Ramón Saldívar argues that "Rodriguez chooses to assimilate without ever considering whether he acted by will or merely submitted to an unquestioned grander scheme of political ideology" (158). Following this, Saldívar writes, "In instance after instance, he [Rodriguez] emphasizes the absolute separation between the private and the public life of men and women, the priority of the individual private inner self over the social public outer self" (158). Saldívar is not alone in suggesting a connection between assimilation and individualism. In her analysis of *Hunger of Memory*, Norma Alarcón centers her critique on the "hyperindividualized project in Rodríguez [sic]," which in turn leads to Rodriguez's "refusal of ethnicity, except as a private phenomenon" (143–44).

The penetrating analyses of Saldívar and Alarcón raise an important question: what is the nature of the connection between individualism and assimilation? Another question logically follows: is it a necessary connection? Readers outside the field of ethnic studies might be inclined to assume the opposite—that individualism and assimilation are opposed to each other because individualists would resist assimilation to a group identity of any sort. For instance, the conventionalism that assimilation to a shared cultural identity entails is underscored by Raymund Paredes in his reading of *Hunger of Memory*. Paredes identifies the literary form of the book as a "conversion narrative" (281), and follows with the remark that "apart from his preference for the traditional Latin liturgy of the Catholic church, nothing reveals Rodriguez's rigid conventionalism more clearly than his adherence to the doctrine of assimilation" (283).[1]

What unites Paredes's critique with that of Alarcón and Saldívar is an awareness that arguments about assimilation have a long history of fomenting nativist sentiments as an instrument for maintaining social inequality. For this reason, Saldívar's critique specifically questions Rodriguez's apparent lack of historical and political consciousness, a criticism echoed by Cristina Beltrán: "Yet the multiplicitous pleasure of transformation in Rodriguez comes at the cost of depoliticizing race and neglecting the past" (60). For the politically conscious, what links individualism with assimilation is an awareness that, historically, the rhetoric of individualism has often been deployed by some on the Right as an ideology for maintaining the status quo—specifically, for preserving and attempting to justify social inequality, the marginalization of minorities, and the ostensibly merit-based foundation of privileged position in society.

What is problematic about *Hunger of Memory* is that the posture Rodriguez adopts associates him with antiprogressive dimensions of conservative ideology, and thus inclines readers to misread his distinction between private and public as aligned with the tradition of maintaining inequality rather than of striving to increase opportunity. The confusion is exacerbated by the effectiveness of a regressive-taxation, corporations-are-people, winner-take-all propaganda machine that appropriates classical liberalism's useful fiction that all people are born equal (as opposed to created equal) and turns it on its head to justify and reproduce the extreme advantages enjoyed by the ultra-wealthy. All of this constitutes the sociopolitical context in which *Hunger of Memory* is read. When Rodriguez makes arguments that oppose private to public, he is easily misread as operating from and endorsing the same assumptions. Likewise, Rodriguez's arguments about the cultural and linguistic dimensions of assimilation are easily misinterpreted as the justification of exclusionary practices predicated on cultural xenophobia. A close reading of *Hunger of Memory* should lead us to reject both of these conclusions. Rather than sanctioning social inequality, Rodriguez's account stresses social mobility; rather than justifying privilege, Rodriguez offers a trenchant critique of socioeconomic disadvantage.

Rodriguez's arguments about assimilation are indeed tied to those about the individual in society, but not in the way heretofore assumed. Specifically, in *Hunger of Memory*, Rodriguez argues unequivocally for recognition as an individual, which is a cornerstone of progressive liberalism. He is not, however, as many critics have read him, advocating a more individualistic culture, libertarian or otherwise. Just the opposite: Rodriguez's analysis of public and private identity inverts both the solipsistic notion of individuals as disconnected monads and the deployment of the rhetoric of individualism to justify inequality. Instead, Rodriguez stresses the intersubjective nature of society, and sees the public-private intersection as vital to both community and greater socioeconomic equality. In short, Rodriguez's individualist stance is a surface posture underneath which lies a more fundamental desire for community. Likewise, Rodriguez's assimilationist surface arguments, as suggested by the opening lines of *Hunger of Memory* ("I have taken Caliban's advice. I have stolen their books. I will have some run of this isle"), reveal a much more trenchant resistance to hegemony, to the potential tyranny of various ethnic, racial, and gendered discourses mapped onto ethnic bodies (3). Taking precedence over subordinate (and often criticized) arguments linking individualism to assimilation are Rodriguez's desire for human connection and his rebellion against ethnic hegemony, which, taken together in his autobiographical works, consistently connect ethnic identity with community.

• ◆ •

Whereas the postmodernist critique emphasizes the extent to which various discourses construct, constrain, and ultimately deny agency to subjects, Rodriguez sees discourses of language and culture as the vehicles through which the ethnic subject gains greater agency. Like Caliban, ethnic subjects acquire agency in acknowledging and then mastering the cultural and linguistic discourses that situate them. For Rodriguez, identity is negotiated through discourse rather than imposed by it, and interpellation is intersubjective rather than wholly subjectivizing. Rodriguez demonstrates these unstated philosophical underpinnings in a most Butleresque manner through the performativity he enacts in his text.[2] To adapt J. A. Marzán's cogent analysis of Rodriguez's "public theatricality," the authorial referent of Richard Rodriguez as he presents himself is "a monument to postmodernism and reinvention" (63–64). Marzán titled his essay "The Art of Being Richard Rodriguez," and, as that title suggests, it is precisely through his posturing that Rodriguez enacts his being.

This performative being, however, is not without limits. Ethnicity, insofar as it is visible to others, is inscribed on the body just as are narratives of race and gender. And though the interpretation of those markers is social, the site of interpretation is always the body. The ethnic self is inescapably an embodied self, and thus always someone whose consciousness and personal identity are inflected by ethnic experiences and filtered through the perceptual lens of alterity. Rodriguez personifies the inescapability of ethnicity. Not only does his presumed authority as a commentator on Latino issues derive from assumptions about his ethnic Hispanic status, but readers also continue to read him as an ethnic author. Rodriguez's very consciousness is informed by the embodiedess of his ethnicity. Indeed, his nostalgia for a lost ethnic past in *Hunger of Memory* reflects the indelible tincture of an ethnic perspective. It not only is one of the most powerful themes in the book, but also inescapably informs his sense of self. Rather than endorsing any solipsistic, Ayn Rand–like individualism, Rodriguez's sense of the self—of the ethnic self—reveals a deeper impulse to forge and nurture community.

In what follows I attempt to engage Rodriguez on his own terms to suss out the nature of the relationship between individualism and assimilation as presented in *Hunger of Memory*. I develop this argument by first flashing forward to the elaboration of Rodriguez's worldview as presented in his two subsequent books, both of which are part of the context in which *Hunger of Memory* is now read. I then turn to a close reading of the summer construction job scene in *Hunger of Memory*, which Rodriguez offers as a critique of racial essentialism but, importantly, does so in the service of the larger aim of both increasing the agency of racial subjects and of expanding community.

My objective in this chapter is to illustrate the extent to which Rodriguez's desire for greater connectedness with others runs far deeper than surface arguments of his that have drawn critical scrutiny—such as his controversial views on bilingual education and the overstated dichotomy he draws between ethnic and mainstream cultures through the stand-ins of private and public identity. Not everyone will agree with the account he offers, or be comfortable with the complicated intellectual genealogy of his ideas (the political impurity of his brown thoughts). However, a close reading of *Hunger of Memory* entails decoupling its arguments from an assumed direct and uncritical inheritance of conservative ideology, especially given that Rodriguez's radically class-based critique subverts—and his communally derived notion of the ethnic self inverts—the individualist rhetoric that favors antiprogressive financial elites and seeks to institutionalize inequality. Far from urging an unquestioning and naïve assimilationism either in tandem with or replaced by an atomized individualism, *Hunger of Memory* is an expression of the desire to link ethnic identity with community.

A COMMUNALLY DERIVED ETHNIC SELF

Much of the critical resistance to Rodriguez's representation of the ethnic self and his use of the word *private* comes from the association of the self with classical liberalism (from which the modern notion of the self sprang) and, more problematic, with the ideology of conservative individualism. Despite its great virtue of enabling the useful political fiction that everyone is equal in a democracy, classical liberalism for most of its long history failed to grant the status of person to all but privileged white males. It is this troubled history that Norma Alarcón alludes to in her analysis of Rodriguez's views when—in reference to the summer construction scene in *Hunger of Memory*—she criticizes Rodriguez for privileging the rights of individuals over those of groups, and for his validation of the "bourgeois classical liberal political subject" (143). The problem with this view, Alarcón explains, is that "(im)migrants are constituted as the other of the bourgeois classical liberal political subject. Thus the political economy's constitution of this grouping (i.e., immigrants) is rejected for the pleasures of the hyperindividualized citizen-subject" (143).

Alarcón's reading also exposes the link between classical liberalism and its misappropriation by the class-protectionist wing of conservative ideology: "Rodríguez [sic] demonstrates that neoconservative liberal cynicism knows no bounds, as it rhetorically feeds its own trope machine by the selective filtering of the discourse of emancipation" (150–51). Such selective filtering takes the form of what behavioral psychologists call *fundamental attribution error* when manifested in the self-congratulatory credo of the wealthiest 1 percent's far Right, the *Atlas Shrugged* type of billionaire whose justification for excessive socioeconomic inequality goes something along the lines of "If I am rich it is not because I have been fortunate or have benefited from socially funded infrastructure, but because of my hard work and individual talent alone." The argument is persuasive for a surprisingly large number of people for two reasons. First is that the other 99 percent cling to the dream that they will be rich themselves someday. Second is that this sophistry can seem true if taking the syllogistic premise that those who work harder do better in life for the conclusion that if you are richer than everyone else, you must have worked harder than everyone else. Although as a society we would want to foster talent and provide incentives for hard work, to believe that any one person can be tens (let alone billions) of times more talented or hardworking than anyone else is a numerical absurdity. What John Galt individualism denies is the inequality of opportunity that is endemic to American society and the extent to which the most affluent and successful tend to be those who have disproportionately benefited from greater social and economic access. Bill Gates could never have become who he did had he been born in the libertarian paradise of Somalia. Without access to the opportunities afforded to him by the society he was born into, his talents would not have developed and the financial rewards of his hard work would have fallen more in line with those of, say, working-class immigrants—who, if wealth were directly proportionate to hard work alone, would be among our wealthiest citizens.

Rodriguez's arguments for class mobility—around which his arguments for assimilation revolve—are the opposite of the solipsistic individualism suggested here. Alarcón's criticism, however, comes from a different intellectual tradition—that of minority discourse. When Alarcón speaks of Rodriguez's individualism, she is contrasting his assimilationist stance to political identification with ethnic community. Most immigrants come from cultures less individualistic than mainstream America, and the marginalized status of Chicana/os inclines many to stress ethnic community (solidarity) over individualism, in part as self-defense against marginalization, discrimination, and exploitation by dominant groups. In respect to Chicana/os and other minorities, the rhetoric of individualism is often deployed as an instrument not only for maintaining current inequalities but also for preserving hierarchies of class, race, gender, and even culture. Given the long association between individualism and assimilation in this context, it is no wonder that Rodriguez's assimilationist stance leads many to read him as a neoconservative even though his arguments about public individuality—which he sees as a means to greater equality and opportunity through recognition as a person—depart radically from that of individualist strains of conservative ideology. Because intellectual traditions intersect in confusing ways here, and because using the same terminology in a different sense presents such an obstacle when it comes to discussing Rodriguez's stance in *Hunger of Memory*, the most penetrating question to ask is whether we read Rodriguez's position as seeking to protect civil liberties, or merely to protect the advantages of the wealthy and privileged.

Perhaps the most conspicuous example of this crucial question—also one of the touchstones where criticism of Rodriguez is most heated—is Rodriguez's opposition to affirmative action in *Hunger of Memory*. His stance on the politicized issue readily associates him with attempts to dismantle equal opportunity programs through an individual-merits argument that protects the status quo by ignoring the existence of disadvantage and obscuring questions of access and opportunity. In this formulation, the criticism of affirmative action easily dovetails with an ideology of individualism that benefits the privileged and their legacies. As it turns out, however, this is not how Rodriguez frames his critique of affirmative action. He focuses instead on the degree to which existing programs fail to accurately distinguish between advantaged and disadvantaged persons, and at what point a person stops being disadvantaged.

The first prong of this critique is evident in remarks that Rodriguez made as late as 2003, in which he faulted programs "for not defining carefully who, in their eyes, was disadvantaged or not" (interview with Torres 178). What stands out in his account is the extent to which he stresses considerations of class, both economic and cultural. "It became easy to underestimate, even to ignore altogether, the importance of *class*. Easy to forget that those whose lives are shaped by poverty and poor education (cultural minorities) are least able to defend themselves against social oppression, whatever its form" (*Hunger* 149–50). "The strategy of affirmative action, finally, did not take seriously the educational dilemma of disadvantaged students. They need good early schooling" (151). In comments framed around a preoccupation with questions of social justice, Rodriguez cites his objection to race-only policies that do not also consider class. "Forget the inadequacies of affirmative action as they pertained to working class Americans. Forget the fact that it was unfair to lower class whites" (interview with Torres 178). Rodriguez continues by raising a point about the difficulties of bureaucratic attempts at racial categorization. "Forget the fact that Hispanic is an absurdity because it's not even a race" (interview with Torres 178).[3]

The second prong of Rodriguez's critique is directed at the assumption that disadvantage is permanent. The standards of socioeconomic disadvantage that Rodriguez emphasizes can change over a lifetime, but affirmative action policies that considered race and gender foremost made it "difficult to distinguish the middle-class victim of social oppression from the lower-class victim. In fact, it became hard to say when a person ever *stops* being disadvantaged" (*Hunger* 150, emphasis in the original). Rodriguez considers himself among those who are no longer socially disadvantaged. Indeed, following his progression from socially disadvantaged child to "middle-class American man. Assimilated" provides the narrative structure of *Hunger of Memory* (3; for additional nuance, see 143–56).

His opposition to affirmative action programs led many readers to assume that Rodriguez was a defender of privilege and entitlements. By opposing programs that sought to narrow the inequality gap between minorities and the rest of society, Rodriguez had inadvertently framed himself as ignoring institutionalized racism and other forms of systemic disadvantage. Adding to this impression was the autobiography's narrative arc, typical of the Benjamin Franklin or Horatio Alger ascent narrative, which depicted its protagonist as triumphing over any environmental obstacles that might put him at a disadvantage. To some readers, this suggested the kind of minority success story (where the exception is taken as the rule) often used by defenders of the status quo to dismiss the force of systemic disadvantage faced by others. Other readers felt that because Rodriguez had benefited from affirmative action himself, that he was guilty of subscribing to a last-one-through-the-gate mentality. Rodriguez's arguments for assimilation and against affirmative action drew reader attention to the surface-level arguments of *Hunger of Memory*, framing reception of the text in a polarizing way, and consigning to neglect a more fundamental concern with opportunity and economic integration for ethnic subjects in a much broader sense—with negotiating an ethnic identity in a world of prejudice, inequality, unequal access, and cultural difference.

PARADIGM SHIFT: CHANGING FRAMES AND THE EVOLUTION OF HOW WE READ *HUNGER OF MEMORY*

Twenty-first-century readers of *Hunger of Memory* read quite a different text than those who read the book when it was first published. In 1982, the book's critique of affirmative action and bilingual education—flash-point issues at the time—had the adverse effect of distracting otherwise sympathetic readers from a much deeper preoccupation with the search for an ethnic identity and the desire for community. Likewise, readers distracted by perceived partisan cant, in this or any text, accordingly frame the text in a biased way. By aligning his stance with the conservative position on politicized ethnic issues—regardless of the different path he took to those conclusions, and regardless of the myriad ways in which he departs from hard-line conservative ideology—Rodriguez led his readers to misread him. The policy issues Rodriguez took up were, and continue to be, particularly polarizing because they are sometimes used as wedge issues to secure the white vote.

Rodriguez further exacerbated unsympathetic readings of *Hunger of Memory* by resorting to reductive binaries, such as that between ethnic and mainstream. Objections to these overdrawn oppositions are a dominant strain of the negative criticism that the book attracted. Saldívar, for example, is just one of many to shine the spotlight on Rodriguez's sharply drawn distinctions between private and public. Alarcón also notes "the deployment of the extremely dichotomized political categories of the private and the public" in *Hunger of Memory* (141). The result, as A. Robert Lee notes, is that the book remains "a jousting-ground for notions of cultural centre and periphery, the canonical as against the ethnic self" (53). The dichotomies continue in Rodriguez's second book, *Days of Obligation* (1992), such as in the metaphorical and rhetorical oppositions drawn between Mexico and the United States and between Catholic and Protestant cultures, prompting Rosaura Sánchez to observe that "the discourses of 'difference' with which he plays in these essays are not the product of social relations but rather mythic/metaphysical and fetishistic 'differences'" (157). The same argument could be made about Rodriguez's association in *Hunger of Memory* of the private with the past (and with his Spanish-speaking family), and the public with the present (and mainstream society). In sum, Rodriguez himself is largely to blame for the charges of hyperindividualism and uncritical assimilation leveled against him.

Later critics offer a major shift in approaches to reading him. Jennifer Browdy de Hernandez, for instance, offers a more nuanced account that sees past the surface binaries to note that "the autobiographical texts of Rodriguez and Naipaul are works of mourning which extend beyond the merely personal, casting light upon the struggles of the postcolonial marginal subject who is caught between the desire to assimilate and the recognition of the losses such assimilation incurs" ("Postcolonial Blues" 152). These texts "attempt to work through their postcolonial ambivalence and alienation" and thus "move beyond the oppositional politics of their critics into a postcolonial space that resists such reductive dualism: not black or white, not love or hate, but both ambivalently" (153). This approach, by modeling the theoretical concept of hybridity, exemplifies the general drift of much of the recent scholarship on Rodriguez and other ethnic authors grappling with identity issues.

Those scholars writing after the release of *Darling* in 2013 have within their critical purview the complete arc of Rodriguez's autobiographical oeuvre, published in ten-year increments. Depending on where one focuses the critical lens, Rodriguez's autobiographical odyssey from *Hunger* to *Days* to *Brown* to *Darling* may seem like either a mere expansion of Rodriguez's thinking or a complete revision of his ideas. In this chapter, I emphasize the consistency of underlying philosophical sentiments in Rodriguez's first three autobiographical books, later installments of which inform our reading or rereading of *Hunger of Memory*. The wider scope offered by the quartet, however, also reveals an evolution in Rodriguez's treatment of what are more proximate themes—such as the specific posture taken in each text when grappling with the issues of ethnicity, race, and sexual orientation. In *Hunger of Memory*, for example, Rodriguez is evasive about his homosexuality. In *Days of Obligation*, however, Rodriguez's identity as a gay male is central to the "Late Victorians" chapter (2), which explores the devastating effects of the AIDS epidemic on his community. Even more striking, the tropological dichotomies so dominant in the first two books are replaced in the third book by the titular trope of brown, a dichotomy-dissolving metaphor for cultural and racial miscegenation.

The critical reception of each successive book in the quartet noted changes in Rodriguez's approach to dominant themes revolving around linguistic and cultural issues. Martha Cutter's insightful analysis of the interlingual voice in Rodriguez, for example, notes a linguistic and cultural progression over the first three books from a direct opposition between English and Spanish in *Hunger of Memory*, through "an uneasy dialectic between English and Spanish" in *Days of Obligation*, to the resolution of this dialectic in *Brown* by "using, yet also refashioning, English, so that English becomes interlingual, miscegenated, brown, and inflected by Mexican Spanish, by ethnicity itself" (190). As I have been alluding to by reference to how we read *Hunger of Memory* in the contemporary context, each subsequent Rodriguez book informs how we read that book today.

As Cutter's account suggests, we now have to read *Hunger of Memory* in light of his later work: for example, the more revised cultural dialectic presented in *Days of Obligation* and the arguments made for racial, cultural, and linguistic miscegenation in *Brown*. But even critics reading *Hunger of Memory* in that updated context are prone to criticizing Rodriguez for his excessive individualism, and linking this to his arguments about assimilation. In raising the possibility of "the false universality behind the ideal of assimilation," Paula Moya follows Alarcón's example in referring to Rodriguez as a "neoconservative," an epithet he earns, in Moya's analysis, by his opposing of "individual to collective identity" (103). Because her book *Learning from Experience* appeared in the same year as *Brown*, Moya did not yet have access to Rodriguez's third installment when writing. Nevertheless, her critique raises two important points: one, that individualism and assimilation are inherently linked persists as a dominant assumption in the field of Latina/o studies; and, two, that Ernesto Laclau's concern about hegemony and the particular masking as the universal is something we must always be on our guard about (21–28). That is, when it comes to negotiating one's identity among different identity groups, how does one avoid the false universality of any single, hegemonic identity group?

It remains an open question as to whether mainstream culture, the same as the dominant narrative of any given minority culture, can ever be fully immune to the possibility of becoming hegemonic. But the conceptualization, in *Brown*, of mainstream culture as the product of continuous cultural miscegenation is an account in which the evolution of cultures inherently resists hegemony. What Rodriguez seems to be seeking is freedom not from belonging to a community, but from hegemonic collective identities. Rodriguez wants ethnic subjects to be free to negotiate the complicated interaction between ascribed and self-identifying aspects of their identity. Thus, in his communally derived individualism (*Brown* 131, 200), Rodriguez has much more in common with his identity-politics critics than conceived of to date. One can easily imagine one of these critics uttering a version of what he writes in *Brown*: "Americans are so individualistic, they do not realize their individualism is a communally derived value.... 'In order to be individualistic, one must have a strong sense of oneself within a group'" (200). In this passage, the notoriously slippery Rodriguez is unequivocal: he rejects the notion of an individual without a community. These ideas rest on the surface in *Brown* and, because they so clearly express Rodriguez's philosophical stance, I cite passages from that later work. But Rodriguez's commitment to the idea of the interdependence of individuals and communities is also found in *Hunger of Memory*, to which I now return.

PUBLIC IDENTITY, OR RECOGNITION AS A PERSON, IN *HUNGER OF MEMORY*

In chapter 4—titled "Complexion"—of *Hunger of Memory*, Rodriguez deconstructs the conflation of race with class using arguments that seek to maximize the agency of ethnic subjects and to emphasize their social connectedness. He does this, characteristically, by offering an anecdotal account of his experiences at a summer construction job. The vivid scene not only illustrates the complex interdependence of race, class, ethnicity, and myriad other aspects of identity, but also underscores the dependence of ethnic selfhood on connection with others. Rodriguez does this by contrasting those recognized as individuals with those known only as members of what is mistakenly perceived as a homogeneous group—a notion of community that is diametrically opposed to that of a diverse society. The overall effect of the scene is to illustrate the importance of community and of recognition by others within communities.

Rodriguez's fascination with the masculine image associated with working men initiates the scene, in which, having just completed his undergraduate degree at Stanford, he hopes to fulfill his yearning to prove himself just as masculine as *los pobres* (the poor, here with the added connotation of disadvantaged) by taking a summer construction job (*Hunger* 136). While on that job, Rodriguez experiences an epiphany, a realization that in having long since crossed discernible class lines he has also, as he sees it, crossed the color line. By the end of the summer, Rodriguez, who had spent much of his childhood ashamed of his dark complexion, has come to reevaluate his racial identity:

> After that summer, a great deal—and not very much really—changed in my life. The curse of physical shame was broken by the sun; I was no longer ashamed of my body. No longer would I deny the pleasing sensations of my maleness. During those years when middle-class black Americans began to assert with pride, "Black is beautiful," I was able to regard my complexion without shame. (*Hunger* 136)

Rodriguez's realization that he has fully entered the middle class—combined with the insight that how one's race is perceived has a lot to do with one's social class—leads him to no longer view his complexion as a mark of shame. His dark skin is no longer shameful, but exotic, completing reversing the social value of his complexion.

That the meaning of race can be transfigured so suddenly gives the lie to the notion that race has any natural and self-evident meaning. The semiotic baggage of skin color is loaded in social space:

> My complexion becomes a mark of my leisure. Yet no one would regard my complexion the same way if I entered such hotels through the service entrance. That is only to say that my complexion assumes its significance from the context of my life. My skin, in itself, means nothing. I stress the point because I know there are people who would label me "disadvantaged" because of my color. (*Hunger* 137)

Rodriguez is unequivocal here in rejecting essentialist notions about skin color, but the chapter is easily misread as a disavowal of racial disadvantage, or of the existence of insidious forms of systemic racism in society. Rodriguez's account does not seek to deny the existence of racism, but rather to stress the means of agency available to racialized subjects. Because the semiotic charge imparted to phenotypic features has more to do with discourse, culture, signification, and relations of power than biological difference, then racial subjects can subvert racial discourses through cultural and linguistic acts. That is not to discount the epistemic value of experience, however. Two decades later, Rodriguez will muse that people of the same race may share enough similar race-based experiences to cast their thoughts in similar hues—that is, to thus engender a racial consciousness through which experience is in turn filtered: "But do we really think that color colors thought? . . . In the case of brown thought, though, I suppose experience becomes the pigment, the grounds, the *mise-en-scène*, the medium of refraction, the impeded passage of otherwise pure thought" (*Brown* 33–34, italics in the original).

Rodriguez's arguments about class also stress the extent to which socioeconomic class is inextricably bound up with fluency in what he sees as the more powerful discourses of language, culture, and education. Aware of the overlap between the two, Rodriguez often makes little effort to explicitly distinguish between social class and economic class. To do so, in part, risks carving out abstractions unnaturally isolated from the intricate web of social reality in which they are enmeshed. Nevertheless, his engagement with class is more cultural than economic.

Rodriguez dubs the other brown-skinned English speakers at the jobsite middle class, though at least some of them are employed in menial and physical labor almost identical to that of the working-class Mexican aliens. These are undocumented workers, but what most strikes Rodriguez is that they are hired as a group: "They came and left in a single old truck. Anonymous men. They were never introduced to the other men at the site" (*Hunger* 134). The brown-skinned men who speak English, in contrast, are not at all anonymous, and are not considered interchangeable. They are not seen only as indistinguishable parts of a homogeneous group. Their individuality is recognized: "[T]here was no single *type* of worker. I am embarrassed to say I had not expected such diversity" (*Hunger* 133, emphasis in the original). For Rodriguez, it is this recognition as an individual that, paradoxically, connects them one to another and to society as a whole. As Rodriguez sees it, the nature and quality of intersubjective relationships hinge on such recognition.

Ironically, it is Rodriguez's initial inclination to lump people into homogeneous groups, by occupation in this case, that leads him to this realization. He takes the summer construction job hoping to affirm his manhood as a "mythical Mexican laborer," to "at last become like a *bracero*" and prove that he knew what real work was (*Hunger* 127, 131, italics in the original). But not long into the job, he realizes "that I was fooling myself if I expected a few weeks of labor to gain me admission to the world of the laborer" (133). Mere participation in similar occupational activities does not make him one of los pobres. He can no longer assume, as he had, that "a disadvantaged life was circumscribed by particular occupations" (137–38).

In noting his failure to experience working-class life truly, despite briefly engaging in genuine physical labor, Rodriguez also offers a caveat about the assumed uniformity and cohesiveness of group identifications. He can no longer justify lumping together people of the same race, gender, or ethnicity: "All Mexican-Americans certainly are not equally Mexican-Americans" (*Hunger* 150). Any minority group is diverse: despite the importance of common experiences among those sharing a race, gender, or ethnicity, shared experiences alone do not guarantee a shared identity, nor do they ensure the cohesiveness of a group. Moreover, as evidenced by the example of the middle-class Mexican American workers at the construction site, identification with a minority group need not exclude one from identification with and within larger society, nor vice versa.

Rodriguez concludes that group identification is most inclusive through the public identity that the shared language of English provides (*Hunger* 25–28). One might argue that identifications that span many languages, such as religious identities, are much more inclusive. However, given his preference for the Latin Mass, Rodriguez would likely stress that those sharing an identity across the language barrier literally have nothing in common to speak of.[4] Rodriguez takes the position that at least minimal fluency in the principal language of a place offers the most satisfying and inclusive means of identification and recognition. The dominant language of a society is so inclusive and expressive that even most freely choosing ethnic individuals would opt to use it as their public language of choice. At least, that is the scenario as Rodriguez painted it, and as modeled by the life he depicts in his autobiography.

Reliance on language as the glue that holds people together in society has a downside, however. It is the most formidable border to cross. One cannot master another tongue, and go back and forth between languages, as easily as Rodriguez is able to cross the color line when invited to an upscale cocktail party in Bel Air. Differences in language proficiency also contribute to differences in class. Class differences among the workers at the construction work site are easily identifiable, though all are doing the same job. English-speaking middle-class workers can fill out their own work sheets (*Hunger* 134). In comparison, Spanish-speaking workers are viewed as a collective and collectively paid by the contractor (*Hunger* 135). The ability to read and fill out the work sheets is symbolic in its capacity to separate racially indistinguishable people into distinct socioeconomic classes. Filling out the work sheets indicates proficiency in the customs and language of the dominant culture. Additionally, because those who cannot fill out their time cards unassisted are paid less, the metaphor demonstrates that economic class is partly determined by cultural class. Class mobility, as is true in similar ways even for those whose mother tongue is English, seldom goes against the current of acculturation and education.

The most problematic part of Rodriguez's reading of the scene is that it downplays the vulnerability that their undocumented legal status imposes on los pobres. When I was a boy, the police came onto our property to arrest a cousin whose backbreaking job moving irrigation pipe on a potato farm would be the rural analogue to the type of work available to los pobres in Rodriguez's tableau. His crime was working without proper documentation. He was deported and I never saw him again because he died prematurely a few years later. He spoke little or no English, but fluency in English would have done him little good in the face of a force as impersonal and systemic as immigration law. Rodriguez's example would be more convincing had the so-called Mexican aliens Rodriguez uses to illustrate his point been U.S. citizens who spoke no English (*Hunger* 134). Nevertheless, his point that class mobility has a cultural or discursive component, and is not strictly economic, is well taken. Undocumented workers who are fluent in English are, among other things, less likely to be conceptualized and treated as noncitizens or as irredeemably culturally other.

Cultural fluency may go a long way toward social integration, but socioeconomic inequality remains sharply demarcated along lines of race, gender, and ethnicity. That the complicated apartheid legacy of economic division follows such contours indicates the extent to which these other aspects of social reality are threaded into the weave. Rodriguez's account offers an explanation for the perpetuation of social inequality, but seems to leave out dimensions of social inequality that others take for granted. Nevertheless, Rodriguez seeks to increase the agency of marginalized subjects in his account, and does so by trying to give them a voice. It is the lack of a voice, Rodriguez insists, that most disadvantages and makes vulnerable the members of marginalized groups. Whether externally imposed by others ("them Mexicans") or an act of self-identification ("*nosotros*," Spanish for *we*), the collective identity of los pobres denotes, along with their silence, the absence of a publicly recognized individual identity—an absence that, as Rodriguez's interpretation of the scene suggests, prevents their being recognized by others as a person. Unable to speak English, los pobres lack a public identity—recognition of which depends on linguistic and cultural aptitude within the social and geographic context they inhabit—and are thus seen as persons apart rather than as persons with the same civic status as everyone else (*Hunger* 138). Rodriguez notes, "If tomorrow I worked at some kind of factory, it would go differently for me. My long education would favor me. I could act as a public person—able to defend my interests, to unionize, to petition, to speak up—to challenge and demand. (I will never know what real work is)" (138). Sociologists make a similar point when distinguishing between generational poverty and situational poverty, between the underclass and the transitory poor. The middle-class divorcée may experience a temporary lowering of income and lifestyle immediately after the divorce, but retains all the cultural knowledge and other hidden advantages of a middle-class upbringing.

 The class divide, as Rodriguez characterizes it, has as much to do with the disparity of cultural knowledge as it does the inequality of incomes. Like Frederick Douglass before him—realizing, in one of the most iconic and inspirational scenes in American literature, that literacy is the key to mental and, in Douglass's case, physical emancipation—Rodriguez recognizes the need to read the letters of social discourse to participate more fully in it and to have any hope of escaping disenfranchisement. As any academic from a working-class background can attest, trying to fit in in academia—with its career-oriented, politically savvy, middle- and upper-class culture—involves profound culture shock. The career prospects of would-be academics are almost directly proportional to their mastery of the dominant culture and discourses of academia, and other analogues of postcolonial mimicry, including writing and speaking fluently in the language of the field and the ability to situate oneself within the academic conversation—both prerequisites to having one's work accepted by colleagues and peer reviewers. So it goes with larger society, argues Rodriguez. The voice that does not speak in the language of shared discourse is not heard. It is participation in the realm of public discourse that Rodriguez advocates when extolling assimilation, and when prophesying its inevitability among the descendants of immigrants.

Assimilation of any kind involves trade-offs, and Rodriguez's title, *Hunger of Memory*, communicates his sense of loss and nostalgia for a culturally ethnic childhood. Poignantly depicted is what was lost—ways of thinking and feeling, fluency in his mother tongue—in order to gain access to something else. In this sense, assimilation can be constricting. But, as Rodriguez notes in *Brown*, assimilation is not a zero-sum game in which one must give up everything in exchange for marginalized and unsatisfactory participation in a dominant culture inherently opposed to one's cultural heritage. The culture and language to which people assimilate is also changed in the process of assimilating diverse cultures, an idea Rodriguez eloquently expresses at public talks using an image he links to the figurative title of his most recent book, *Brown*: when different crayons melt in the sun they become one color, the culturally and racially blended hue of brown.

Yet most of the emotional power of *Hunger of Memory*, as the title indicates, comes precisely from the pathos with which Rodriguez depicts what he has lost in the process of being assimilated: "I remember what was so grievously lost to define what was necessarily gained" (*Hunger* 6). In *Brown*, Rodriguez thematizes the ways in which minority and majority cultures shape each other—contaminate each other. In *Hunger of Memory*, he focuses on personal experiences revolving around the loss of one in exchange for the other: "As I grew fluent in English, I no longer could speak Spanish with confidence" (28). On an emotional level, Rodriguez fetishizes the loss, but on other levels he appeals to his readers to focus on the gain: "If I rehearse here the changes in my private life after my Americanization, it is finally to emphasize the public gain" (27). Through his assimilation to the English-speaking middle class, Rodriguez has options not available to the unassimilated pobres, collectively marked by their silence. He will never know what real work is because real work is the absence of choice, being bound to an occupation by dint of a narrow education or the inability to speak in society (133–35). The way to help the Spanish-speaking laborers, as Rodriguez would have it, would be to assimilate them (if not them, their children) through the classroom and the English language. This would open more options for them—options that flow from participating in a shared language, culture and, for better or for worse, mass society.

The power inequalities in what Mary Louise Pratt would call the contact zone—"social spaces where disparate cultures meet, clash, and grapple with each other, often in highly asymmetrical relations of domination and subordination" (4)—of the construction jobsite have, as Rodriguez describes it, nothing to do with race per se (dark-skinned Rodriguez and the other assimilated Mexican-American workers get the going wage), something to do with recourse to political and legal power (the right to organize without risk of deportation, for example), and everything to do with cultural and linguistic dominance. At least, this appraisal follows from Rodriguez's depiction of the scene. On the California side of the Mexican-American border, English paves the roads to education, public discourse, and recognition as a full member of society. One need not cease to live a culturally ethnic life, but forsaking participation in mainstream culture carries certain disadvantages. Social benefits derive from public recognition, which in turn derives from minimal literacy in the dominant language and culture. From Rodriguez's point of view, it is not enough to assert an imbalance of power between cultures within the contact zone. The very medium in which relations of power are forged is thoroughly and ineradicably cultural, and culture itself is primarily linguistic.[5] Rodriguez sees learning English as the prerequisite to both joining society and being recognized as a person.

Rather than urging ethnic minorities to act hyper individualistically, Rodriguez's arguments for assimilation advocate greater community through fuller participation in the society around them. For Rodriguez, the ethnic self is inescapably a communally derived self, which is how the ethnic self is portrayed in *Hunger of Memory*. Only in *Brown* does it becomes clear that Rodriguez's notion of the ethnic self is also a culturally miscegenated self, and that the ethnic subject need not forsake ethnic community to participate in society at large. The problematic dichotomies of *Hunger of Memory* and *Days of Obligation* are dissolved in *Brown*, where Rodriguez offers an account in which he no longer gives the impression that ethnic heritage and mainstream culture are mutually exclusive. This reconsideration of Rodriguez is a reading of *Hunger of Memory* that adjusts our interpretive lens in light of a greater appreciation for the philosophical assumptions underlying his public—we might say with some irony—stance, arguments, and terminology in that text. Elucidating such a reading are the contours of

Rodriguez's shifting postures and emphases over subsequent books relative to more fundamental and consistent philosophical views, an example of which I have foregrounded here in tracing *Hunger of Memory*'s surface arguments for individualism to Rodriguez's more fundamental desire for greater community. The emphasis on recognition as an individual and Rodriguez's assimilationist arguments in *Hunger of Memory* are indeed linked. The linkage, however, is far removed from formulations of individualism used as a tool for repression, and from paradigms of assimilation invoked as a justification for the exclusion of cultural minorities. Rodriguez imagines just the opposite: cultural and linguistic fluency as a means of agency, inclusion, and opportunity for ethnic subjects. *Hunger of Memory* offers a performance of these principles, its author resisting with words the discourses that situate and constrain ethnic bodies. The ways in which those discourses of ethnicity play out in print culture is the subject of the next chapter, in which we turn to Rodriguez's second book, *Days of Obligation*, and the use of the ethnic father as the manikin of autobiography.

4

En el Nombre del Padre

The Immigrant Father as the Manikin of Autobiography, and Its Agon with the Print Culture Self in Richard Rodriguez's *Days of Obligation: An Argument with My Mexican Father*

EXORDIUM: ENCOUNTER WITH THE BANK ROBBER

Not long after the publication of his second book, *Days of Obligation* (1992), Richard Rodriguez began to correspond with a convicted bank robber serving the last of his seven-year term in a Massachusetts federal prison. The man's name was Joe Loya, and the correspondence continued for two years until Loya's release from prison in 1996. Loya had initiated the correspondence, writing to Rodriguez from his prison cell and, once an epistolary relationship had been established, urging Rodriguez to visit him in prison. As Rodriguez recounts in his introduction to Loya's memoir, *The Man Who Outgrew His Prison Cell*, he demurred, preferring to keep open the ontological gap between the man he knew only in letters—a "secret sharer"—and the embodied referent of the literary self in those letters: "No. No. The letters were everything" (introduction xi–xii). Precisely because it places you at a physical remove, correspondence with another person through space-negating media such as letters or e-mail offers a unique intimacy. Counterintuitively, such intimacy can be lost when standing face-to-face, when meeting your Conradian "secret sharer" in the flesh—a truism borne out by the readiness with which people share intimate thoughts and feelings in e-mail correspondence and through social media that they wouldn't so readily share in person. In a related insight, Rodriguez had mused in *Hunger of Memory*, that "works of literature ... are so often among the most personal statements we hear in our lives.... *written* words heighten the feeling of privacy" (187–88, emphasis in the original).

The personal connection of the page, paradoxically, can be lost or diminished when the author walks onto the stage. At the time of his correspondence with Loya, Rodriguez is keenly aware of all of this and strives to maintain the intimacy of their personal correspondence by refusing to meet Loya in person. In fastidiously repressing the reality of the referent of the literary ethnic self with whom he is corresponding, Rodriguez splits Loya's subjectivity, just as he had done with himself in *Hunger of Memory*: "My brother and sisters recognize a different person, not the Richard Rodriguez in this book" (190). The two Loyas—the literary self and the real-life referent—cannot be kept apart indefinitely, however. The irrepressible Loya will have his audience with Rodriguez, and the two do eventually meet shortly after Loya's release from prison. Their encounter, as much in its belatedness as in its irrepressibility, is an apt metaphor for Rodriguez's revisiting of his ethnic roots and the undead past in *Days of Obligation*. It is also emblematic of the reconciliation of the ethnic self with the literary self, a reconciliation not only of the self to that other self narrated on the page, but also of the ethnic self to the self shaped by print culture.

The performative self that Rodriguez enacts in *Hunger of Memory* emphasizes the agency of ethnic subjects in part by suggesting that ethnic culture can be relegated to the private sphere or to the dead past. The corporeal Rodriguez, however, finds himself doggedly confronted by the reality of the visibility of ethnicity in the public sphere. Rodriguez's ethnicity is integral to the framing and reception of his books, and to his status as an author—with readers perceiving Rodriguez as a Hispanic author. No matter how fictionalized the self on the page, the divided self of the two Rodriguezes (the literary self and the biological self) cannot long stand divided because it is continually sutured together again by readers who make epistemological assumptions based on what they think they know about the referent. The biological being of the ethnic author cannot be denied or repressed—its spectral presence persists despite its ontological absence from the text. Rodriguez's ethnicity haunts and inhabits his texts no matter how much that ethnicity is relegated to the past or denied within the public sphere. This haunting is demonstrated by the way in which Loya comes to Rodriguez as a reader only by first coming to him as a viewer. It was the text of race—the semiotics of race in America—that led Joe Loya to first contact Rodriguez when seeing on television the "dark-skinned essayist Richard Rodriguez, his face Indian like mine" (301). Echoing the pattern, Rodriguez's autobiographical books are supplemented with a picture of their ethnically marked subject on the front or back covers of paperback and trade paperback editions, underscoring the visibility of ethnicity in society and its role in the reading and interpretation of books by ethnic authors.

The visibility of ethnicity is prior to reading, just as it is prior to the ethnic subjects who are born into discourses such as race, gender, and ethnicity. This observation about the always-already nature of ethnic visibility in society is not meant to suggest that such visibility is relegated entirely to the visual sphere nor is it meant to suggest that linguistic texts follow a wholly visual logic. The not-just-visual visibility of ethnicity precedes the text and the ethnic author in consequential and meaningful ways, but the text itself is wholly linguistic in ontology. Additionally, Rodriguez would argue, it is only through "public language" and English-language print culture that the two ethnic selves (Loya and Rodriguez) are able to become Conradian "secret sharers." Until meeting Loya in the flesh, Rodriguez knows only the textual self, but with their first encounter what might previously have been taken as an ontological gap (between corporeal self and narrative self) is revealed to be merely epistemological—a gap bridged by language. The significance of language to identity (to the very being of subjects) is figured by Rodriguez in salvific terms: "Words can save you" (introduction xiii).

As Rodriguez's appraisal suggests, language is far more than something merely additive or supplemental. Rather, language is integral to the self, constitutive of the self. Indeed, it is through language that we both narrate the self and express higher-order thoughts. Personal identity, by extension, is indelibly stamped not only by our mother tongue, but also by the imprint of our reading. Of the embodied Joe Loya he has by then come to know, Rodriguez will proclaim that "[r]eading saved him," emphatically privileging the written word over the spoken word (introduction xiv). The question, then, is how we reconcile, for instance, the self who reads and writes predominantly in English with the self who speaks to family in Spanish? Rodriguez would stress that he and Loya would never have connected in the first place without the English language and its print culture as intermediary. Rather than severing the two from their ethnic culture, the dominant language serves here as the means by which they "descended further and further into the past" and as the prerequisite to the discovery of any shared ethnic experiences that the two might have in common (introduction xii).

What Rodriguez expresses in his introduction to Loya's memoir resonates as a thematic chord throughout his work. Namely, the identity formation of ethnic subjects not only bears the tincture of the printed page but also largely takes place through print culture, which in turn becomes the medium through which authors articulate the literary ethnic self. Not only must any account of narratives of the ethnic self include some consideration of the role of print culture, but without a shared print culture, minority voices are not likely to be heard by the larger reading public. Completing the circuit, we must also take into account the ways in which readers come to these texts through the interpretive lens of conventions and expectations surrounding ethnic genres, interpretive practices that are inseparable from the extratextual visibility of ethnicity in society. Embedded in this triangulation of text, self, and society, *Days of Obligation* explores the tension not only between ethnic cultures coexisting within the self (the mestizaje, or cultural mixing, inherent to identity itself), but also between ethnic authors and the ethnic expectations of their readers. What is more, to those wary readers of *Hunger of Memory* who felt that Rodriguez was posturing for the page while ignoring how ethnicity (and the then-closet drama of Rodriguez's gay identity) plays out on the stage of the real world, *Days of Obligation* is an invitation to a more personal encounter with the conman we have been corresponding with.

ON MEXICAN FATHERS AND THE MANIKIN OF AUTOBIOGRAPHY

Richard Rodriguez describes the focus of *Days of Obligation* as "the influence of Mexican ethnicity on my American life" (*Brown* xiv). If, in *Hunger of Memory*, Rodriguez had seemed to overemphasize the extent of his assimilation to Anglo culture, now, in *Days of Obligation*, he would reveal the ethnic roots of his American self. The subtitle of Rodriguez's second autobiographical book, *An Argument with My Mexican Father*, heralded this encounter with the Mexican ethnicity of Rodriguez's parents as well as his own formative years.[1] In *Hunger of Memory*, Rodriguez had depicted that familial ethnic culture as private, and as conducted in a "private language"—something that was lost, or at least repressed, as the price of assimilation to mainstream society (15). In *Days of Obligation*, Rodriguez explores the return of the repressed—the benthic upwellings of the strong ties to ethnic culture instilled by immigrant parents—and the tension, or "argument," on which the identity and experiences of the ethnic subject balance between the dominant culture and an ethnic subculture.

In *Hunger of Memory*, Rodriguez uses himself as the manikin of autobiography, following the example of Henry Adams, and dressing himself, the scholarship boy, in the robes of education across episodic chapters that trace the arc of his education—an arc that maps almost perfectly onto the path of his assimilation (66).[2] Rodriguez disrupts the perfect harmony of those tandem arcs in *Days of Obligation* by also at times having his immigrant father stand in as the manikin of autobiography, particularly in the last chapter, "Nothing Lasts a Hundred Years." "My father remains Mexican in California," writes Rodriguez. "Much in life is failure or compromise; like father, like son" (*Days* 219). The title of this chapter alludes to the ritual of concluding a prayer, supplication, or blessing with the paternal invocation, "in the Name of the Father." That is exactly what Rodriguez does in ending his second book with his father, adapting the religious ritual as autobiographical literary convention. Likewise, the book's introductory chapter, "My Parents' Village," adapts as literary device the invocation prayer offered at the beginning of ritualistic ceremonies, such as college graduations—thus entwining ethnic, literary, and spiritual dimensions of his identity.

Through the invocation of parental proxies, Rodriguez is able to excavate, even to sacralize, what was buried as repressed memory in *Hunger of Memory*—an ethnic identity. In America "you will find yourself a stranger to your parents, a stranger to your own memory of yourself," Rodriguez tells us, but in Mexico you will find a "tabernacle of memory" (*Days* 161, 79). Rodriguez even goes so far as to personify Mexico as memory ("Mexico is memory") and, through the metonymy of Mexico, to characterize ethnic roots as memory (73, 67). On one level, characterizing one's ethnic roots as memory might seem dismissive of ethnic culture, something relegated to the past and thus banished from any significant role in the present. Indeed, that is how many critics read *Hunger of Memory*: ethnic identity seemed to be that which Rodriguez sacrificed in order to assimilate, the mandate to assimilate being the basis of his controversial arguments against bilingual education. Nostalgia for the past is a dominant theme in *Hunger of Memory*, however. Likewise, in *Days of Obligation*, Rodriguez is critical of American amnesia, of "the severing of memory" and its link to "the belief that one can choose to be free of American culture" (171). This same belief about the hold of culture and of the past extends to Rodriguez's religious identity, as well as to the Mexican perspective inherited from his parents. The last Rodriguez explores through the proxy of his father. This approach allows Rodriguez to hold in suspension the "tension that describes my life," to balance his defense of a common American culture with the personal insight that "[n]ow that I am middle-aged, I incline more toward the Mexican point of view" (*Days* xvii).

The depiction of the tension between opposites is a persistent theme in Rodriguez's work, the drawing of those oppositions always courting the charge that he misrepresents by starting from reductive binaries. In *Days of Obligation*, Rodriguez's emphasis on the tension between the "Protestant north" (comic, individualist, and optimistic) and the "Catholic south" (tragic, communal, and cynical) cultures that coexist within him suggests, however, something beyond the initial gesture toward overly generalized cultural differences. Rather than binarist, Rodriguez's approach here is dialectical. Many scholars have focused on the reductiveness of Rodriguez's binaries, but I emphasize the synthesis that comes out of that dialectical approach. *Days of Obligation* continues, as did *Hunger of Memory*, in the tradition of the autobiographical mode of Saint Augustine's *Confessions*, bookending the "Late Victorians" chapter (2) with allusions to Augustine in its first and last sentences. The Augustinian frame story suggests other borrowing from Augustine, including self-consciously situating himself loosely within the tradition of spiritual autobiography as well as importing that genre's use of the dialectical mode. As Thomas Cooley writes, "Saint Augustine's *Confessions* is constructed on a principle of dialectic. Augustine's tendency to arrive at order through warring contraries shows up in his narrator's fondness for dialogue, in his antithetical style, and in recurring contrast between images of light and darkness" (31).

So it is with the dialectic between Protestant America and Catholic Mexico in *Days of Obligation*, the synthesis of which is found throughout the culturally fluid and permeable *frontera*—in border spaces such as Tijuana. "Whereas San Diego remains provincial and retiring, the intrusion of the United States has galvanized Tijuana to cosmopolitanism" (*Days* 84–85). Rodriguez chastises Anglo America for fixing the dialectic and failing to achieve such a synthesis. "In New England the European and the Indian drew apart to regard each other with suspicion over centuries. Miscegenation was a sin against Protestant individualism" (13). It is with an awareness of Rodriguez's deployment of an

Augustinian and Hegelian dialectical approach that we must read the book's subtitle, *An Argument with My Mexican Father*. We must read Rodriguez's dramatization of oppositions in the text with an understanding that warring contrasts not only coexist in tension but also are the beginning point to a possible synthesis.

The desire for achieving such a synthesis can be seen in the way Rodriguez carries arguments about the force of assimilation over from his first book: "Language is *the* lesson of grammar school.... Grammar school teachers forged a nation" (*Days* 163, emphasis in the original). In this second iteration, Rodriguez advances the dialectic by expanding on his earlier sense, easily overlooked in *Hunger of Memory*, of American culture as dynamic and inclusive, mirroring the perpetual fluidity and the assimilation of opposites that Hegelian synthesis entails: "To be an American is to belong to black history. To argue for a common culture is not to propose an exclusionary culture or a static culture" (*Days* 170). His defense of the idea that a multicultural nation of immigrants can share a culture stems in large part from an awareness that his identity has been molded as much by print culture as by his first-generation Mexican parents, to whom he dedicates *Hunger of Memory*: "For her and for him—to honor them."

The synthesis that is the self, Rodriguez realizes, arises from the dialectic of contrasting cultures. It is not only fitting, then, but almost inevitable that the introduction to *Days of Obligation* should be "My Parents' Village." Neither, however, can Rodriguez's identity, particularly as a writer, be separated from his identity as a reader, no more than the reading of Rodriguez can be separated from his public identity as an ethnic author. In turning back to his ethnic roots in *Days of Obligation*, Rodriguez expands the definition of *full public individuality* as he uses the term in *Hunger of Memory* (27). Cultural assimilation to a shared public culture—even a dynamic and inclusive one—may bridge or conceal some ethnic differences, but public identity remains associated with a visibly marked body. And though Rodriguez's visibility as an ethnic subject may be wholly determinative of neither ethnic nor personal experience, it nonetheless informs the ways in which readers read his books. Ethnic experiences and the attending ethnic expectations of society, however, often exist in great tension with the print culture narratives that are constitutive of the ethnic self. This tension is played out in *Days of Obligation* by numerous allusions to a largely Anglo American literary tradition in chapters that primarily address ethnic topics. What follows is an exploration of the intersection of the ethnic subject with print culture.

READING CONVENTIONS AND THE LITERARY ETHNIC SELF

Print culture can be approached from several angles, three of which are particularly salient to this analysis: content, form, and social practice. These classifications can be put more concretely as what we read, genre, and reading conventions. Rodriguez invokes a sophisticated understanding of distinctions in genre, and the reading conventions that accompany them, when associating theater with communal experience and novels with the rise of individualism: "When Hamlet leaves the play behind him, *Hamlet* becomes a novel" (*Days* 177). The use of each genre as a metaphor for community and individualism is developed throughout the "Latin American Novel" chapter (9) as a theme, and as a warning against excessive individualism. "I went to England to pursue a study of Puritanism and the rise of the novel. . . . Then I was recalled by the Catholic necessity to avert my soul's eye from a Protestant logic that would make mere individualism a virtue" (*Days* 193–94). So intertwined are the content, genre, and reading conventions facets of print culture, and so integrated is print culture with the larger culture, that Rodriguez is able to offer a much broader cultural analysis simply by reflecting on the kinds of books we produce and read as a society.

In the pages that follow, I begin with the last of these three interlocking aspects of print culture, reading conventions, and work my way backward to ethnic genres (including superimposed genres) and print culture (what we read) as formative of ethnic identity. Genre and reading conventions are two sides of the same coin, and it is as a genre that readers frame autobiographical texts by ethnic authors. Genres, for the most part, are not mutually exclusive, nor are reading conventions. Rodriguez's texts are read variously—or simultaneously, depending on the reader—as essay, autobiography, cultural criticism, regionalism, or ethnic literature (a lengthy list but by no means an exhaustive one).

Literary conventions place boundaries on texts in much more formal ways than similar discursive framing does in interpersonal oral exchanges. Insofar as we are reading Rodriguez's books, and reading them as autobiographical, we are constrained by them. Conventions that encourage the articulation of ethnicity can also corral ethnic texts and the representation of ethnic selves more severely than the daily experiences of the author. Rodriguez is treated as a whole person by his friends, but readers of his books expect him to be representatively ethnic in much more limited ways. The textual self may thus brush up against constraints not encountered by the real-world referent. In the next chapter, I take up one such constraint—one that need not be—in addressing the discourse of ethnic authenticity through a close reading of Rodriguez's *Brown*. In discussing reading conventions here, I begin by treating life writing as a genre and finish with a cautionary word about the relationship between ethnic author and the literary self—and the need to distinguish between the two.

Jonathan Culler offers a clear, concise, and powerful definition of genre: "A genre, one might say, is a conventional function of language, a particular relation to the world which serves as norm or expectation to guide the reader in his encounter with the text. . . . the sets of expectations which have enabled readers to naturalize texts" (*Structuralist Poetics* 136). Unpacking what he means by "to naturalize texts," Culler elaborates:

> What we speak of as conventions of a genre or an *écriture* are essentially possibilities of meaning, ways of naturalizing the text and giving it a place in the world which our culture defines. To assimilate or interpret something is to bring it within the modes of order which culture makes available, and this is usually done by talking about it in a mode of discourse which a culture takes as natural. This process goes by various names in structuralist writing: recuperation, naturalization, motivation, *vraisemblablisation*. (*Structuralist Poetics* 137, italics in the original)

Meaning is communicated through shared conventions, conventions about (though not restricted to) the relationship of text to world. That is how language works and how texts produce meaning.

Autobiography is read and interpreted differently than other necessarily fictionalized accounts or even an autobiographical court deposition, in part because disparate readerly conventions are brought to each genre. These discursive practices depend on knowledge outside of the text, on context, as does meaning itself. Changing the genre changes the context. Indeed, genre often functions as the signifier of a meaning-making context. It is knowledge of the extratextual context in which it is situated—a juridical one—that leads readers to read the court deposition differently than they would the identical document in an alternate context. Gracing the court deposition with a cover and placing it on a publisher's list of fiction titles would, by giving it an entirely new context, make it a significantly different text.

Context, therefore, is neither ancillary nor merely supplemental to texts. Rather, the meaning of texts—or at least meaning in any sense of the word beyond the purely solipsistic—is radically contingent on context. We invite serious misreading when dismissing reading conventions as arbitrary constraints imposed on a detached and transcendent text—something existing up there in Plato's world of ideal forms. There is no transcendent text. Additionally, adopting a grounded account avoids essentialized notions of genre, instead defining a genre by, following Wittgenstein, family resemblances between texts rather than by a list of indispensable features. Such an account also resists textual materialism and naïve correspondence theories of language. In place of such notions, textuality is seen as a product of language—whether on clay tablets, ink and paper, or digital screens—relying on a critical mass of shared signs, conventions, and experiences in order to signify. Conventions, such as those of genre, form part of the text, at least in the sense that valid interpretation of the text hinges on recognition of the conventions. A strong version of genre theory might argue that the meaning-making structures (or grammar) are embedded in the text, as early structuralist approaches assumed. A more modest account, a weak version, will suffice, however. Namely, texts need not embed information in an information-theory sense to convey universal patterns of meaning; rather, we need only say that some particular patterns of meaning emerge whenever authors and readers share genre conventions of meaning-making.

The constraints of genre and convention in fact pose relatively few constraints on the imagination. Texts, like language, are capable of infinite expression, however constrained by the demands of conventional usage. As a mode of interpreting experience, autobiography is likewise unbounded in its capacity for imagination and self-creation. The textual self might metaphorically fly or, when convalescing after a childhood beating, see "huge wobbly white bags, like the full udders of cows, suspended from the ceiling above," as Wright does in *Black Boy* (7). Literary texts, that is, far exceed the bounds of literal truth, historical fact, or material reality. "All autobiographers are unreliable narrators, all humans are liars," writes Timothy Dow Adams (ix), and "critics of autobiography must also distinguish between historical truth, propositional truth, personal truth, psychological truth, narrative truth, and conditional truth" (8). When Rodriguez echoes Whitman by pronouncing "*Of every hue and caste am I*," the reader does not fault him for claiming something that is biologically impossible, but accepts the statement as a poetic truth about human connectedness (*Brown* 230, emphasis in the original).

Because autobiography begins with a personal narrative of identity, Adams compares it with the oral tradition: "Like the mythology of a community, or of a nation, autobiography seeks to refine the self's folk stories, those successive versions of events we tell ourselves, consciously and unconsciously" (169). Human memory is not a written text; instead "what constitutes a self or an identity is a set of memories-turned-into-stories" (169).[3] Autobiography has its genesis in memory, its exodus in migrating inchoate thoughts to folk stories, and its literary ascension through committing the spoken word to the page. In transmuting memories into the contours of speech and consigning speech to the exigencies of print—selecting memories, ordering them, vetting them rhetorically, and inflecting them to the logic of print capitalism (what the market demands)—self-narrative becomes something quite different from its origins. Through this metamorphosis, the autobiography transcends death, and a version of the self as narrative—if not the soul itself, as Vladimir Nabokov so poignantly yearns for in his memoir, *Speak, Memory*—lives on.

Autobiography, nevertheless, remains a "referential art" as Paul John Eakin reminds us (*Touching* 28). Life writing relies on readily recognizable conventions of genre to turn subjective experience into something intelligible to the reader as outside observer.[4] Among these conventions are realism, referentiality, and basic fidelity to historical facts. At the same time, though, "for the autobiographer, part of the game includes trying to keep the reader off balance, trying to disturb what Philippe Lejeune calls 'The Autobiographical Pact'" (Adams 8). Lejeune's autobiographical pact is, as Eakin describes it, a "reader-based" approach (foreword xi), or a "reader-based poetics of autobiography" (ix):

> the notion of a contract between author and reader in which autobiographers explicitly commit themselves not to some impossible historical exactitude but rather to the sincere effort to come to terms with and understand their own lives. The formal mark of this commitment to autobiographical discourse is the identity posited among author, narrator, and protagonist, who share the same name. (*Touching* 24)

This holy trinity of author, narrator, and protagonist is the referential linchpin of Lejeune's account, Eakin tells us:

a *textual* criterion by which to distinguish between autobiography and fiction, namely the identity of the proper name shared by author, narrator, and protagonist. With an evident sigh of relief, he could abandon an author-based perspective that had required the reader's knowledge of a finally unknowable authorial consciousness. Putting the slippery ethic of sincerity safely behind him (or so he must have thought) as he shifted the fulcrum of the genre from the extratextual state of authorial intention to *the sign of that intention* present in the text.... (foreword ix, emphasis in the original)

Lejeune's shift away from any claims of epistemic knowledge of "authorial intention" to merely the textual "sign of [that] intention" promotes close reading of "the text itself" and of "the language of the text." Importantly, however, as Eakin stresses, this is not so formalist an account as to deny reality and the referentiality of the author:

Lejeune parts company with those contemporary theorists who take a more limited view of the possibility of reference and the existence of the self beyond language, [theorists such as Paul de Man] insisting on the concept of a person as a linguistic structure and holding reference to be a problematical, secondary rhetorical effect. (foreword x)

The autobiographical mode is inherently referential, though Lejeune's focus is on the "mode[s] of reading" rather than the extratextual referent (29).[5] Autobiography is based on "the implicit or explicit contract proposed by the *author* to the *reader*, a contract which determines the modes of reading of the text and engenders the effects which, attributed to the text, seem to us to define it as autobiography" (29, emphasis in the original). The framing of a text within the dyad of reader-writer contract (genre, or modes of reading and writing), as well as within the larger context of reality, means that authorial intentionality still matters for Lejeune, if only to insist that autobiographers write with a particular genre in mind, and are otherwise mindful of reader expectations.

Autobiography, as with textual meaning, emerges from a hermeneutic circle in which the reader is very much a part of the construction of the text and the author creates the textual self in relation to the limits of the genre as recognized by readers.[6] Readers expect the autobiographical self to refer to its biological referent and to not depart from the corporeal self in ways that any reasonable and prudent person would deem deceptive.[7] The impetus for maintaining such autobiographical referentiality derives partly from the fact that "ethically speaking, the reader is part of the game." For example, "Testimonial life writing . . . makes direct and obvious claims on the reader as moral agent," writes Eakin (foreword 14).[8] More generally, all readers take autobiography seriously (though not always literally) because, as Eakin reminds us, "We are crypto-autobiographers, asking questions about our selves and our life stories indirectly by observing others as they struggle to find answers" (14).

THE REFERENT (AND THE REFERENTIAL GAP) OF ETHNIC AUTOBIOGRAPHY

Readers take life lessons from texts. They also expect nonfiction to be true to life, largely because more is at stake in texts whose truths are taken as referential truths, as accurate representations of the actual experiences of others. Though at first counterintuitive, a theory of reading and interpretation that centered around nonfiction texts would make even stronger claims than phenomenological and reader-response theories of literary interpretation about the role readers play in completing the meaning of texts. More directly than in other genres, readers of nonfiction exert pressure in the form of readerly expectations on authors to present a historically, referentially, and experientially accurate rendering of reality as they perceive it. Readers of autobiography especially expect authorial honesty in biographical details—such as race, sex, and sometimes even whether the author had sex with a particular person—whose omission or misrepresentation risks corroding epistemically vital links between objective knowledge about the real-life referent and the self depicted in autobiography. In short, the reality and reliability of the connection between the referent and the textual self is an essential part of the narrative, and constitutes a large part of the meaningfulness of the text for readers.

When making narrative choices, writers—influenced by reader expectations—are aware that how the text is framed will incline it to be read through existing formal and informal reading conventions. This extends to self-identification, and the author's choice to conceal or reveal various facets of the autobiographical referent in print. In initially failing to disclose his homosexuality, Rodriguez is aware that he may be thwarting readers from reading his autobiography through the lens of gay narrative or queer theory. He cannot, however, keep his ethnicity in the closet, and even his protestations that he is not writing ethnic literature are easily understood by readers for what they are—an attempt to preserve his individuality, a disavowal of the self as representative of other members of the ethnic group, as well as resistance to literary categorization in a subgenre.

As is true of other identity choices, a sober-minded awareness of social reality is indispensable to ethnic identification. Greater agency is possible through self-conscious reflection and response to that reality. Denying or obscuring the ways in which one is ethnically marked, however, is not a valid or effective option. It fails to increase the agency of ethnic subjects because society does not allow it: the absence of references to the author's ethnicity (particularly in texts that readers approach as ethnic literature) is always a conspicuous absence. Ethnic passing in autobiography is not a reality-based response, however long the author might be able to conceal the fact of her actual ethnicity before it is exposed. Why this should be the case with ethnicity when other aspects of identity are concealable can be summed up in one word: visibility.

The referent of ethnic autobiography is a corporeal self, whose body is visibly marked as ethnic, though the author may wish to deemphasize ethnicity in order to emphasize other self-identifications. Vexing as it may be to the author, many of these may be difficult to reconcile—both on the page and in life—with ethnicity, given the assumptions and preconceptions that follow from the dominant paradigms of social structuring. Despite the referentiality of autobiography, the author—ethnic or otherwise—and the self on the page are not fungible. And although the conventions of autobiography match the central character with the author, the autobiographical self is not identical to the author that is its referent. Furthermore, though honesty about reality matters, the genre is shot through with traces of the fictional. Eakin points this out in describing the "referential aesthetic" of autobiography. Even in regard to historical or biographical facts, the "repetition of the facts of a life can never merely mirror them but always transforms them. In this sense all mimesis is necessarily the work of fiction" (*Touching* 29, 51).

Aware of the referential gap, Rodriguez rightly draws a sharp distinction between the textual self and its referent. The Rodriguez who has written three autobiographical books is not the same man as the one seen on television or in the lecture hall, in large part because "within Western culture there are crucial differences between the conventions of oral communication and those of literature" (Culler, *Structuralist Poetics* 133). Rodriguez notes that people who know him intimately do not recognize him as the mournful author of *Hunger of Memory*: "That's why I wrote that book, because I wanted to be mournful, because I could not be mournful among my normal acquaintances.... I needed the reader to let me have that part of myself.... There are things that you can only tell a stranger" ("Violating" 429). Later in the interview, Rodriguez adds, "'I was pretending an intimacy that is the artifice of my work. That's all it is. It isn't true intimacy because I don't know who you are. If it was intimate I would have used your name in a letter directed to you.' On the other hand I tell my true intimates that what I write is not intended for them. In fact I'd prefer they never read it" ("Violating" 445). Rodriguez, that is, self-consciously writes to readerly conventions even as he writes against the ethnic genres that frame, signal, and accompany the set of reading conventions brought to autobiographical essays by an author of his surname, complexion, and ethnic heritage—of his ethnic visibility.

ETHNIC GENRES

Rodriguez's resistance to ethnic genres might seem inconsistent with his understanding of readerly conventions, given the close connection between the two. Certainly, one could simply note that Rodriguez is an author of many paradoxes, and leave it at that. This particular paradox, however, can be readily understood through the most parsimonious of explanations. Namely, though mindful of readerly conventions, Rodriguez writes against the notion of ethnic genres because he fears that classifying his books as ethnic literature will place overly constrictive reader expectations on his work:

> Let the bookstore clerk puzzle over where it should be placed. (Rodriguez? Rodriguez?) Probably he will shelve it alongside specimens of that exotic new genre, "ethnic literature." Mistaken, the gullible reader will—in sympathy or in anger—take it that I intend to model my life as the typical Hispanic-American life. (*Hunger* 7)

Rodriguez laments the vagaries of classification, which concretize natural and artificial differences alike. He objects, furthermore, to the fragmentation of American print culture, the impulse to segregate works of literature without full consideration of the effects of such practices: "How a society orders its bookshelves is as telling as the books a society writes and reads. American bookshelves of the twenty-first century describe fractiousness, reduction, hurt" (*Brown* 11).

Ethnic genres or subgenres might be a good idea for several reasons Rodriguez does not address, not least of which is that it helps readers interested in the culture and experiences of others quite different from themselves identify titles of interest to them. Literary profiling (labeling, classifying, or otherwise grouping) of this sort has its downsides too, as I will elaborate, but it is also true that it is not just the familiar that readers seek. They also place a premium on novelty, and hence the exoticism factor: ethnic lit read as cultural tourism. It could be argued that Rodriguez tries to have it both ways, resisting categorization as ethnic literature even as he invites it through, for example, the ethnically coded reference "My Mexican Father" in the subtitle of *Days of Obligation*.

In his zeal to disavow the limitations of overclassification, Rodriguez might seem to reject all generic classification. The paradoxical result of a prohibition on classification, however, would be that all books would be classifiably the same, each would be simply and equally a book: from cookbooks to classics, and sacred texts to profane ones—they would all be the same. It is not, of course, the undifferentiated lumping of all books as simply books that Rodriguez desires. What he is arguing for is just the opposite: even greater particularism, for the uniqueness of each book. "Books should confuse. Literature abhors the typical. Literature flows to the particular, the mundane" (*Brown* 12). Rodriguez further elaborates in a 1999 interview with Timothy Sedore: "It [literature] looks for the particular, and then it seeks the universal through the particular rather than the other way around [as sociology does]" ("Violating" 430). "There is only one subject: What it feels like to be alive. Nothing is irrelevant. Nothing is typical"—each is a "particular life" (*Brown* 12). The force of authorial afflatus, as Rodriguez sees it, endows each book with a soul, each possessing a unique identity.

Unquestionably, if literature sought only to systematically classify all experience under general categories, it would be drained of much of its vitality. Take imported literature. Having one's books promoted and read as ethnographic, as often happens to ethnic and foreign authors, rather than naturalized as simply literary can place unwanted constraints on the author. This is not to suggest that one cannot achieve literary recognition when writing to such expectations—witness Chinua Achebe's *Things Fall Apart*, for example—but it is to acknowledge the existence of constraints not imposed on other authors. When read abroad, authors (particularly those most culturally distant from their readers) are frequently read as representing the quintessence of whatever ethnonational background the author happens to have. After the release of the translation of her novel *Delirio* in 2007, the Colombian author Laura Restrepo noted that Terrance Rafferty's review of the translation in the *New York Times Book Review* prominently featured an outline map of Colombia as the icon most readily identifiable with the book. Restrepo, however, resists expectations that she be representative of Colombian-ness in her work, and argues that writers should not try to write to a stereotype or, for example, "from a 'Latina' point of view." Rather, one should write as an individual, and eschew writing for "cultural tourists" (panel discussion 2007).

Such is the quagmire of book classification and how it affects both writers and the ways in which readers approach books. I argue neither for nor against particular forms of classification. I do maintain, however, that with or without formal classification readers make certain distinctions, and a primary axis along these internal lines is the ethnicity of the author. These schemata cannot be ignored in literary criticism because the full meaningfulness of a work of literature is actualized only through the semantic interaction that occurs when the reader encounters the text. It is readers who arc the epistemological gap from ontological text-object to epistemologically meaningful text—meaningful only to the extent that reader and text share a degree of linguistic referentiality to external reality—completing the circuit by bringing their experiences, thoughts, and parole to it. The same book is thus to some extent a particular text to each reader, differing also for each reader at different times in her life: "[B]ooks must be reimagined, misunderstood, read. Readers repair to books as men and women to monasteries, none with an identical motive" (*Brown* 13-14).

Just as the meanings of a text vary with what readers bring to it, so the extratextual ethnicity of the author provides much of the text's meaning to readers. Readers make different judgments about the meanings of a text, particularly autobiographical texts, based on what they know about the ethnicity, gender, race, and class of the person who wrote it. The same is true of other biographical information available to them about the author, particularly whenever such information is highly visible in society. The ethnicity of the author matters a great deal to readers when reading about immigration, ethnic experience, or race relations. The referent matters when authors refer to themselves, and when they write about race and ethnicity. Readers evince a particular epistemic hunger along those lines, desiring to know more about the race and ethnicity of the writer. Something similar, but not equivalent, happens with gender. This certainly does not mean that writers cannot write about races, ethnicities, and genders other than their own but, certainly, they do breach a tacit contract when deceiving readers about their race, ethnicity, or gender. Even writers of fiction risk breaching the reader's trust if adopting a pen name of someone of the opposite gender or different ethnicity than their own.

I have made certain epistemological assumptions about reference that I have so far addressed only briefly. That authors can so easily deceive readers about their race, gender, or ethnicity might seem to undermine the very notion of any significant connection between the textual self and its referent. Against that view, I argue that the connection between the author's ethnicity—which tends to trigger salient and often stereotypical associations prevalent within the social context in which reader and text are imbricated—and the text is meaningful for readers. It is social and epistemological rather than strictly ontological, and follows the logic of a genre. Clearly, such an account puts great emphasis on the reader's response to the text. As we have seen, however, the author's mindfulness of reading conventions and genre is also indispensable. It is perhaps the author's role that most needs emphasis here, given that though it is common today to speak of ligatures between readers and texts, the connection between author and text has been greatly contested in recent decades. As a skeptical realist, I assume a necessary triangulation of author, text, and reader, all three embedded in the same social and natural world. This realist approach forces us to consider yet one more connection, one often occluded from literary investigation: the ways in which authors and readers are joined by a shared social context that can bypass the text.

ON INTENTIONALITY: SHARED BELIEFS ABOUT REFERENTS AND SOCIAL REALITY

Joe Loya came to Rodriguez's texts only after first seeing the author's image on television. A certain extratextual relationship thus preceded any textually mediated one between them, a relationship that began, as Loya recounts, with ethnic identification. The anteriority of world and society also framed the text for Loya in certain ways, and did so long before he ever set eyes on it. Likewise, the Mexican American reader's perception that Rodriguez is either an inspiration or a sellout has everything to do with the social context shared by reader and writer. Of course, these examples assume that the author is contemporaneous with the reader. In certain ways, though, an extratextual relationship between author and reader can exist even when the author is dead. Cultural myths about Shakespeare, for example, live on as part of the extratextual cultural landscape that precedes the reading or hearing of any of his plays. Allusions to Shakespearean drama, for example, are sprinkled throughout *Days of Obligation*—"Caliban eyeing his master's books"; "I am the class wit. Like Falstaff" (23, 179). They are also likely recognizable as such even to those who have not read the specific plays alluded to. As with other literary icons, people often know many famous lines, incidents, or plotlines from a given Shakespearean work without ever having actually read the play. What they do know, if nothing else, is that the line can be attributed to Shakespeare, a writer for whom they have a biographical script (however partial and inaccurate) in their mind's eye. That so much of the purported biography of an author such as Shakespeare—of whose life we have only scant biographical evidence—is so extensively imagined rather than known is precisely why many critics argue for the "death of the author." To proponents of such a view, it would seem that the real biography of the author does not matter. The author, the argument goes, is no more than a product or a projection of the culture.

Such arguments oversimplify the case. They do, however, offer a welcome caveat about the need to distinguish, on some level, between the biographical writer and the cultural projection that is the author. That does not mean, however, that there is no connection between the writer and the author. Shakespeare is not an invention. In fact, because he was a prominent figure in literary circles, enough biographical evidence about him was known by his acquaintances to prevent attributing just any biographical figure—or none—to the authorship of his plays. More to the point, the person who penned the lines (or the bulk of them, given the collaborative nature of theater and the vagaries of editing) of *Hamlet* and *Romeo and Juliet* was not some incorporeal cultural fable but a flesh-and-blood man. What little we do know about that man, and the degree to which biographical information is judged to be accurate, matters to readers of his texts when they come to know of it.

The same is true of ethnic authors, bringing us back to my epistemological claim about the correspondence between biological selves and textual selves.

I have already suggested some of the difficulties of making such a claim: writers can fool readers about themselves; the ontological gap between biological selves and textual representations of those selves is vast; we are often less influenced by what we actually know about writers than by what we think we know about them. There is, in short, no necessary connection between the self and the self on the page. Acknowledging the ontological fact of the matter does not—as some would have it—settle the matter epistemologically, however. Significant epistemological correspondence remains between texts and their writers. The problem, as it turns out, is a familiar one.

We need look no further than not-so-recent but continually renewed debates about the presence or absence of any correspondence between words and their referents. What we know about the relationship between signifiers and signifieds must necessarily shed light on the relationship between texts—as linguistic objects—and world. Although popular in academic literary critical circles, theories of language and literature that would deny any such correspondence, or the capacity to know anything about it, leave language incomprehensible because the meanings of most words depend a great deal on extralinguistic knowledge about the world, knowledge that goes beyond the information in the utterance. More convincing are theories that treat language as part of the natural world rather than as separate from it. Included in that world, to be perfectly clear, are humans and their need for communication.

John Searle, Hilary Putnam, W. V. O. Quine, and other philosophers of language and mind have persuasively argued that language partly depends on shared referents—or, at least, shared beliefs about those referents—to function as communication. In his essay, "Reference and Understanding," Putnam demonstrates the need for the word *tiger* to correspond with its referent and for speakers to share a belief that it does: "How could *discussion* take place if we could assume *nothing* about what all speakers believe? Could I safely use the word 'tiger' in talking to you if, for all I knew, you believed that tigers are a kind of *'clam'*?" (215, emphasis in the original). Searle, in *The Construction of Social Reality*, underscores the role of intentionality—"the feature of representations by which they are *about* something or *directed at* something"—and its role in distinguishing between "brute facts" and "institutional facts" (7, emphasis in the original).

Conventional usage, rather than the arbitrariness of words, indicates the capacity to agree on some shared referent, whether that be an object, a mental conceptualization, or something else altogether. Language's reliance on conventions—even those that perpetually shift over time, as they do—to communicate meaning constitutes, at a minimum, significant correspondence between the labels assigned to objects and mental images, and shared beliefs about what those labels, or words, refer to. Such beliefs can be hazy and imperfect as well as perpetually revisable, but such knowledge is both possible and necessary. Thus, despite the slippage of language, necessary links between the words on the page (or at least some of the words on the page) and extratextual referents keep written language meaningful. Only in such ways can print culture link writers and readers.

Similar arguments can be made about the nature of the ontological gap between the literary self and its referent. Ontologically, the literary self is no more than wood pulp and ink stains, whereas the author is a superorganism of biological cells contiguous within a defined space. An epistemological bridge, mediated through language, connects the two in social reality. Thus we can not only know something about the superorganism from the ink stains on the page but also (through the conventions of autobiography in social reality) be reasonably assured that in most instances the ink stains represent (though are not identical to) the superorganism. As is apparent in reading Rodriguez, the referent of ethnic autobiography is a self that has a biological body, the social visibility of which is integral to the meaning of the text.

For argumentative coda on the correspondence between literary selves and their referents, I refer the reader to Satya Mohanty's *Literary Theory and the Claims of History*. Mohanty offers a realist—what he calls a postpositivist realist—synthesis of literary theory with insights from the fields of philosophy of language and the philosophy of mind and, in particular, from the philosophy of science. Those literary critics loath to consider philosophical arguments outside the Continental school of thought will find in Mohanty's work a compendious account of interdisciplinary insights not otherwise available to them, and framed in terms and debates with which they are familiar. In explaining and developing the indispensable concepts of background theory (or background knowledge), revisability, and the holistic nature of objective knowledge (162, 192–93), and by bringing the grievously neglected work of analytic philosophers such as Quine and Putnam to the attention of literary critics, Mohanty offers a redoubtable defense of the referentiality of the minority subject as author.

SATIRIZING LATINO IDENTITY AND ETHNIC GENRES

As I have argued, ethnic literature is a genre in certain key respects. We adjust our reading conventions depending on the assumed ethnicity of the author. Readers also tend to rely on ethnic stereotypes from experiences outside print culture as part of the interpretive framing of any text they read by an author associated with a recognizable ethnic group. The conventions of genre, whether formalized or not, provide the readers of ethnic literature with one of the interpretive frameworks (for good or for ill) through which they approach the literary work.

Also integral to framing a text is the further recognition of tonal, stylistic, and rhetorical modes. This is a version of situating the text in the most fitting genre or genres, though often doing so over the much shorter span of a phrase or passage rather than of an entire book. When taking satirical, tongue-in-cheek, or figurative moments too literally, it is easy to misread Rodriguez. More so than less ludic writers, Rodriguez's poetics sometimes lead him to playful overstatement or—like fellow critic of ethnic authenticity Stanley Crouch—to hyperbole for rhetorical effect. "I am crying from my mouth in Mexico City," Rodriguez writes on the opening page of *Days of Obligation*, a poetic rendering of a more graphic image for which he was criticized: "All the badly pronounced Spanish words I have forced myself to sound during the day, bits and pieces of Mexico spew from my mouth" (xv). Such moments lead to the frequent labeling of Rodriguez as a provocative writer. Audacious statements cloaked in ambiguity, paradox, or the scandalous turn of phrase can easily be misperceived as wholesale earnestness. Against such readings, I argue that Rodriguez is too often taken in earnest when he is instead writing figuratively or playfully. This is characteristic of his prose: frequently ironic, more poetic than literal, and not shy of using hyperbole for rhetorical and stylistic effect. Crucial to a fuller and more subtle reading of Rodriguez's texts, then, is the recognition of moments of irony, hyperbole, figurativeness, and other such polyvocal modes and nuances.

Satirical moments—such as when he begins a sentence with "Surviving Chicanos (one still meets them)" (*Brown* 108)—are among the multifarious modes featured in Rodriguez's writing. Though not a dominant form, the satiric mode is more illustrative than most for its ability to completely change the interpretive lens through which a text is understood. Perhaps the most frequently misrecognized genre, satire is often dismissed or lambasted, as are its authors, when readers miss the wink behind the words. A brief look at the long-standing misreading of one of Rodriguez's literary precursors, a Chicano satirist who seems to have had no direct literary influence on Rodriguez, exemplifies the importance of genre as well as the political fallout of its misrecognition when ethnic literature is among the multiple genres or modes through which the text can be read.

Oscar "Zeta" Acosta, the legendary Chicano lawyer and pioneering Chicano autobiographer, is widely read among non-Chicanos. Perhaps this in part because—unlike later writers who would deploy code-switching with the express intent of having non-Spanish-speaking readers experience the marginality of ethnic subjects—Acosta presents the reader with untranslated Spanish terms in a way that avoids alienating or excluding a wide readership. This is not to say that the linguistic borderline should not be tested anew by each generation of writers, but simply that Acosta leaves no one hanging on the fence. More to the point, the critical reception of Acosta's first book, *The Autobiography of a Brown Buffalo*, demonstrates the importance of reading conventions—the interpretive lenses through which we read the text—when approaching a text. As we have seen, different meanings are extracted from the same text when read in alternate genres, such as Chicano literature as opposed to satire or compound identification such as satirical Chicano literature. Each identification of genre, for better or for worse, elicits distinct readerly expectations. To contravene being saddled with expectations that he perform as an authentic Chicano, Acosta satirically refers to himself—and indeed his racial features are routinely mismatched with a variety of ethnic and racial identities depending on the social context that others encounter him in—as a brown buffalo and a Samoan.[9] "I hate for people to assume I'm an authority on Mexicans. Just because I'm a brown buffalo doesn't mean I'm the son of Moctezuma, does it? Anyway, I told her I was a Samoan by the name of Henry Hawk" (101).

Of particular note is that Acosta satirizes himself and the ethnicity he is most affiliated with. In his seminal work, *The Difference Satire Makes: Rhetoric and Reading from Johnson to Byron*, Frederic Bogel makes an important correction to the long-held "sighted repellent object, sank same" theory of satire:

> In this revised scenario, the crucial fact is not that satirists find folly or wickedness in the world and then wish to expose that alien something. Instead, satirists identify in the world something or someone that is both unattractive and curiously or dangerously like them, or

like the culture or subculture that they identify with or speak for, or sympathetic even as it is repellent—something, then, that is *not alien enough*. (41, emphasis in the original)

Acosta's self-satirizing references to himself as a Samoan (a pun on his body shape and size) and a brown buffalo (a more obviously satirical reference to his obesity and skin color) mark the self as an axis point. Around it, the satirical mace is swung to create some distance between himself and any subsuming group identification pressing close enough to threaten the autonomy and personal identity of the self. What Acosta beats back out of range is a fetishized and monolithic account of Chicano identity, and the expectation that all Chicanos are, by virtue of blood and ethnicity alone, homogeneous. Essentializing narratives are inimical to the self, and Latino literature critic Ilan Stavans notes in his mixed-genre biography of Acosta that the author was equally critical of exclusionary racial essentializing on either side of the fence, as is evident in his only published work of short fiction "Perla the Pig." This, in depicting the discrimination against the light-skinned *huero*—which translates as blond, but is often used derogatorily to refer to Anglos and light-skinned people—in a Mexican barrio "contains an underlying critique of the Mexican character that refuses to accept otherness" (Stavans, *Bandido* 54).

Michael Hames-García argues that "emphasiz[ing] essentialist notions of authenticity" and reading Acosta's two "works as novels, autobiographies, or some hybrid of the two" leads to "interpreting Acosta's writing as ethnic autobiographical self-revelation" (463). Instead, Hames-García suggests, the two books should be read "in the context of the author's legal work as well as considering them in relation to the genres of grotesque satire [as first suggested by Héctor Calderón in 1982] and *testimonio*" (463, italics in the original). Hames-García argues that Acosta "advocated neither essentialist nationalism nor unstable and indeterminate identities. Rather, he supported a realist approach to justice and identity that rejected inadequate conceptions of both while articulating better alternatives" (463–64). Acosta's public identity is thus validated when his writing, both legal and fictional, is read through conventional Pan-American genres, which are indispensable to understanding the text, whereas ethnic compartmentalization, when interpreting Acosta's texts literally, distorts the narrative as well as the personal identity of the author.

In his search for identity, Acosta routinely skewers notions of ethnic authenticity but nevertheless endorses ethnic and racial affiliations as a strategic response to the racialized organization of society. Fragmentation within supposedly homogeneous ethnic identities is encountered by the young Acosta when moving from Texas to California, where the local Mexican Americans "said we weren't *real* Mexicans because we wore long, black patent leather boots and short pants, which my mother bought for us in Juarez" (77, emphasis in the original). It is such ethnic authenticating that frustrates Acosta's search for personal identity. "One sonofabitch tells me I'm not a Mexican and the other one says I'm not an American," leading him to conclude that "[m]y single mistake has been to seek an identity with any one person or nation or with any part of history" (196–99).

Acosta proposes a "new identity. A name and a language all our own. . . . I propose we call ourselves the Brown Buffalo people" (198). Acosta is in satirical mode and should not be taken too literally, as is evidenced on the following page where he switches back to referring to himself a world-famous Chicano lawyer rather than a Brown Buffalo lawyer. What should be taken seriously, however, are the earnest undertones that motivate his deployment of satire. Among these is a call for participation in a wider public identity than that circumscribed by any particular race, ethnicity, gender, or language. The dramatization of this cosmopolitan, multicultural sentiment constitutes the narrative motivation for Acosta's candid revelation that "I never went out with the few Mexican girls in school because they always stuck to themselves and refused to participate in the various activities" (112). This is not a rejection of Chicano culture. It is, rather, in the larger context of the text, a repudiation of Chicano nationalism qua exclusivist ethnic chauvinism (for further comparison between Acosta and Rodriguez in the context of Chicano nationalism, see Paul Guajardo's *Chicano Controversy*). Acosta's new identity is hybridized, but not in a binarist way. It rejects a linear spectrum between either-or poles in favor of a reticulate and somewhat universalist notion of identity, one with "world-famous" aspirations.

BROWN READERS IN BLACK AND WHITE: PRINT CULTURE AND ETHNIC IDENTITY

Print culture, by simultaneously universalizing and particularizing, plays an inordinately large role in the production of modern selves. This is no less true for ethnic selves. Rodriguez's privileging of English-language print culture over the Spanish-language oral culture of his childhood can induce an initial reaction against and resistance to his description of the role that print culture plays in the formation of the ethnic self. Ethnic readers might also espouse concerns about the extent to which the dominant language and culture excludes or has historically excluded minority voices, cultures, and languages. Many Americans rely on languages other than English to express the self to intimates. Rodriguez's formulation of this important relationship between ethnic identity and minority languages—as inhabiting a "private language" that excludes them from "public society"—troubled Chicana/o readers of *Hunger of Memory* (19–27). *Days of Obligation*, however, is peppered with Spanish, from *vete* (you go) to *el otro cachete* (the other buttock), through which Rodriguez is able to incorporate his mother tongue into his literary representation of the ethnic self (50, 2, 85). Perhaps equally significant is that written language follows a different logic than spoken language does, as is clear in the use of Latin as the universal language of print culture throughout the Middle Ages even as vernacular languages dominated oral culture. Although both are integral to modern identities, scholars of ethnic studies have to date placed much more emphasis on spoken language than on written. In what follows, I turn that approach on its head, inverting the conventional emphasis to explore the role of print culture in shaping ethnic identity and consciousness.

Vexing questions present themselves when one undertakes accounting for the role of written language in shaping ethnic consciousness. Among these is the question of hegemony. Can a print culture–dominant language—be it Latin, English, or something else—truly be inclusive? For Rodriguez, the answer to that question is an unequivocal yes. Although we may be more likely to suspect hegemonic tendencies in a print culture in the dominant language than we would a print culture in a language other than the local vernacular, Rodriguez attempts to dispel fears about both. As with his views on assimilation, Rodriguez believes that the gains outweigh the costs. A poignant example can be seen in his arguments in favor of the Latin Mass (codified in and recited from printed texts), which Rodriguez believes would bring together diverse ethnic communities, such as Latino and Vietnamese, who would otherwise attend separate masses and continue along a "path of ethnic separation" (*Days* 195). As Rodriguez sees it, what Jeehyun Lim identifies as a "third language" (the Latin Mass, here) would thus be more inclusive rather than less so (Lim 519).

In Rodriguez's view, English-language print culture is equally inclusive as a third language, perhaps more so given that readers also share a spoken language. Rodriguez attempts to demonstrate the validity of this view through his life writing, including within the purview of *Days of Obligation* everything from Mexican culture to gay identity and Asian parents. No topic is too profane (too other), and nothing is unapproachable through his pen. Nor is the ethnicity of the referent (the ethnic author) peremptorily expurgated in articulating the self in print culture through the dominant language. Just the contrary, it is print culture (in this case the dominant print culture) that allows ethnic authors to more fully express the self. Neither is one's ethnicity erased simply through immersion in the texts and language of the majority culture. Although Rodriguez emphasizes how far removed he is from his ethnic origins, the traces of those early experiences remain part of the self that he projects to the world. Also, how others react to him still has much to do with his race, class, gender, and family name. Details about these aspects of his ethnicity are sought out by those who read him. The ways in which the text is meaningful to readers depends significantly on these details, on the reader's knowledge of the writer's ethnic background and the visibility of his racial features. Identity (including the author's ethnicity or gender) can be obscured in print, if that is what an author sets out to do. However, the ethnic identity of an author who already reads and writes in English is by no means erased simply by electing to write in English rather than some other language.

Rodriguez's rejoinder to such doubts is made, again, through the example of his memoirs: "I was a student of language. Obsessed by the way it determined my public identity. The way it permits me here to describe myself, writing" (*Hunger* 7). In reading the classics, Rodriguez discovers himself: "Huck was the archetypal bilingual child" (*Days* 163). In all of Rodriguez's books, one finds an expression of the ethnic self through the English-language print culture, which for Rodriguez offers ample space and inclusivity for the articulation of the self—ethnic, gay, and defiant of constrictive identity narratives. Indeed, a predominantly print culture–based education, though it initially caused him to have "grown culturally separated from my parents," is ultimately compensatory in endowing Rodriguez with "ways of speaking and caring about the fact" (*Hunger* 72). What is more, rather than thwarting the articulation of alterity, the dominant print culture—by bridging the gap between otherwise segregated subcultures—creates a larger and freer space both for the construction of the self and for acceptance of that self by others. In such ways, mainstream print culture allows for a more expansive articulation of the self than either spoken language alone or exclusive reliance on a written language that is not dominant in that society.

Although counterintuitive, Rodriguez's forewarning that he writes of "one life only" turns out to be similarly expansive rather than overly reductive, because he sees the particular as the road to the universal (*Hunger* 7). Consistent with his distinction between the language of intimates and the language of society, Rodriguez finds fuller expression of the self available only through the ways print culture universalizes: "I write today for a reader who exists in my mind only phantasmagorically. Someone with a face erased; someone of no particular race or sex or age or weather. A gray presence. Unknown, unfamiliar. All that I know about him is that he has had a long education and that his society, like mine, is often public (*un gringo*)" (182). Instrumental to its capacity to universalize are print culture's naturalizing conventions: "Dickens tried to incorporate the voice of the working-class man within his novel and never succeeded within the novel, because when the miner begins to speak, all of his speech is misspelled" (interview with Torres 179). Speaking of the multilingual writings of Nabokov, Rodriguez maintains that one can "never [be] bilingual in the same period of time" (interview with Torres 180). You cannot speak in the language your universal readers are familiar with but have your character speak in an incomprehensibly rendered brogue (of the miner, say). As someone who writes "essays intended for readers I never expected to meet" (*Hunger* 182), Rodriguez is arguing that an assimilated or naturalized aesthetics in print culture is inherently more universal than, in this case, an overdone dialect because "there's never that grid or haze over [the character's] speech. It is invisible when you read it" (interview with Torres 179). For Rodriguez, print culture is tied to the public language, whereas dialect is a kind of private language (the language of intimates).[10] Extending his arguments, Rodriguez suggests that reading conventions oriented toward the universal not only make possible articulation of the ethnic self to an audience wider than one's familiars and intimates but also expand self-expression and self-conceptualization.

The obverse side of the universalizing tendencies of print culture, however, cannot be ignored. For all that is gained, much is also lost. Lacking the additional inflections of tone, body language, and other signifying accoutrements, texts do not have dialects the way that people do. And though written language has the capacity for generating vast dialectal permutations of its own, such tendencies are constrained by the pressure to standardize. The more standard the writing, the greater its potential reach. In addition, much of the practicality and usefulness of written language comes precisely from its facility in making writers and readers of various regional and ethnic dialects even more mutually comprehensible to each other than when speaking in person. Shaped by forces such as these, the conventions of written language are more uniform—though not necessarily and ineluctably so—than those of spoken language. In contrast, dialects generated by social or geographic separation, along with lexical and other linguistic inflections or markers, are often a highly visible part of one's identity. These dialects and other linguistic markers are often elided in a text, particularly one set down in standard written English, or one that is self-consciously poetic: "I did not know until this year that Keats spoke with a cockney accent" (*Brown* 14). This significant, and highly visible, aspect of the poet's identity could not be missed if one were to speak with Keats in person. Although other features of the author's ethnic and regional identity remain visible to readers, his accent has been lost in the transliteration from spoken to written language. The accent, of course, can be rendered and incorporated into the text as dialect, but doing so would come, Rodriguez is arguing, at the cost of more universal accessibility.

If Keats's accent can be erased somewhere between the person and the page (between biographical fact and reading conventions), it might be assumed that ethnic origins can be just as easily expunged. Race, gender, and ethnicity, beyond all doubt, can be erased from texts in ways that are not possible in face-to-face encounters. George Sand can turn out to be a woman. The reader of a book has no ocular proof of the author's gender, something that can be erased in writing to strip readers of the "gender goggles" through which they would otherwise read the text. Print culture may even involve hegemonic occurrences of the particular-masking-as-the-universal variety that Ernesto Laclau warns of (28). One such example is the use of the pronoun *he* in a gender-neutral way because no effective gender-neutral pronoun exists in English, something that happens much more frequently in writing than in conversation. Examples of other such erasures—ethnic, racial, gendered, and otherwise—are legion. The Armenian American author of a paper published in an academic journal might turn out to be a computer, or more accurately, a hoaxer's collage of computer-generated academic catchphrases and jargon.[11] Likewise, the influence of the Spanish and French languages on William Carlos Williams—whose mother was Puerto Rican and who spent two years of study in Geneva and Paris—can become so etiolated on the page, especially given that he scrupulously eschewed foreign literary and linguistic allusions in deference to concrete imagery conveyed in "plain" American English, that many readers will never know their importance to his identity, nor resituate their reading of his poetry in the way that they would his spoken words had they previously heard him speak in perfect Spanish.

Print culture, in other words, can elide or conceal otherwise inescapable details about the ethnicity of the author. This is not to say that print culture is color-blind. What readers do know about the author's ethnicity will be interpreted in such a way that it will change how they read the text, thus changing meaning. The literary corpus (the body of print culture) does not escape the signification imposed on the corporeal self (the ethnic body in society) to which it is connected. Given this connectedness—the inescapability of ethnic situatedness—the revisability of the ethnic self in print is a strength rather than a weakness of ethnic literature as a genre. This revisability allows the ethnic subject to subject in turn the prevailing ethnic narratives to revision, both in the world and in the literary tradition: "I have taken Caliban's advice. I have stolen their books. I will have some run of this isle" (*Hunger* 3).

• ◆ •

In *Days of Obligation*, Rodriguez seeks to reconcile the print culture self with the ethnic self, to square the influence of Shakespeare with that of his Mexican heritage: "Come away from the window, Shylock commands. I hear my father's voice" (160). The postcolonial image of Caliban stealing his master's books, the genesis trope with which *Hunger of Memory* begins, is reiterated early in *Days of Obligation* (23), reaffirming the double consciousness of ethnic identity. In the minds of his readers, Rodriguez's ethnic identity is "given"—assumed to be both natural and inherent (if not essential) in some way. What they do not fully comprehend is the extent to which that identity has been molded by print culture. To jolt readers out of their misperceptions, Rodriguez downplays ethnic heritage in *Hunger of Memory* while, like Richard Wright before him, conscientiously listing a litany of titles from his English-language and Great Books reading program, the books that shaped his identity from an early age: "*The Scarlet Letter* and Franklin's *Autobiography*. . . . the *Iliad*, *Moby Dick*" (61). Having distanced himself from ethnic pigeonholing in his first collection of autobiographical essays, Rodriguez feels free to more openly embrace his ethnic heritage—as well as a gay identity—in *Days of Obligation*. *Brown* features ethnicity conspicuously in the title, while the opening chapter of *Darling* is titled with a Spanish word: *Ojalá*. In all four books, the stamp of print culture on the autobiographer's mind is not only inescapable but also inescapably prominent.

Readers inevitably filter much of their experience through what they have read—avid readers all the more so. Though, lamentably, we cannot assume that all life writers—and memoirists in particular—read as widely and deeply as good writers must, when it comes to Rodriguez there can be no doubt. As a scholarship boy and insatiable reader, Rodriguez's identity has been significantly molded by the conventions of reading, right down to getting many of his early notions about sex and sexuality from books rather than from experience. "Through my reading, I developed a fabulous and sophisticated sexual imagination" (*Hunger* 127). All of this, however, is often invisible to others, part of an interior life that is known only if self-consciously revealed. Ethnicity, by contrast, is highly visible in society, so much so that self-conscious concealment of it in autobiography is viewed by readers as not only self-defeating but also deceptive. Almost inevitably, the truth will come out and the author's ethnicity will be exposed. The homogenizing effects of print culture can extirpate a cockney accent but, at least in ethnic autobiography, the biological referent—ethnic, racial, and gendered attributes inclusive—is so socially significant as to be comparatively immune to the kind of erasure that Keats undergoes in his poetry. The author's ethnicity, even when not addressed in the narrative, is part of what makes the autobiographical text meaningful to readers. It is not his ethnicity that is at risk of being erased in his autobiography, but the identity-stamping mark of print culture. To tell the story of his own life, Rodriguez must also tell us about the books he has read. Both *Brown* the autobiographical book and brown as metaphor for the complexity of ethnic identity, that is, must be understood partly in black and white—not just the black and white of American racial history (a binary Rodriguez urges us to break free from), but also the black and white of ink on paper.

MANY AMERICAS

In returning to his ethnic roots in *Days of Obligation*, Rodriguez establishes a rapprochement between his ethnic heritage and the stamp of print culture. As forcefully presented in *Brown*, doing so opens the door to the wide embrace of a complex identity and its inherent contradictions. Indeed, a subsequent rereading of *Days* reveals evidence of Rodriguez's pluralism long before the full-bodied mestizaje promulgated in *Brown*. A retrospective reading of Rodriguez's early work reorients binarism into a dialectic that promises a synthesis, even if only by holding inevitable contradictions in equilibrium. The tensions and conflicts of identity explored by Rodriguez, however, are by no means exclusive to ethnic identities. Certainly, everyone who participates in print culture also participates in some other, often predominantly oral, culture. Rodriguez embodies this multiplicity of identity. Growing up in an immigrant household, Rodriguez was immersed in an oral Mexican American culture. Racially, he describes himself as "darkish reddish, terra-cotta-ish, dirt-like, burnt Sienna in the manner of the middle Bellini" (*Brown* 126). Society sees him as Latino. But he is also a reader and, as we have seen, his consciousness was from an early age significantly informed by, filtered through, and expanded by wide and prolific reading. There is little mystery, then, to Rodriguez's strongly identifying with the English language, English-language print culture, and the Anglo American culture most reflected in that print culture. By the time his first book was published, Rodriguez had spent the majority of his life in school—an educational odyssey that began at parochial school, passed through Stanford, Columbia, and Berkeley, and on to a Fulbright sojourn as a Renaissance scholar at the British Museum Library. The ethnic self, however, is more than the sum of the books one reads or the formal education one receives.

In using his immigrant father as the manikin of autobiography in *Days*, Rodriguez expands his notion of public identity, reflecting the extent to which languages once relegated to the private, familial sphere are making gains on English as public languages in U.S. society. Advances in media, technology, and human mobility also link the global diaspora. To an unprecedented extent, the "common language" and "shared culture" that Rodriguez argues for in *Days*—chapter 8, "Asians"—is possible despite geographical remoteness, and it might not be English (163–64). Pan-American Latinos participate in both a common language and a shared culture as channeled through Spanish-language satellite television. If television does not allow two-way conversation in the sense that Rodriguez thinks a public language should, it does nonetheless offer a significantly inclusive culture for those who share a non-English mother tongue.

Román de la Campa calls this phenomena the split-state predicament: "the ontological plurality that comes from deriving an identity from more than one American imaginary, an aspect that has specific importance for all

Latino groups, regardless of national, racial, or ethnic origin" (377). The split state follows from the "postnational imaginary" of the "post-melting-pot period of American history. New ethnic enclaves in the United States (Asian, West Indian, as well as Hispanic or Latino) respond to migratory pressures that have rendered meaningless many of the legal, psychological and literary categories that define one's sense of belonging to a nation" (384, 381).[12] De la Campa's analysis is an academic counterpart to Rodriguez's rhetorical and metaphorical descriptions of contemporary American culture in *Brown*. As early as *Hunger of Memory*, Rodriguez illustrates what de la Campa offers as a friendly reminder, "that amongst Latinos racial markers seem secondary to cultural affinities." By *Brown*, Rodriguez fully engages the important clause that follows, "and, as such, they might contribute to a critique of a deeply rooted binary of essentialized whiteness and blackness" (381). His finger on the pulse of cultural evolution in the trendsetting state of California, Rodriguez has argued with increasing vigor in each book that culture trumps race. For some, the culture line has already replaced the color line as the principle binary in the national imagination.

Also delineated in academic terms by de la Campa is Rodriguez's metaphor of the browning of America:

> Today's Latino, for example, must speak more Spanish than ten or fifteen years ago. Newly arriving Latin Americans, on the other hand, find a U.S. Latino Culture that precedes them, largely articulated in English.... Latin and Anglo-American literatures, another example, can no longer ignore the wealth of an in-between culture for which English may have become a linguistic home, but whose cultural references and tonalities require interpreters skilled in Spanish language and Latin American cultures. (381)

This cultural snapshot echoes Rodriguez's view that print culture will remain English, which will also remain the national spoken language, however much inflected by other tongues: "The Laotian kids were all speaking English with a Spanish accent" ("Remarks" 6; see also "Invention" 4–6). But one must wonder what direction English-language print culture will take as the Spanish language and bilingual presses continue to grow and significant numbers of Americans read their American literature in Spanish. New theoretical models will be needed to explain the impact on identity formation when large numbers of Americans are reading a large body of American literature that has never been translated into English. If these books are subsequently translated into English, the theoretical models will require even more retooling. Theorists will also have to consider the emergence of bilingual presses in the myriad other languages spoken by Americans as a mother tongue or as a second language.

In consideration of these cultural and communication trends, de la Campa expects to see some form of hybridity in texts by ethnic writers. He calls for a "cross-over aesthetic" situated between mainstream culture and the particular ethnic culture the writer is grouped with. As this study suggests, one potentially deleterious by-product of readerly conventions and ethnic expectations is the often unconscious assumption that ethnic authenticity is a given or inherent set of traits rather than a cultural narrative that is perpetually evolving. Ethnic identities are far more complex than the description of them given by essentialist accounts. In addition, ethnic identity cannot be considered in isolation, as if existing in a cultural vacuum. Social relations are negotiated both inside the ethnic group and within the greater social matrix, resulting in myriad individual subject positions and identifications. It is with these kinds of social interactions in mind that de la Campa attributes to *Days of Obligation* a crossover aesthetic, classifying it as the product of an "in-between culture" in which "he in turn seems to have discovered a new America in which he can be a Latino writer after all. I'm inclined to believe that the literary vigor of his second book seduced the ethnic fears of his first" (382). Social relations and realities justify his use of the category Latino, but de la Campa is also careful to note the fragmentation and inherent "indeterminacy" of Latino cultures and ethnic labels, or designators, such as Latino and Hispanic (384, 377). In doing so, de la Campa resists the essentializing project of ethnic authenticity. And it is to that subject that we turn in the next chapter.

5

The Inauthentic Ethnic

Richard Rodriguez's *Brown* and Resisting
Essentialist Narratives of Ethnic Identity

• ◆ •

"'You are idle shallow things. I am not of your element,' Malvolio shrieks to the pit, to the beggars and molls in the pit, even—it must be—at the actor playing himself" (*Brown* 50). In this compressed theatrical rendition of *Twelfth Night*, Rodriguez struts the Puritan, Malvolio, across the stage as he chides the playgoers of that era. As it was for Shakespeare before him, the actual object of Rodriguez's critique is not (as it is for Malvolio) the hapless recipient of the Puritan's invective but, rather, puritanism itself. His most theatrical book to date, *Brown* is saturated with allusions to theater, cinema, musicals, and performances of all kinds. Prominent among these are the identity performances of characters such as Richard Nixon, the Stanford mascot, and professional wrestlers. Rather than dismiss the phoniness of their performances, Rodriguez explores the limits of performativity through a Whitmanesque celebration of "the theatrical invention" of the self (*Brown* 57). By once again intertwining identity, religion, and ethnicity, he also extends the sacralization of identity suggested in his earlier book, *Days of Obligation*. Theatricality is central to identity, particularly public, ethnic identities, and "[t]heatrics were an offshoot of liturgy—of the Mass, of the Passion and miracle plays and the lewd plays that preceded Lent," he reminds his readers (*Brown* 50). True to this genealogy of theatrics, Rodriguez embraces both the sacred and profane, what the Puritans approve of as well as what they reject. Given his comfort with the contradictions of identity, it is at times difficult to tell when Rodriguez is in earnest and when, "as regards identity," he is engaged in "parody or, indeed, ... self-parody" (*Brown* 70). It is in this ludic spirit as regards the inscrutable complexity of ethnic identities that this chapter is titled "The Inauthentic Ethnic."

THE POLITICS OF POLITICAL LABELS: NEOCONS, CHICANOS, AND "ALL/NONE OF THE ABOVE"

Provocative is, perhaps, the word most often invoked in describing Richard Rodriguez. The early Rodriguez was especially provocative (invoking here the full euphemistic sense of the word) to Chicana/o scholars. Having struggled through and beyond the civil rights era to affirm the value of a minority identity, Chicana/o scholars were particularly troubled by the assimilationist arguments in Rodriguez's first book, *Hunger of Memory* (1982).[1] To critics who did not self-identify as Chicana or Chicano, the tone of the criticism directed at Rodriguez suggested the vitriol of a family quarrel, the deep sources of which would always be beyond full comprehension by outsiders.[2] Criticism of this timbre leveled at Rodriguez seemed to be more about identity politics than about the specifics of his opposition to affirmative action and bilingual education programs—not, that is, about how best to achieve assimilation and social integration for minorities, but about which communities and community-defined identities one is to assimilate to, and who is define them.[3] To the many critics who framed Rodriguez's texts primarily in terms of political identification, attaching a political label to him seemed an indispensable cognitive heuristic with which to equip other readers approaching his texts. Early critics often simply referred to Rodriguez as a conservative minority, but of late the term *neoconservative* has come into use. Distinguished Chicana scholar Norma Alarcón seems to have originated the use of this political label when arguing in a 1995 essay that "Rodriguez demonstrates that neoconservative liberal cynicism knows no bounds" (150). Paula Moya cemented the use of the term in her rigorously identity-focused 2002 analysis: "Richard Rodriguez exemplifies the situation of the neoconservative intellectual in the United States" (101–2).[4] Both Alarcón and Moya invoke the neoconservative classification to emphasize Rodriguez's political individualism, specifically what might be called his ethnic individualism: his "hyperindividualized citizen-subject," his resistance to "collective racial identities," and his "refusal of ethnicity, except as a private phenomenon" (Alarcón 143; Moya

103; Alarcón 142). Given the politically unconventional combination of Rodriguez's liberalism with his contrarian stance on the highly politicized minority issues of affirmative action and bilingual education[5]—a stance that, particularly in the midst of the culture wars of the 1980s, seemed to dovetail with a conservative political platform that sometimes used race as a wedge issue—one can see why Alarcón, Moya, and other scholars found the neoconservative tag so convenient. Rodriguez confounded conventional political identities by refusing to reconcile the contradictions of a complex ethnic identity—classifying him as a neoconservative affixed an existing (and therefore epistemically useful) identity marker, allowing critics to more easily conceptualize his politics.

The popularity of the term *neoconservative* as applied to Rodriguez raises interesting questions. First is whether conceptualizing him as such focalizes more than it distorts our understanding of him, his thought, and his texts. Even a resistant reading of his four autobiographical books offers a multitude of examples that complicate the categorization of the author as a conservative of any stripe. To the textual evidence, one must add Rodriguez's open support of gay marriage and the liberalness of his Catholicism.[6] What is more, he publicly identifies as "left of center" (interview with Gillespie and Postrel). Adding to the confusion is the dominant sense of *neoconservative* today—namely, as a designation for a person or position that advocates an activist, unilateral, and militaristic foreign policy, as in the neocons William Kristol and Paul Wolfowitz and the neoconservative ideology that helped sway the Bush administration to invade Iraq in 2003. By this definition, thinking of Rodriguez as a neoconservative—when his foreign policy might best be described as cosmopolitan, and though he is a sharp critic of America's us-versus-them racial and cultural logic—would seem to cloud our conception of his views more than to clarify them.

A second and related question is whether our present understanding of Rodriguez's texts justifies the neoconservative label. Much has changed since Rodriguez's first book appeared. In the three that followed, his notions of ethnic American identity widened and became more multidimensional, as did those of the ever more inclusive Chicano, then Chicana/o, and now Latino community.[7] Not either-or, but both . . . and more. Of the evolution of Rodriguez's thought, it is important to note that his political views do not take the characteristic forms of political activism. What Rodriguez expresses in his books and in public appearances is, at most, qualified advocacy greatly nuanced by irony and ambiguity.[8] Above all else, he is a reflective, peripatetic essayist in the tradition of Montaigne—more interested in exploring the contours of a theme than (despite his polemical bravado) in didactic conclusions. Like Montaigne, Rodriguez's essays—pensive and poignant—scintillate with the prismatic refraction of complex thought, tacking one direction and then another in a style that resists a literalist reading.[9] In his essays, many of which approach the status of prose poems, Rodriguez frequently, and readily, acknowledges personal and political contradictions. Paradoxes tumble from the page: "[Y]ou will often find brown in this book as the cement between leaves of paradox" (*Brown* xi). In addition, assimilationist sentiments conveyed in *Hunger of Memory* are substantially revised in *Days of Obligation* (1992) and *Brown* (2002). In those two later texts, Rodriguez reorients his thinking to reflect the evolution of race relations and American culture over the two decades since the publication of *Hunger* in 1982. In *Brown*, Rodriguez cuts across the grain of the conventional notion of assimilation (as a one-way march toward a static and monolithic mainstream culture) to instead underscore the fluid, mestizo nature of the mainstream and to herald the triumph of the interpenetration of cultures, for which the very title *Brown* is a metaphor. Brown is cultural impurity. It is, to invoke the image offered by Rodriguez at speaking engagements, and in an interview with Gregory Wolfe (65), the color of crayons melting together in the sun.

Rodriguez identifies the different emphasis of each of his first three books as—in chronological order—class, ethnicity, and race (*Brown* xiv). In the first instance, Rodriguez's class consciousness entails a conception of socioeconomic disadvantage and the possibility for class mobility that acknowledges the role of cultural differences (of socialization by socioeconomic class, such as that described in Annette Lareau's *Unequal Childhoods*) inculcated not only by formal education and the hidden curriculum but also by print culture. Foregrounding ethnicity in *Days of Obligation*, Rodriguez's reductively binary representation of the cultural differences between Protestant North (the United States) and Catholic South (Mexico) serves not only for narrative and rhetorical contrast but also to strengthen the emphasis on cultural differences over racial ones. In *Brown*, the much-criticized cultural dichotomies found in *Hunger of Memory* and *Days of Obligation* merge into syntheses as Rodriquez emphasizes not so much race as racial and cultural miscegenation. Through his arguments about the profound and irredeemable interpenetration of cultures (racial as well as ethnic), Rodriguez hopes to do nothing less than to "undermin[e] the notion of race in America" (*Brown* xi).

My aim in this chapter is to take that hope one step further: to undermine overdetermined notions of "ethnic authenticity." Rodriguez, I argue, offers an example of resistance to those narratives of ethnic identity that have transmuted into hegemonic discourses of ethnic authenticity. I begin with a critique of ethnic authenticity that aims to explain both its eternal recurrence and the logic by which it operates. A subsequent section extends the critique of ethnic authenticity by recapitulating much of Rodriguez's decades-long criticism of it and laying the groundwork for understanding his philosophical worldview and why he takes—notoriously so for his detractors—some of the stances he does. After sketching Rodriguez's views, I briefly trace the change in tenor of the critical response to Rodriguez following the publication of his second and third books before turning to a critique of the ways in which lingering traces of ethnic authenticity can creep into conceptualizations of even such ostensibly antiessentialist theorizations of identity as hybridity.

AGAINST ETHNIC AUTHENTICITY

In debates over identity politics and ethnic literature, one finds a persistent return to essentialist notions of identity. Although most theorists of identity are rightly wary of the essentialist turn in the form of something like Richard Herrnstein's and Charles Murray's *The Bell Curve*, essentialist notions such as collective consciousness and racial memory continue to have particular appeal for projects heavily invested in collective ethnic and racial identities.[10] In his essay "Ghosts of Essentialism," John Su traces the persistence of essentialism in ethnic literature and theories of ethnic identity. He explains the eternal recurrence of essentialism by noting the enticing appeal of progressive notions such as strategic essentialism, concluding that "the hope for achieving greater social objectivity ironically guarantees that essence will continue to be a haunting presence in academic scholarship as well as in ethnic American fiction" (380).[11] Whereas Su is interested in explaining or explaining away racial memory, my interest here is with similarly essentialist narratives of ethnic authenticity. Ethnic authenticity transmutes essentialist logic into ethnic terms, trading biological claims for mostly cultural ones. Although scholars as prominent as Werner Sollors have called attention to the fallacy of ethnic authenticity, and though contrarian critics such as Walter Benn Michaels have noted and denounced the trend from biological to cultural essentialism, the tempting expediency of nonbiological essentialist claims ensures their persistence.[12] Such temptation is particularly alluring in any discussion of Latino identity. Latino is not a racial categorization, and thus excludes categorically all claims to either biological or mythical (and mystical) ties along racial lines. Ethnic authenticity, however, readily fills the void for identity claims that would otherwise be staked out through recourse to racial essentialism. The assumption, for example, that Latino identity must be oppositional to American culture serves the political and practical goal of uniting Latinos as a minority community in the absence of any inherent and everlasting essential sameness. Such expectations, though, resurrect the ghost of essentialism by defining in cultural terms Latino ethnicity as perpetually and irrevocably opposed to some cultural other.

To take a literary example, we might consider the expectation held by some that the Latino reader's literary consciousness must necessarily be significantly shaped by Latino literature, perhaps even to a greater extent than by the disparagingly dubbed "dead white male" canon. Similarly, Rodriguez comes to be thought of as a "coconut" (brown on the outside, white on the inside) by his Berkeley students when resisting the idea of minority literature as separate from American literature (*Hunger* 161–62).[13] Fortunately, today's avid ethnic readers resist such dichotomies, just as they resist the constraints of ethnic authenticity. They want both and reject neither. They read Tómas Rivera through Sherwood Anderson and Ernest Hemingway—who, in turn, they read alongside Walt Whitman, Toni Morrison, Sherman Alexie, and Sandra Cisneros. The literary canon thus becomes more diverse and inclusive as readers read—read widely, read without borders.

Denunciations of ethnic inauthenticity have the opposite effect. Rather than recognize the intransigent heterogeneity of ethnic communities and the complexity of actual minority identities, ethnic authenticity strives for hegemony. This is the first danger of essentialist claims. Expectations about ethnic authenticity impose a single ethnic narrative on each member of the community, as if everyone had the same experiences and interpreted those experiences in the same way.[14] This is patently not the case and, as Satya Mohanty notes, "Simply put, the essentialist view would be that the identity common to members of a social group is stable and more or less unchanging, since it is based on the experiences they share" (202).[15] The second danger of essentialist claims is that, regardless of intention, they have the unwanted effect of justifying and reifying existing social prejudices that are themselves myths and stereotypes. That is, if you believe in racial memory (an essentialist form of epistemic privilege), for instance, you must also believe in significant intellectual differences between the races. Similarly, if you believe that the otherwise mythical ties that bind imagined communities together are real and unchanging (and follow ethnic lines), you must logically also believe that ethnic identities are mutually exclusive rather than overlapping and interpenetrating. What unites the criticism of Rodriguez are (often unspoken) assumptions along similar lines about what it means to be Latino in the United States, assumptions that frequently have the unintended consequence of inherently opposing hybridity, mestizaje, in-betweeness, borderland identities, and the interpenetration of cultures.[16] That criticism of Rodriguez is most heated when directed at his views on assimilation, affirmative action, bilingual education, and the relation of ethnic individuals to the ethnic community—and that these criticisms so often cast Rodriguez as an inauthentic ethnic—attests to the persistence of latent notions of ethnic authenticity. At the same time, a counter-discourse of cultural mestizaje has long been central to Latino identity—and, despite their contradictory natures, notions of ethnic authenticity often coexist alongside notions of cultural interpenetration. It is to Rodriguez's notion of the interpenetration of cultures, and the changing reception of Rodriguez's texts in recent scholarship, that the next section turns.

TURNING THE BLACK SUIT INSIDE OUT: ETHNICITY-AS-CULTURE

The "Poor Richard" chapter (4) of *Brown* is a picaresque tale in miniature. The narrative, however, includes more than one *pícaro*: Rodriguez, Richard Nixon, and a black suit. Like other picaresque heroes, the black suit glides from one social milieu to another, offering trenchant social commentary wherever it goes. Rodriguez uses it to drift across the topoi of American society.[17] It unlocks doors otherwise closed to him and allows him to observe American culture from inside the room. It is sartorial minimum for upward social mobility: "One puts on the black suit. In the distance lies the city—the Ivy League, the lukewarm cocktail; the good, worn carpet; the unwelcoming rich" (*Brown* 87). The black suit is the only attire one can be seen in in such social spaces. It also allows one to go unseen, however: "My black suit made me invisible and that was its point. Respectably shabby, and that was its point. I could go to the opera. I could go to New York" (2). As these two passages suggest, the black suit can be many things. As a metaphor, it is intentionally protean, its figurative sense shifting throughout the essay. Like ethnicity and race—which can render one, simultaneously or by turns, both hypervisible and invisible—the meaning of the black suit changes with the social context in which it is worn.

The very image of the black suit recalls the opening scene from *Hunger of Memory*, where Rodriguez notes that "at a cocktail party in Bel Air" he looks "exotic in a tuxedo," though he is "dark-skinned" with "Indian features which would pass notice on the page of a *National Geographic*" (3). A woman at the upscale party is not surprised to hear that he is a writer; someone else suggests the possibility of a modeling job. This opening tableau introduces the writer—it is Rodriguez's first book—to the reader by disrupting some of the expectations the reader may have brought to the text. The reader may find the book shelved under ethnic literature, but its "dark-skinned" author disavows representing any "typical Hispanic-American life" (7). The photograph of the author on the book cover frames the autobiography as that of a visibly Latino male, but Rodriguez chooses to open the narrative by subverting reader expectations about how their awareness of the author's race and ethnicity informs their reading of the text. That he looks exotic in a tuxedo as an invited guest at a cocktail party in Bel Air demonstrates to the reader that the social meanings of his racial features change with the social landscape. That readers are interested in such features indicates the extent to which they use what they know about the author to interpret the text. That Rodriguez addresses this impulse reflects his awareness of the visibility of race, gender, and ethnicity in society. His intervention emphasizes the extent to which the meanings imposed on racial, gendered, and ethnic features are always subject to revision—particularly as the social context changes.

In depicting personal experiences, Rodriguez resists the essentialization of race and interrogates notions of what belonging to a particular race means. Racial features may be biological, unchangeable rather than constructed, but interpretations of race are, in John Searle's terms, social facts, the meanings of which are determined in social reality (xi–xii). That the social meanings of race are so monolithic compared with the diversity of their billions of biological referents testifies to the constructed and discursive nature of the interpretation of race as a biological fact. Race, in short, is all too often just a bad story, a narrative too implausible to continue taking seriously in today's increasingly multiracial world. If race is such a dark and shabby suit it may be time to "lose the black suit" (*Brown* 93).

In the post–civil rights era, Rodriguez suggests, culture is much more important than race. He has been making this argument from the beginning. Indeed, the thrust of chapter 4—"Complexion"—of *Hunger of Memory* is that class (by which, here, Rodriguez means something more like middle-class culture than purely economic class) trumps race in American society. It trumps because culture, and the language through which it is transmitted, shapes consciousness. Culture, that is, colors a person's thoughts, whereas race colors only the skin. Contact with another culture can change one's cultural self-identification, regardless of one's race. This holds true despite the power of race and ascribed racial narratives in America. That, at least, is the thrust of the arguments made about race and culture in *Hunger of Memory*, in which Rodriguez offers a poignant example of his personal struggle with the power of racial narratives as a young man when, in response to the "shame and sexual inferiority I was to feel in later years because of my dark complexion," he scrapes a razor over his arms "to see if I could get out, somehow lessen, the dark" (124).

In *Brown*, however, Rodriguez adds greater nuance and complexity to these views. In chapter 2, "In the Brown Study," he ponders the idea that "color colors thoughts," concluding that "I think I probably do. (Have brown thoughts)" (33, 46). The sentiment is bracketed not only by the disclaimer of the subjunctive mood—probably—but also through figurative language (starting with the titular trope of the brown study, a phrase roughly synonymous with melancholy and dating back to at least the sixteenth century).[18] A similar mode of assertion and erasure is used to suggest as plausible, rather than to stake as a claim, the role of experience in mediating racial and ethnic identities: "In the case of brown thought, though, I suppose experience becomes the pigment, the grounds, the *mise-en-scène*, the medium of refraction, the impeded passage of otherwise pure thought" (33–34, italics in the original). The lack of closure, the unwillingness to make an unequivocal pronouncement, is characteristic of Rodriguez's distinctively nuanced style: polyvalent, often figurative, always elusive.

Throughout his oeuvre, however, Rodriguez consistently gives more weight to culture than to race in the formation of the ethnic self. An emphasis on cultural identities rather than racial ones does not, in itself, slip the noose of essentialism, however. Much of the narrative of race in America has been transferred to ethnicity and culture, or ethnicity-as-culture, maintaining old social divisions and creating new ones. Characteristically, Rodriguez dissects just what this new development entails. "Whereas whites regarded their Americanization as a freedom from culture, black was fated because black was blood. Blood was essence; black was essence.... So 'black,' once a restriction imposed by whites in defiance of obvious history, black now is a culture (in the fated sense) imposed by blacks" (*Brown* 141). Such whole-cloth models of culture—whereby culture or ethnicity is defined as mutually exclusive of other cultures—are zero-sum games. They preclude any overlapping of cultures, leaving out, for instance, an account of participation in what then become, by definition, nonethnic and nonracial cultures, such as popular culture, and print culture. Such cultural narratives—separately laundered, heavily starched—cannot account for the strong identification of white middle-class teens with hip-hop, or the trilingual menus and wait staff of Chinese Cuban (or is it Cuban Chinese?) restaurants in Manhattan.

This is not to suggest that ethnicity does not, at times, follow the same logic as race. But neither are ethnic narratives as fluid as cultural ones. In her rigorous philosophical investigation of identity, Linda Martín Alcoff warns the reader of *Visible Identities*:

> At times I will address race/ethnicity and sex/gender as if these each represent a common entity. This is because, as I shall argue, race and ethnicity often slip into one another's shoes, as some ethnicities (or cultural identities) are perpetually and relentlessly raced even as race (as bodily entity) is made to stand in for ethnicity. (10)

The duality of ethnicity—at times functioning like race, and at other times like culture—confounds ready agreement on a definition of the term. By way of offering a working conceptualization of ethnicity, I invoke from Alcoff's formulation what I take to be the key feature of ethnicity, its visibility. What distinguishes ethnicity from culture is that one's ethnicity is perceived and recognized as ethnic by others.[19] At first glance, this may appear to be a tautology. It is not. Rather, the phrasing is meant to stress the semiotic aspect of ethnicity as something that involves the recognition and interpretation of, for lack of a better term, cultural signs. Culture comprises much that is, in general, not clearly and immediately apparent (visible) to others, such as knowledge, ideas, beliefs, values, customs, practices, perceptions, and the like.[20] Ethnicity, however culturally based, tends to be more recognizable—recognizable as pertaining to a culturally other group, whose otherness is typically characterized by regional, linguistic, biological, and similar forms of difference. One's ethnicity, of course, signifies differently—because it is largely based on the recognition and interpretation of such differences from a particular social reference point—in different cultural contexts. But ethnicity, unlike race, is not universally held to be immutable and indelibly manifest in biological features. Rather, its visibility emanates from a broad array of sources, such as accent, surname, proclaimed ancestry, body language, and the like. Such an account recognizes ethnicity's entanglement with both race and culture. It recognizes that ethnicity is often employed not only as a surrogate for race, and vice versa, but also for culture. That is, it notes the extensive overlap between race and ethnicity and between ethnicity and culture, but—equally important—resists conflating all three. Such an account has practical as well as theoretical value, providing, for example, an explanation for the scant attention given to white ethnics (Irish, Italian, Polish, and others) these days in academic scholarship and in American society at large: in the modern era, their ethnicity is less visible.

In full appreciation of its capacity to operate in the borderlands between race and culture, the depiction of ethnicity in this chapter at times reveals ethnicity's affinity with race, and at other times emphasizes its overlap with culture. Rodriguez's exploration stresses the ethnicity-as-culture mode. Lest the black suit of ethnicity become a straitjacket, he deemphasizes ethnicity-as-race in order to present ethnicity as tending to have the malleability and porosity of cultures. The underlying motivation for this is to gain for ethnic individuals the "white freedom" enjoyed by those whose ethnicity is less visible. It is to grant—through "a more playful notion of culture. Culture as freedom"—to racial and ethnic subjects the same capacity for reinvention that everyone else has (*Brown* 142). Besides excluding others from participating in the culture, and thwarting understanding between cultures, a dress code that permits only one "ethnic suit" to be worn by everyone who shares a similar background or a given set of racial traits, greatly restricts the self-expression and self-realization of people who happen to possess those traits. Ethnic cultures are more miscible, Rodriguez reminds us, than the dominant narratives of ethnicity or ethnic heritage suggest. There are no pure cultural heritages, ruling out supposedly innate connections linking all Latinos (or any other ethnic group) by virtue of shared origins. Nor are there any pure cultures, hermetically sealed off from all the other cultures: "National borders do not hold. Ethnic borders. Religious borders. Aesthetic borders, certainly. Sexual borders. Allergenic borders" (213). Cultures rub up against each other in acts of mutual frottage. Inescapably, like races, cultures frequently merge: "I write of blood that is blended. I write of brown as complete freedom of substance of narrative. I extol impurity" (xi). Everyone belongs to more than one culture.

This is the Rodriguez who Juan de Castro describes as having "evolved towards a celebration of hybridity," pairing Rodriguez with Gloria Anzaldúa and José David Saldívar as a "theorist of the borderlands" (116, 102).[21] In the penetrating analysis of Rodriguez and his work that introduces her 2003 interview with him, Claudia Milian Arias also now compares Rodriguez with Gloria Anzaldúa. "Regardless of whether or not he has achieved 'white freedom,' or whether he no longer desires it, one cannot help but turn to Gloria Anzaldúa's foundational book, *Borderlands/La Frontera: The New Mestiza.* Anzaldúa (1999, 101), perhaps the most renowned theorist of Chicana mestizaje, notes that she wants 'the freedom to carve and chisel my own face'" (Milian Arias 273; for other insightful interviews of Rodriguez, see those with Cooper, Sedore, and Wolfe). As this comparison indicates, Rodriguez's conceptualization of brown clearly resonates with Anzaldúa's theorization of mestizaje: "The new mestiza copes by developing a tolerance for contradictions, a tolerance for ambiguity.... She learns to juggle cultures. She has a plural personality, she operates in a pluralistic mode—nothing is thrust out, the good the bad and the ugly, nothing is rejected, nothing abandoned" (101). Writing in 2001, Maarten van Delden concurs in arguing that Rodriguez's "work has clear affinities with the work of border theorists" (120). Saldívar, in his book *Border Matters*, dubs *Days of Obligation* a "borderland 'text'" (12). "If Richard Rodriguez remains an 'assimilated man,'" writes Rubén Martínez in his review of *Days of Obligation*, "then the terms of assimilation—American 'culture' itself—have changed" (19). And Kevin McNamara argues that Rodriguez "enacts a poetics of cultural miscegenation" (106). To this reappraisal following the publication of *Days of Obligation* in 1992 and *Brown* in 2002, Frederick Luis Aldama adds, "Rodriguez re-visions himself neither simply as *activo* nor *pasivo*, *gringo* nor *hispano*, Chicano nor *indio*, but as a confluence of coexisting identities" (*Brown on Brown* 78, italics in the original). Even more recently, Nidesh Lawtoo sets out to reassess *Hunger of Memory* and "Rodriguez's epistemology of in-between identities," explaining Rodriguez's troubling dichotomies, particularly between public and private, as manifestations of a "kind of writing which allows for the expression of different and contradictory voices" (220, 240). Gustavo Pérez-Firmat recovers the Spanish voice in Rodriguez in arguing that, because Spanish was his mother tongue, Rodriguez's writing is indelibly stamped with the imprint of that language: "Contrary to what *Hunger of Memory* wants to assert, however, the contest between Spanish and English is resolved in favor of the former, for *lenguajes* cannot rival *lenguas* or *idiomas* in their hold on individual speakers, including Rodriguez"; that is, "Rodriguez abandons his mother tongue, but he cannot escape her," yet again alluding to the largely unexcavated mosaic of voices and identities to be found in Rodriguez's writings (*Tongue Ties* 19, 155, italics in the original). Further profound linguistic reevaluation of Rodriguez's texts is offered by Martha Cutter, who traces the interlingual voice in Rodriguez from the binary opposition of English and Spanish presented in *Hunger of Memory* to Rodriguez's "using, yet also refashioning, English," in *Brown* "so that English becomes interlingual, miscegenated, brown, and inflected by Mexican Spanish, by ethnicity itself" (190).

I do not mean, in cataloguing charitable evaluations of his recent work, to suggest anything like a critical consensus on Rodriguez's writing.[22] On the contrary, much work remains to be done in recuperating Rodriguez's texts, not only within the academic community, but also for much of the Latino community at large. What José Limón observed in 1998 is to a troubling extent still true today. "There is no intellectual or political love lost between him [Rodriguez] and the Chicano and post-Chicano and Chicana movement intelligentsia. They remain uniformly critical and in rejection of his work since the publication of the preliminary essays that appeared later as *Hunger of Memory*" (392).[23] "Critics have failed to notice the multiple 'selves' Rodriguez re-presents in his texts," explains Laura Fine, "and have not come to terms with his re-writing/righting of his identities" (120). Critical engagement with Rodriguez's work continues to be constrained by the legacy of, as Randy Rodríguez describes it, "the political and ideological demands of cultural nationalist movements of the 1960s and 1970s, such as the Chicano movement, which prescribed loyalty to racial and ethnic identification" (396).[24] A common refrain is to sing the praises of *Brown* while denouncing his first book, but *Hunger of Memory* is simply too important of a book and Rodriguez too important of a writer to dismiss in such a manner. Rather, *Hunger of Memory* needs to be reread—as Nidesh Lawtoo and Randy Rodríguez, for example, have begun to do—in light of Rodriguez's later work.

THE INAUTHENTIC ETHNIC

From an early age, Rodriguez notes being painfully conscious of authenticating ethnic narratives—"the Puritans' insistence upon deathless identity" (*Brown* 51):

> There was not another noun in my childish Spanish vocabulary that made me more uneasy than the word *"cultura"* (which was always used against me, but as indistinguishable from me—something I had betrayed). I did not shrink from culture's cousin-noun, *"costumbre"*—custom, habit—which was visible, tangible, comestible, conditional.
>
> In Spanish, culture is indissoluble; culture is everything that connects me with the past and with a sense of myself as beyond myself. (129, italics in the original)

In the last sentence, Rodriguez is ventriloquizing indictments made against those who have "lost" their (Mexican, or more generally, Spanish-language) culture. Those who fault Rodriguez for losing his cultura conflate culture with the visibility of ethnicity: one's family background, mother tongue, surname . . . race. But Rodriguez exposes the essentializing assumptions—the fetishized link between ethnic origins or racial features and culture—behind the charge: "If culture is so fated, how could I have lost it?" (*Brown* 129). He rejects both the conflation of the self with any particular culture and the notion that personal identity is historically determined by that culture. Nor does anyone ever belong exclusively to only one culture, wholly free of other cultural influences.

Rodriguez would instead complicate ethnic identities, noting how each culture rubs off on the other, changing the tincture of each: "From the inception of America, interracial desire proceeded apace with segregated history" (*Brown* 139, 134). Americans persistently ignored "[o]ne of the first lessons in America, the color-book lesson, [which] instructs that color should stay within the lines" (135). Old discourses of race may stubbornly dichotomize the world into black and white, suppressing consciousness of the "erotic history of America," but miscegenation and waves of new immigrants cause ruptures in such tidy categories: a "brown intrusion into the tragic dialectic of America, the black and white conversation" (134, 126). Rodriguez reminds us that miscegenation, rather than racial difference, should be the dominant American metaphor:

The last white freedom in American will be the freedom of the African American to admit brown. Miscegenation. To speak freely of ancestors, of Indian and Scots and German and plantation owner. To speak the truth of themselves. That is the great advantage I can see for blacks in the rise of the so-called Hispanic. (*Brown* 142)

Likewise, there is no pure ethnic identity, and though the ethnic costume hopes to cover up such indecent revelations it turns out that the emperor has no clothes: "What Latin America might give the United States is a playful notion of race. . . . / What the United States might give Latin America is a more playful notion of culture. Culture as freedom. Culture as invitation. Culture as lure. . . . / Only further confusion can save us" (*Brown* 142).

Most critics would agree with Rodriguez's critique of racial essentialism. When narratives of identity are framed in cultural terms, however, many find him guilty of ethnic inauthenticity—a modern-day race traitor. Petra Fachinger, for example, criticizes Rodriguez for resisting "hybridization and double-voicedness" in *Hunger of Memory* (111). What is problematic, writes Fachinger, is that Rodriguez "mak[es] mainstream culture the center of [his] perception" (124). This, she argues, causes him to "view reality in terms of dichotomies" (124). What is more, he writes for mainstream readers, who see him as an "insider informant of a [minority] culture," and he "essentialize[s] 'English' as a monolithic structure that opens the door to privilege" (124).

Where Rodriguez stresses that "literature flows from the particular" (*Brown* 12), and that he "write[s] of one life only" (*Hunger* 7), Fachinger stresses the ways in which Rodriguez is representative, arguing that he "assumes a representative voice by claiming that his experience is a typically American one" (120). Rodriguez's autobiography, Fachinger argues, is already more than the atomized one life only that it claims to be in the prologue. The book is, after all, classifiably about American immigrant experience, though it rejects classification as being representative of minority or ethnic experience. It is not only for his resistance to the expectation that he be ethnically representative that Fachinger criticizes Rodriguez, but also for indulging in apolitical nostalgia and longing "for a pastoral past" (124). "Rodriguez's texts are problematic," writes Fachinger, "because they avoid the 'politicization of memory'" (124). Other critics have noted precisely the opposite: Rodriguez's politicization of memory in the service of, for example, his views on affirmative action and bilingual education.[25] It is clear, then, that what Fachinger is really critiquing is not a lack of political engagement per se, but Rodriguez's failure to conform to a particular narrative about ethnicity. It is not that Rodriguez is a politically detached art-for-art's-sake voluptuary, as Vladimir Nabokov is often characterized as, but that his identity politics do not conform with certain expectations about what a minority writer's self-identification should be. Such expectations lead Fachinger to conclude that his "nostalgia prevents [Rodriguez] from linking collective ethnic memory and individual memory in a dialogue, a narrative strategy that, according to Jennifer Browdy de Hernandez, is characteristic of 'ethnic autobiography'" (124). Although Fachinger does not explicitly invoke ethnic inauthenticity, implicit in her faulting of the text for resisting "cultural hybridization and double-voicedness" is a criticism of the text's failure to be "authentically ethnic" given the ethnic background of its author.[26] I have chosen to single out Fachinger's critique of Rodriguez precisely because it is an example of the subtle ways in which expectations of ethnic authenticity can reinscribe themselves even when one is scrupulously endeavoring to avoid ethnic essentialization by engaging something—hybridity and compound identities—that is on its surface antithetical to essentialist claims.

In writing about women writers on both sides of the U.S.-Mexican border, and interrogating the dominant modes of border theory, Debra Castillo and María Tabuenca Córdoba identify and critique a similar essentialization of hybrid identities as "either ideal types," or "seen through a Bakhtinian theoretical perspective on 'border culture,' according to which any and all [border] readers and writers are border residents; therefore they are bicultural in the broadest and most inclusive sense of the term *culture*" (14–15). A form of what social scientists call the ecological error—assuming that traits characterizing the group statistically, or as a whole, are equally true for individuals—leads to mistakenly categorizing all border writers as "uniformly bilingual, [and] runs the risk of excluding a large number of primary referents" (14). Sweeping away the clouding mists of overly generalized and abstract theorizations of border identities, and grounding their observations and analysis firmly in the intractable reality of actual border people, Castillo and Tabuenca Córdoba remind us that "there are few bilingual writers on Mexico's border with the United States and even fewer who are bicultural" (14).

Even through border theory or a Bakhtinian dialogic approach, then, the anti-authenticating gesture of extolling bicultural or hybrid identities can become reinscribed as an expectation that ethnic subjects fit one mold or another of ethnic authenticity. The Hydra-like resurgence of various forms of this expectation, and its imposition on ethnic authors, is fueled in part by impulses at the core of identity discourse: "[A] sense that identity, especially ethnic identity, grounds claims to authenticity and cannot represent a complex or problematic affiliation. Ethnic identity must be limited, contained, 'insular.' It should represent a single unproblematically authentic Otherness" (Castillo and Tabuenca Córdoba 231–32). As Castillo and Tabuenca Córdoba make abundantly clear in *Border Women*, resistance to "complex or problematic affiliation" can place the ethnic author under attack from all sides, ducking the petards of ethnic inauthenticity (from the dominant ethnic culture and minority ethnic culture alike, from both *los gabachos* and *los mexicanos*) only to turn right into the charge of being inauthentically hybrid.[27] Of course, hybridity does not mean the same thing for Fachinger as it does for Rodriguez, or as it would for most people who consider their identities to be characterized by hybridity. Again, Fachinger specifically cites Rodriguez as an anomalous exception to Browdy de Hernandez's claim that "ethnic autobiographers create a hybridized, double-voiced form of autobiography in which collective ethnic memory and individual memory are linked in a dialogue" (qtd. in Fachinger 111).[28]

Browdy de Hernandez's term, *collective ethnic memory*, suggests strong essentializing or authenticating notions about ethnic identity, mystically imputing to all ethnic writers the innate possession of the same sort of heritable collective consciousness as that implied by the notion of racial memory.[29] Fachinger is more cautious here, bracketing antiessentializing terminology in quotation marks to hang her arguments on the framework of a Bakhtinian theory of hybridization and doubled-voicedness:

> "ethnic" discourse could consequently be read as the discourse of an "ethnic" writer who dialogizes the dominant language by self-consciously resorting to "ethnic" form and language to express his or her intentions in a "refracted" way through the dominant language. Since autobiography is traditionally both a "western" and an "androcentric" genre, "double-voicedness" in "ethnic" autobiography would be apparent in the "refraction" of conventional discourse, that is, in its rewriting, or, at least, in its self-reflexive questioning of autobiographical conventions. (111–12)

Fachinger makes no direct pronouncements about collective ethnic memory or collective consciousness. She does, however, endorse claims about the existence and value of such notions by making their perceived absence in

Rodriguez's text the departure point for her critique of the autobiographical self presented in *Hunger of Memory*. Rodriguez is deemed an inauthentic ethnic because, in Fachinger's reading, he lacks the double-voicedness that characterizes all ethnic autobiographers.

The critique of ethnic authenticity offered in this chapter, it is hoped, will serve as a reminder of the need to continually be on our guard against the eternal recurrence of old essentialist claims in new guises. Few academic fields would not profit from regular self-examination in this regard, but scholarship in the comparatively young and vibrant field of ethnic studies would particularly benefit from constant vigilance against taking an essentialist turn, especially given John Su's astute analysis and prediction that "essence will continue to be a haunting presence in academic scholarship" (380). Any stroll down the essentialist path, regardless of how noble or strategic the reasons for doing so, is likely to engender more problems than it resolves. Moreover, narratives of ethnicity that avoid essentialist trappings have greater resonance and power than those that do not. John Alba Cutler reminds us of this reality when appraising Chicana/o literature of the Vietnam War: "The power of these texts ultimately lies in eschewing traditional notions of authenticity as essential inheritance. In Benjamin's terms authentic empowerment is an intersubjective process" (607). As Latino iconoclast, the early Rodriguez was a magnet for the label of inauthentic ethnic. As a queer, brown, church-going Catholic, perhaps Rodriguez's example (especially in *Brown*) will inspire us to celebrate the irredeemable complexity of identity—the intersubjective, contradiction-laden brown-ness of us all.

EPILOGUE

The Hermeneutic Consequences of Writing While Ethnic

A devoted voluptuary of the aesthetic, narrative, and imaginative dimensions of literature, I have throughout this study nonetheless refused to relinquish a persistent connection to the extratextuality of texts. I have done so because it is only in social context that texts—particularly nonfiction texts—are meaningful. Those who remain resistant to the idea that extratextual features such as the ethnicity of the author are at all relevant to how readers interpret texts would, I believe, at least concede the more modest claim that readers alter their readings of autobiographical texts when they are aware of discrepancies between biographical facts about the author and the presentation of that self on the page. Readers also expect other nonfiction narratives to correspond with historical and biographical facts, and revise their readings of those texts when their awareness of these facts changes.

Few contemporary critics would deny that extratextual elements inform the reading of texts in such ways. Nevertheless, some formalist and textual-materialist critics might insist that we must distinguish between how a text is read and what a text is. Extratextual features do not change the language of the text itself. That is true, but thinking of a text as nonfiction rather than fiction does not change it either. Nothing I propose here changes the status of the text in its material form. What changes, rather, is the text-object's triangulation with readers and extratextual context. The text's presumed genre—fiction versus nonfiction, ethnic literature versus nonethnic literature—is a categorization of the text's relationship to the world, a relationship that has large repercussions for how the text is read and the ways in which it is meaningful. In short, the extratextual feature of correspondence with the world is integral to what the text, as social artifact, is. The language of the text matters, but so does the situatedness of that language—of the text—in social context.

THE ETHNIC SELF IN FICTION

In previous chapters, I limited myself to a discussion of autobiographical texts in analyzing narratives of the ethnic self. In this epilogue, I turn briefly to a consideration of the ethnic self in fiction. Fiction does not make the same referential claims as autobiography and nonfiction. Fictionalizing through narrative liberates nonfiction texts from an account of reality dulled by excessive literalism and a lack of imagination; fiction, however, imposes no referential limits on the imagination. In fiction, anything goes. One should not, then, some would argue, concern oneself with such things as the ethnicity of the author when analyzing works of fiction. If anything goes, then nothing is certain, including the ostensible biography of the author—even if that biography is embedded as part of the book's promotional apparatus. All this is true. Fiction and nonfiction are very different creatures indeed. Readers approach works presented to them as fiction with different expectations than they do nonfiction texts. Authors can be more imaginative in fiction. Readers can be less literal.

The ethnicity of the author, however, cannot be (nor is) completely ignored when discussing fiction. Two things happen to ethnic authors when they write fiction. First, their texts are more likely to be read as at least partially autobiographical. Second, they are read as ethnically representative. Readers, in other words, tend to read works of fiction by ethnic authors with essentially the same framework of ethnic expectations that they bring to ethnic autobiography. That is not to say, however, that such expectations are applied in the same measure. Certainly, there are differences of degree, if not of kind. Nevertheless, the fictional works of ethnic authors are read much differently than are those of authors assumed by readers to be nonethnic.

Those who have read Richard Wright at all have usually read one of two texts, *Black Boy* or *Native Son*. What most stands out when comparing these two texts is the stark contrast between the two protagonists. *Black Boy*'s is an avid reader, nonviolent (though confrontational), and ultimately sympathetic. *Native Son*'s Bigger Thomas, in contrast, is uneducated, excessively violent, and hard to sympathize with. On most counts, he is the anti-Wright. A critic interested in talking about Bigger Thomas as Wright's alter ego might be better off, it would seem, describing him as Wright's nemesis. But that, too, is a basis for comparison. The fictional protagonist is still, in some way, read as reflective of the ethnic author, if only as—like Poe's fictional doppelgänger in "William Wilson"—an inverted mirror image of the self. Indeed, a persuasive argument could be made for reading Bigger as Wright's existential double: "what I killed for I am" (*Native Son* 429). As we have seen, Wright was an existentialist before existentialism came to America. Even so, as much as his experiences growing up in the Jim Crow South may have led him to conclude that hell is other people, he does not need to kill to experience true freedom and creativity. His fictional dark other, however, does precisely that, allowing Wright to depict the explosive violence that can follow from racism and its social, economic, and psychological effects on black subjects. Wright eludes the naturalistic determinism that is Bigger's fate, but he makes sure that Bigger does not find a similar escape. In so doing, he deepens his indictment of a society that continues to ignore discrimination and inequality. Bigger Thomas is Richard Wright denied all but the slenderest thread of agency. In such ways, a comparison between the author and his volatile fictional protagonist can be made, and is more than persuasive. The point, to be clear, is not that no such comparisons can be made. Rather, it is that readers are more likely to make such comparisons when the fictional protagonist is the same race, gender, and ethnicity as the author.

Early critics of *Native Son* offer quite a different interpretation. What they saw was not Wright's dark double, but a symbol of the black masses. Writing in the *Atlantic Monthly*, David Cohn argued that "Wright elects to portray his hero not as an individual merely but as a symbol of twelve million American Negroes" (91). What is striking is what these widely divergent readings have in common. In both interpretations, the author's ethnicity, though read differently at different times and by different readers, is the most prominent feature. What is more, in the second interpretation, critics balked at the negative depiction of Bigger because they knew that he would be read as, on some level, representative of the race:

> He [Wright] certainly did not pick the average unemployed Negro youth, who does not become a rapist, a murderer, and fall into the

> pitfall of crime, as Bigger did[,] despite the pressure on the average youth exerted by his white ruling class oppressors. In fact one of the serious weaknesses of the book, particularly in the third part, is that the author overwrites Bigger into a symbol of the whole Negro people, a native son to the Negro people. (Davis 71)

As with autobiography, the ethnic novel and its characters are framed by expectations about their racial representativeness. Indeed, much of the power of the novel comes from knowing that the author is a black man. Not only would the depiction of Bigger Thomas's character in *Native Son* have been even more controversial had readers thought that the author of the book was white, but readers would have been more skeptical about the accuracy of the novel's representation of Bigger's psychological state.[1]

Regardless of what is possible in fiction, it is often assumed that only a black author can take us inside the mind of a fictional black character. The logic stems from the real-life intuition that an African American author can best tell us about the experience of being an African American in this country. A similar reasoning runs in the opposite direction: readers expect that anything an ethnic author writes will be representative of the ethnic group. Again, the genealogy of this logic has its roots in everyday life. In real life, people who share an ethnicity are similarly situated in society as well as in the minds of the public generally. Stereotypes are routinely referenced in social reality, and readily carry over to the reading of fictional texts: most Mexicans fit a certain stereotype for the reader, so the reader assumes that a fictional Mexican character will stereotypically inform them about most Mexicans. Given these social and psychological realities, the depiction of Bigger as a sociopath is potentially problematic because mainstream readers will, on some level, think of him as typical.

Because meaning in a text is triangulated between the author, text, and readers, the situatedness of the triangle and each of its legs in the world—of which society is a part—is indispensable to the ways a text can be meaningful. Not only do readers bring their own experiences to the text, but they also make certain assumptions about the kinds of experiences the author can impart or translate to the text. These assumptions are framed by what readers know about those features of the author's identity that are, as with the *Native Son* example, most visible in society. The ways in which works of fiction are meaningful to readers, that is, are informed—as is autobiography—by what readers think they know about the author. Among the more visible of such features, as I have been arguing, is the author's ethnicity.

Many critics resist such notions completely. Following thinkers—or social constructs posing as individual thinkers, if we are to take interpretation of their claims as literally as do their more fundamentalist followers—such as Roland Barthes and Michel Foucault, they take the "death of the author" as a given (see Barthes and Foucault). To acknowledge the ways in which the author's ethnicity informs our reading of the text, however, is not to bar the distinction between author (or implied author) and writer (the individual who produced the text) that such critics make (see also Nehamas 99–100). Nor is it to claim that the author has absolute authority over meaning in the text. Some, such as Walter Benn Michaels in *The Shape of the Signifier*, would conflate authorial intention with the text's meaning. I do not.[2] I do, however, claim that texts are produced by individuals and that how those individuals are situated in social reality engenders a great deal of the meaning—or meanings—that readers take away from those texts.

THE ETHNIC ALTER EGO: AN INVITATION TO FURTHER INQUIRY

Among the avenues of future inquiry this book opens up is the ethnic alter ego. Ethnic authors, even when writing fiction, must deal with reader expectations that their characters will be ethnically representative as well as partly autobiographical. One might ask, then, if self-consciously creating a character that will be readily seen as an alter ego lessens authorial power over fictional creations. Or can doing so increase authorial power in unexpected ways?

Helena María Viramontes's characters are often read as alter egos, particularly of the author in her youth. Her protagonists tend to be young (not yet adults), rebellious, and Latina. Estrella, the main character of *Under the Feet of Jesus*, is certainly all of these. Even readers who know little of the author's biography feel some impulse to associate the Chicana protagonist with the Chicana author, whose Hispanic name is prominently displayed on the book's cover. Readers who are more familiar with Viramontes's biography may be even more apt to map what they know about the author onto Estrella. Although Viramontes distances herself from Estrella by age, it would take changing the gender and ethnicity of the character to significantly insulate her from such associations. That these features are so integral to association or dissociation with the author merely reflects their visibility in social reality, which in turn affirms the extent to which the author's gender and ethnicity inform the ways in which the text is meaningful to readers.

Reading Estrella as Viramontes's alter ego does not, however, make her the writer's autobiographical self. Decidedly not. Yet, as we have seen, readers often approach such novels—those with ethnic characters, and written by an ethnic author—with the same kinds of expectations with which they approach ethnic autobiography. Much can be explored along these lines. What nuanced distinctions do readers make between the expected representativeness of ethnic fiction and that of nonfiction? How do ethnic authors write to and against such expectations? Analysis of the ethnic alter ego requires granting wide latitude to the role of the imagination and, at the same time, exercising more restraint than when conducting similar analysis of the autobiographical self. Authors have almost unlimited freedom to imagine alternate lives through their fictional alter egos, so any comparison between author and character requires greater moderation than when considering works of nonfiction.

As Wright intended with *Native Son*, Viramontes seeks to motivate her readers to change—to do something about the kinds of social injustice depicted in the book. Because she writes in this vein, *Under the Feet of Jesus* is often referred to as social realism, lending the novel to typological comparison with Steinbeck's *The Grapes of Wrath*. To be compelled to social change, however, readers must first believe that the novel realistically depicts the world of migrant workers. This Viramontes accomplishes, as Ellen McCracken confirms. "Viramontes' novel brings the true story of ordinary people like her parents and their fellow migrant workers into the social conscience of the mainstream U.S. public" (*New Latina Narrative* 184). The novel's depiction of the plight of migrant workers is more apt to ring true with readers in part because they assume that Viramontes's Hispanic name indicates personal experience with migrant labor, or at least some personal acquaintance with migrant laborers. This assumption comes from the brute facts of the social context in which the text is read: most migrant farmworkers are Latino. At the very least, the author's ethnically inflected name adds resonance to a text about Latino farm laborers.

These notions suggest future avenues of investigation. Many of the arguments about autobiographical texts could be extended to works of fiction, though some of these extrapolations would have to be modified to distinguish what is true of fiction from what is true only of autobiography. Future investigations along such lines would have to consider the ways in which readers approach works by ethnic authors, the ways in which ethnic authors are situated in society, and the production and marketing of their work. Though one might frame such investigations by using the term *ethnic alter ego*, one might also take a wider approach through the analysis of the broader category of representations of the ethnic protagonist in fiction. Either way, much can be learned from such investigations, particularly those that would give full consideration to the ways in which readings of fictional texts are informed by the embodiedness of ethnic authors and their situatedness in social reality. The book you hold in your hands takes as subject matter that embodiedness and situatedness but, in considering only the much narrower scope of ethnic autobiography, offers only the faintest glimpse of much more illuminating scholarship to come. This parting note is an invitation to other scholars to bring us more fully into the light.

CODA: *DARLING*

Long after this book had been conceptualized and written, Rodriguez's fourth autobiographical book, *Darling: A Spiritual Autobiography*, was released. The manuscript for this book was complete at that time, and all but in proofs. I considered replacing this epilogue with a brief overview of Rodriguez's latest installment. But such a gesture, though extending the coverage of Rodriguez, would not further the comparative and theoretical aims of this study. Indeed, theorization of the ethnic self in literature would be better underscored and extended by keeping the current epilogue, which shifts the discussion to fiction as a way to explore limitations of the approach as well as to suggest avenues of further inquiry. What is more, nothing in *Darling* contradicts or problematizes what has been argued here. Far better, then, to defer discussion of *Darling* to a later date.

That said, allow me to highlight two points of departure from *Darling* that particularly reinforce the spirit of this epilogue and some of the possible directions it suggests. One of these is the theme of gender, expanding the discussion of masculinity to place it in the larger context in which it is meaningful. The beneficial feminization of religion, and of our culture, is a powerful theme in *Darling*, the titular chapter of which ends with these lines: "I cannot imagine my freedom as a homosexual man without women in veils. ... Without women. / Without you." (132). Rodriguez is referring, in part, and on the most literal level, to the Irish Catholic nuns who educated him, and to their altruistic selflessness, compassion, and empathy. By the "feminine way," Rodriguez means "selfless" (131). Interwoven with this conception of what it means to feminize a culture is Rodriguez's humanistic view of religion: "[R]eligion gives me a sense—no, not a sense, a reason, no, not exactly a reason, an understanding—that everyone matters" (225). And it is this liberal pluralist sentiment that underlies any discussion of narratives of the ethnic self, and why literature produced by authors of ethnicities other than our own should matter to the rest of us—to all of us.

Notes

Preface

1. Literature departments, in part due to their own geographic lines of disciplinary division, generally distinguish between American literature and authors (by which they mean those writers and texts associated with the U.S. context) and literature of the Americas (which can include authors and writing from Tierra del Fuego to the Yukon). When I speak of Wright and Rodriguez as American writers, and their writing as American literature, I am referring almost exclusively to the U.S. context. I would note, however, that both writers traveled to Mexico, each has written about their experiences abroad, and each, in varying degrees, was aware of (though not nearly as influenced by) the Latin American literary tradition. Of much greater influence on the consciousness and writing of Wright and Rodriguez is the Anglo American tradition of British and U.S. literature, followed by that of western European provenance more broadly. Each author grew increasingly aware of other global literatures after establishing himself as a writer. Wright, for instance, lived in France and turned to the non-Western poetic form of haiku in his last years.
2. Ethnic literature conceptualized as a genre, that is.

Introduction

1. On the self as narrative but contingent on an embodied substrate see, for example, Daniel Dennett's *Consciousness Explained*. Antirealist and constructivist accounts of the self as discourse are prevalent among influential literary theorists such as Lacan, Derrida, and Foucault, whose respective arguments range widely

but run to varying degrees counter to realist accounts grounded in the embodiedness of the self.
2. A specifically nongenetic formulation of ethnicity is invoked here to stress that ethnicity is distinct from race—though the two terms are often used interchangeably—in that a person can be recognized as ethnic though devoid of racial markers.
3. In *We Have Never Been Modern*, Bruno Latour proposes that we speak only of "natures-cultures," rather than committing either the naïve empiricist or absolute relativist's error of conceptualizing culture as separate from nature "by bracketing Nature off" (104). *Biocultural* is the term used by Brian Boyd in *On the Origin of Stories* (25).
4. Postmodernism and poststructuralism share an affinity with ludic and ironic modes of philosophizing. I sometimes use postmodernism, poststructuralism, and literary theory somewhat interchangeably, here, as all three question or ironize notions of an objective reality or an embodied self.
5. For a critique of methodological individualism and American overreliance on it "when they think about social problems," see Cyrus Patell's *Negative Liberties* (xiii). In addition to exploring the concept of positive liberty in the liberal philosophies of John Stuart Mill and Isaiah Berlin, Kwame Anthony Appiah eloquently makes the case for the social self in *The Ethics of Identity*, arguing that "[t]o value individuality properly just *is* to acknowledge the dependence of the good for each of us on relationships with others. Without these bonds, as I say, we could not come to be free selves, not least because we could not come to be selves at all" (21, 27, emphasis in the original).
6. Although her precise position on the embodiedness of subjects is often debated, in *Gender Trouble*, Butler stresses discourse over the corporeality of subjects—"gender norms are finally phantasmatic, impossible to embody"—and does so despite gestures such as calling gender "a corporeal style" (190–92).
7. This project limits its inquiry to Rodriguez's autobiographical books, but Rodriguez is known to many primarily in his capacity as a journalist for the Pacific News Service and former television essayist for the PBS *NewsHour*. In both his autobiographies and his role as media commentator on Latino and ethnic issues, Rodriguez's authority on ethnic topics is based partly on his visibly ethnic status: he is the brown face on the back of the book cover or framed in your television.
8. Tempering the demerits of tribalism, and any notion of belonging exclusively to a single tribe, is the reality that each of us belongs to many tribes, and the modern assumption that at least one tribe or family can be extended to include all of humanity, and perhaps even more. But still one must ask, What are my tribes?
9. Adams writes, "Olney's idea that the central figure be treated as a single person referred to as 'black boy,' a literary character representing the actual author both as child and as an adult—the famous writer imagining himself as representative

of inarticulate black children—is finally convincing" (74). See also Olney's "Some Versions of Memory / Some Versions of Bios."

Chapter 1

1. All citations refer to the 1998 Perennial Classics "restored text" edition of *Black Boy*, with notes by Arnold Rampersad and introduction by Jerry W. Ward Jr. The restored text was first published by the Library of America in 1991 and is based on Wright's 1944 page proofs, reuniting the first and second halves of Wright's original autobiography. The Book-of-the-Month Club agreed to adopt the Harper and Brothers book in 1945 only if the second section, "The Horror and the Glory," were dropped. Wright agreed and, though excerpts from the expurgated text appeared in magazines in 1944 and 1945, it was published in its entirety only posthumously in 1977 under the title of *American Hunger*. Thus, for three decades, readers of *Black Boy* were deprived of Wright's description of his Chicago years, which included his account of personal battles and ideological differences with the Communist Party over the uses of art and how best to address the "Negro Question" (346).
2. See Webb 197–98. Reynolds's father, Paul Reynolds Sr., had represented Paul Laurence Dunbar, as well as Jack London, Winston Churchill, and Stephen Crane.
3. First appearing in 1937 in the Works Progress Administration anthology *American Stuff*, the essay was subsequently included in the expanded 1940 edition of Wright's first collection of short stories, *Uncle Tom's Children*, and later incorporated into *Black Boy*.
4. Wright's bleak depiction of African American life is in service to his primary objective of using his autobiography as a vehicle for critiquing racial injustice, a theme further explored in chapter 2.
5. Some critics read the Dalton name as an allusion to the medical term *Daltonism*, or color blindness. All three Daltons feel that they have enlightened views about race relations. Mary's mother is physically blind and wants Bigger to get an education. Mary's father fails to see that his philanthropy—such as his donations to colored schools—alone won't undo the effects of racism on the psyche. Mary and her communist boyfriend, Jan, want to organize African Americans to join in the class struggle, but are blind to their demeaning expectations that members of the race perform some sort of minstrelsy. Specifically, Daltonism refers to red-green color blindness.
6. In part because exacerbated by the Communist Party's disregard for racial issues and its unequivocal support of the war effort even as the military maintained segregation among its troops, Wright officially quit the party in 1946.
7. See chapter 4, this volume, on Richard Rodriguez's *Days of Obligation* for a fuller discussion of Philippe LeJeune's conception of the autobiographical pact.

8. Timothy Dow Adams writes, "The lying that [readers] sense centers on these three concerns: 'black boy' is never wrong, falsely naive, and melodramatic" (75).
9. Cited in Adams (73–74). Adams refers to pages 244–45 in Olney, *Autobiography*.
10. Though qualified with the disclaimer that only some of us feel this way, Wright's mention of separatist sentiments and the suggestion that Japanese rule might be better for the "darker races" (*12 Million* 143) was classified as possible "sedition" in the communiqué from FBI Director Hoover to the New York Field Division dated December 1, 1942. Hysteria over the content of *12 Million Black Voices* and suspicion of its author had begun with a single letter written by a white man in Washington to Secretary of War Henry Stimson. This letter had been relayed to the Military Intelligence Service, and then sent on to the FBI (see Gayle 138–39, 146–47; Rowley 275–76). The full quote is "There are others of us who feel the need of the protection of a strong nation so keenly that we admire the harsh and imperialistic policies of Japan and ardently hope that the Japanese will assume the leadership of the 'darker races.'" This sentiment was frequently expressed by African Americans at the time, as World War II was being waged. Reference to sentiments of black sympathy with the Japanese on the basis of color also appears in Ellison's *Invisible Man* and Ernest Gaines's *The Autobiography of Miss Jane Pittman*, when blacks in Louisiana are told that in firefights the Japanese direct their fire only at white soldiers and deliberately away from black troops.
11. Margaret Walker had met Wright during his Chicago years, and knew him when he was in his twenties. Her romantic interest in Wright was unreciprocated. Years later, when in her seventies, she became one of Wright's biographers.
12. I refer to the half of the autobiography rejected by the Book-of-the-Month Club, and which did not appear in book form until published under the title of *American Hunger* in 1977. In part, Wright seems to have been more willing to divulge formative sexual experiences of his adult years than those of his teens. One of the few Book-of-the-Month Club expurgations of part 1 of the autobiography, however, is sexual. Ironically, it is only because the text of part 2 was rejected whole cloth that it survived Book-of-the-Month Club bowdlerization unscathed. As to why the Book-of-the-Month Club would be squeamish about a passage that begins "Richard, how long is your thing?" (*Black Boy* 188, 411), but not about passages depicting venereal disease and naked prostitutes, one explanation (among others) that comes readily to mind is the fickle and arbitrary nature of censorship.
13. A lifestyle at the narrative core of his first novel, published posthumously, *Lawd Today*.
14. Segregation restricted social mobility to a single racial community. In his childhood, Wright often went long periods without seeing a single white face. It is no wonder, then, that he encountered more conflict and witnessed more deviance in his own race than in other races. The distorting effects of economic apartheid were also a factor: "Each of us depended upon the whites for the bread we ate, and we

actually trusted the whites more than we did each other. Yet there existed in us a longing to trust men of our own color" (*Black Boy* 239). Internecine distrust is played out in a scene where the protagonist—despite his awareness of what is happening—and another black boy are maneuvered into fighting each other for the amusement of their white coworkers. The parallel scene in *Invisible Man* is the surrealistic and uproariously ludic battle royal scene of the first chapter. If Wright was going to borrow from Ellison, Ellison would in turn borrow from Wright.
15. After Wright's death, Cayton began work on a biography of Wright. Wright's widow, Ellen Wright, was uncooperative, however. Cayton's biography remained incomplete at the time of his death in Paris in 1970.

Chapter 2

1. The suggested homology morphs into a more explicit association of *Native Son* with *Uncle Tom's Cabin* as Baldwin's rebellion against "protest fiction," in his *Notes of a Native Son* collection, progresses—from the first words of "Everybody's Protest Novel" to baldly stating that "Bigger is Uncle Tom's descendant" (22) and on to a continuation of the critique on page 34 following the next essay, "Many Thousand's Gone."

    Ralph Ellison also characterized Wright as letting his social agenda compromise aesthetic considerations. As Tamara Denissova writes, "[I]n the late 1940s James Baldwin and Ralph Ellison accused Wright in their 'new wave' manifestoes of being a socially engaged writer and of creating, as a result, a simplified and one-dimensional image of the Negro" (239). For a defense of socially engaged literature, including the sentimental novel, see Jane Tompkins's *Sensational Designs*. Tompkins argues that "the work of sentimental writers is complex and significant in ways *other than* those that characterize the established masterpieces," and describes the sentimental novel as "a political enterprise, halfway between sermon and social theory, that both codifies and attempts to mold the values of its time" (126, emphasis in the original).
2. It could be argued that *Black Boy*'s hybrid existentialist and sociological nature both recapitulates old debates in the African American literary tradition and is emblematic of ongoing discussions about ethnic literature: the sense that the categorization and perception of ethnic literature as sociological ghettoize the genre and belie the intense engagement of ethnic authors with aesthetic and narrative concerns.
3. Wright would meet Jean-Paul Sartre in 1946, after the publication of *Black Boy* (Webb 279).
4. "The Ethics of Living Jim Crow" appeared in a WPA anthology in 1937, but Wright later incorporated the essay into both *Uncle Tom's Children* and, in modified form, *Black Boy* (392). See, for example, the scene depicted on pages 187–93 in *Black Boy*.

Of "The Man Who Lived Underground," Carla Cappetti writes that "[i]t is a modern version of the fugitive slave narrative, a literary form whose most famous representative, Frederick Douglass, is honored through the initials of Fred Daniels, the novella's African American protagonist," and also that "[t]he initials of the protagonist's name are those of Fyodor Dostoyevsky, whose novella *Notes from the Underground* (1864) inspired Wright" (41n22).
5. Ellison also wrote extensively about *Black Boy* in two other articles: the 1971 lecture "Remembering Richard Wright" and what had originally been two articles later merged into one two-part essay titled "The World and the Jug" in *The Collected Essays of Ralph Ellison*. All three essays are included in *The Collected Essays*, and it is to that volume's page numbers that all citations refer.
6. This quote is from the published 1945 ending of *Black Boy*, also included in a special notes section of the 1989 HarperPerennial restored text edition. The 1945 edition passages are of particular interest here because they include additional references by Wright to the influence of print culture in shaping his consciousness.
7. The doubleconsciousness described by Du Bois in 1903 is that of a different era, and accordingly places greater emphasis on the internal and external conflict that double consciousness entails: "One ever feels his twoness,—an American, a Negro; two souls, two thoughts, two unreconciled strivings; two warring ideals in one dark body, whose dogged strength alone keeps it from being torn asunder" (5).
8. The word *imagined* here is intended to invoke Benedict Anderson's theorization of the mechanisms by which "imagined communities" are formed.

Chapter 3

1. For an insightful, extended critique of Rodriguez's assimilationist arguments, see chapter 3 of Paula Moya's *Learning from Experience*.
2. Judith Butler is often read as arguing that gender identity is completely constructed and therefore can be shed each day at will, but her account stresses the continuity of identity—identity as a social performance that is reiterated: "[T]he action of gender requires a performance that is *repeated*" (*Gender Trouble* 191).
3. This last point raises the question of whether Rodriguez would consider race as a factor, or whether he sees class as the only legitimate criteria to consider in regard to opportunity programs. Given his failure to explicitly endorse a modified program of some sort, some readers might even wonder whether Rodriguez would be opposed to any type of opportunity program.
4. Rodriguez writes in *Days of Obligation* that replacing the Latin Mass with English or other languages has led to "ethnic separation" (195).
5. Although principally linguistic, neither culture nor the transmission of culture are exclusively so. The persistence of racial and gender narratives and the readiness with which new narratives of race emerge when long-separated groups encounter each other are both demonstrative—as such narratives anchor themselves primarily in visually observable differences—of the power of visual culture, an insightful analysis of which can be found in Shirley Samuels's *Facing America*.

Chapter 4

1. None of Rodriguez's four autobiographical books take the characteristic form or narrative arc of a traditional autobiography. Rather, as Jerzy Durczak writes of *Hunger of Memory*, Rodriguez's books are "basically a collection of autobiographical essays wherein . . . the complex nature of the author's self revealed in his life-story is only one of several different subjects" (109).
2. Rodriguez's arguments about assimilation shift somewhat in *Days of Obligation*, in which he abandons normative aspects of his arguments for an emphasis on the inevitability of assimilation. Paula Moya notes this shift when comparing *Hunger of Memory* with *Days of Obligation*: "Rodriguez, for his part, starts out by arguing that assimilation is a necessary good and ends up by viewing it as inevitable" (111).

    In *Migrant Imaginaries*, Alicia Schmidt Camacho also notes shifts in Rodriguez's posture between books. During the 1980s, she argues, "Rodriguez embraced the fiction of 'unmarked' citizenship, in willful denial of the ways that the state's ideal of assimilation produced racial, gender, and sexual difference in order to maintain class hierarchies." She then observes that "in *Days of Obligation*, Rodriguez remade himself as the interlocutor for the new migrants; their presence, he believed, would remake the nation and expose the insufficiency of the category of 'the minority'" (196–97). Although critical of some of Rodriguez's stances, Camacho insists that his critics also heed the extent to which he "contended with liberal racism during the Reagan and then the Bush era of neoliberal reform and conservative retrenchment" (197). Also central to Camacho's arguments is her declaration that "the author's career as a public intellectual has exposed the failures of liberalism to deliver on its promises of equality amid the global restructuring of racialized classes in the past quarter century" (197).
3. Philosophers of mind such as Daniel Dennett and Douglas Hofstadter offer similar narrative views about the nature of consciousness. Dennett describes the "Self as the Center of Narrative Gravity" (430) in *Consciousness Explained*, whereas Hofstadter invokes as an analogy of human consciousness the perspectival illusion that an ant colony has holistic intelligence ("Prelude" 149–91). Both philosophers make arguments for Strong AI (the belief that artificial intelligence could be capable of the same kind of consciousness as humans possess, an idea that John Searle attempts to refute with his Chinese Room thought experiment). Hofstadter also argues that thinking itself is done by "analogical reasoning"—giving center stage to what could be described as the narrative role of analogy in the "process of cognition" ("Analogy" 136)—and that "all communication, all language, is metaphorical" (141).
4. This intelligibility is a form of Rodriguez's notion of having a public voice. On the reader as outside observer, see Timothy Dow Adam's analysis of Stephen Spender and Shirley Newman (11).
5. Conventions of reading create a clearer distinction between genres, such as fiction and autobiography, than formalist attempts (such as that of stylistics) to distinguish between literary and nonliterary language, rhetorical effects, and the like. The observation is not meant to undervalue the importance of formalist,

stylistic, and rhetorical modes of literary analysis themselves, but to emphasize the signal importance of context—not only to understanding texts but to the very possibility of semantics at all, as even an ostensibly private language, as Wittgenstein noted, relies on words that get their meaning socially.

A text found by the proverbial Martian archaeologist would be virtually meaningless (though it would still serve anthropologically as an artifact of material culture) until the archaeologist learned the language the text was written in. Even then, the meaningfulness of the scribbles of ink on square sheets of paper would not be for the archaeologist what they were for readers in the society that produced that language. With the larger context of that social reality gone the archaeologist's understanding of the language, and therefore of the text, would always be woefully incomplete, despite having full access to the text-object fetishized by textual materialism.

6. Rodriguez has said of reading, in the context of discussing his autobiographical work, "Emerson said that reading is reciprocal. It takes a good reader to make a good book. It seems to me that you have to ask a question about yourself as much as you have to ask a question about the text" ("Violating" 446).

7. One lesson of the 2006 James Frey–Oprah Winfrey controversy is that readers hold memoirs to stronger standards of truth than publishers do. Commercial pressures can incline publishers to a lax sense of exactly where the line between fictionalizing and pure fiction lies. For readers, however, the line between poetic license and false memoir is quite distinct. Readers also hold autobiography to stricter standards of historical truth than they do books presented as memoir.

8. In his *Of Space and Mind*, Patrick Hamilton argues for a similar ethical engagement with Chicana/o texts, because each ethnic "text 'maps' and communicates particular ethical positioning in regard to cultural difference" (2).

9. Calling himself Samoan distances Acosta from being cast as an authentic "son of Moctezuma" while firmly connecting the autobiographical self to its referent—because the Samoan label is a running joke between the real-life Acosta and his friends. This biographical detail is also referred to by his friend Hunter S. Thompson, who includes Acosta in the autobiographical *Fear and Loathing in Las Vegas* as a semifictional character whom he frequently introduces as "my Samoan friend." As a result, the intertextual resonance between the two texts, which are mostly read by very separate reader bases, stems not only from literary influence but also from shared reference to extratextual reality. Each book thus spirals down through smaller and smaller circles of shared social context: racialized American society, the Western states, and real-life companionship between the two autobiographical referents.

10. Rodriguez's arguments for national assimilation reflect the partial autobiographical conflation of print culture and public identity, and call to mind Benedict Anderson's influential observations about the relation between print capitalism and nationalism in *Imagined Communities* as well as Jonathan Culler's analysis

of "what we are claiming when we cite his [Anderson's] authority to discuss the role of fiction in the construction of nations" ("Anderson and the Novel" 32).

11. Although not computer-generated, physicist Alan Sokal's parody article "Transgressing the Boundaries" is largely a pastiche of fashionable ideas and quotes from Derrida, Lacan, and other postmodern thinkers. It interestingly garnered a favorable reception from many of the journal's editors and readers by catering to their ideological preconceptions. In submitting the article, Sokal intended to satirize obscurantism in academic publications and to demonstrate that, in denying external reality, relativistic stances risk dispensing with the need for evidence and logic when asserting political, scientific, and philosophical claims.

To see an actual computer-generated text produced by a postmodern generator, see http://www.elsewhere.org/pomo.

12. See Avtar Brah's "Diaspora, Border and Transnational Identities" in *Cartographies of Diaspora* for a deft analysis of the "new diasporas." "Inscribed within the idea of diaspora is the notion of 'border,'" Brah explains, touching on the disadvantages of "conceptualizing social relations primarily in terms of dichotomous oppositions," and describing "the politics of location *as a position of multi-axial locationality*" by which "the same geographical space comes to articulate different histories and meanings" for subjects differently positioned in social and discursive space (178–210, emphasis in the original). Brah's account problematizes Rodriguez's emphasis on the commonalities of class across racial, ethnic, linguistic, and gender positionalities in social discourse. Rodriguez's account does, however, pay attention to the temporal dimensions of diaspora neglected in accounts that look exclusively at its spatial dimensions: "I realize my book will never be equal to the play of the young" (*Brown* xiv).

Chapter 5

1. Of Rodriguez's four books, criticism of his first has been the sharpest. Earlier versions of many of the essays in *Hunger of Memory* had been in print from as early as 1973. Thus, by the time the autobiography was published in the early 1980s, Rodriguez had already gained notoriety in some academic circles for his views on the political issues of bilingual education and affirmative action. This, coupled with the volatile political context in which Rodriguez situated his narrative of the self, framed the reception and early criticism of *Hunger of Memory* and partly accounts for the avalanche of negative criticism. Rodriguez's second book, *Days of Obligation* followed ten years later. Another decade passed before the publication of *Brown*, and eleven more years before *Darling*. For a sustained critique of Rodriguez's assimilationist stance, see chapter 3 of Paula Moya (100–135). See also Ramón Saldívar, Raymund Paredes, and Norma Alarcón.

2. Aureliano Maria DeSoto perceptively notes that in the identity-politics debates

over assimilation the most contested sites are just as likely, if not more so, to occur within the minority community as between minority communities and the public at large: "The paradox of Rodriguez's mainstream prominence and the almost universal loathing of his work among Chicana/o intellectuals and cultural producers is indicative of the battle over who defines Chicana/o identity, and how such an identity is understood both within Chicano communities and by the public at large" (52–53).

It is the context of these identity-politics debates that accounts for Rodriguez's status as, in the words of Manuel Gonzalez, a "celebrated though controversial Mexican American writer" (27).

3. This formulation is itself fraught, in that it suggests an either-or dichotomy between mainstream and minority identities. The terrible beauty of identities and of communities is that they are, to misappropriate the terminology of creationist pseudoscience, irreducibly complex. Despite perennial attempts to boil identities down to reductive precipitates of their racial, gendered, ethnic, regional, socioeconomic, and ideological elements, our analysis is more penetrating when the interaction of the various aspects of a person's identity, as well as the heterogeneous composition of communities and the complex interrelationship between individuals and communities, is kept in mind. Nancy Miller speaks to this point in squarely framing autobiography as the product of a complex, relational self. "In autobiography the relational is not optional," she writes. "Autobiography's story is about the web of entanglement in which we find ourselves" (544). Miller's emphasis on entanglement and the relational is particularly instructive for any discussion of Rodriguez's autobiographical writings and of his description of the ways in which we are often unable to reconcile various aspects of our identities and the communities to which we belong. The self embodies contradiction: "Brown forms at the border of contradiction (the ability of language to express two or several things at once, the ability of bodies to experience two or several things at once)" (*Brown* xi).

4. Jeehyun Lim also notes that "'neoconservative' seems to be the word most often used to describe Rodriguez today (Camacho 197; Parikh 64–95)." She too—like this analysis—raises questions about the epistemic and hermeneutic usefulness of the label: "What explanatory value this word has for interpreting Rodriguez's writing, however, is open to question" (518). Moving beyond the outdated not-one-of-us interpretive lens, Lim offers a complex, dichotomy-dissolving reading of Rodriguez, insightfully noting how the writer slips the yoke of his public-private binaries by appealing to a third language: "His third language tropologically relates to postcolonial scholarship on 'Third Space,' and provides an alternative to the binary view of the public and private so prominent in the debates on bilingualism in the 1990s. Characterizing the language of the lovers in D. H. Lawrence's *Lady Chatterley's Lover* and liturgical Latin as third languages, Rodriguez removes the binary of the private and public languages from cultural and political contexts, and instead writes it into a universal narrative of American individualism" (520).

The two scholarly texts cited by Lim are Alicia Schmidt Camacho's *Migrant Imaginaries* and Crystal Parikh's *An Ethics of Betrayal*. Parikh argues that "the assimilatory betrayals of the minority neoconservative—the model minority and the *pocho* [read, Rodriguez]—must be read as betrayals compelled by the structural configurations of race, ethnicity, class, and diaspora in late-twentieth-century America" (67). Camacho's sense of various political labels and how these might or might not apply to Rodriguez is more nuanced. "Despite Rodriguez's long flirtation with the neoconservative demand for a 'color-blind' society, his reflections on the migrant presence undo his personal accommodations to the liberal ideal. Rodriguez's aspirations to full, unmarked citizenship notwithstanding, his interest in the undocumented reveals the continued salience of Latina/o critiques of liberalism, when delivered from another quarter, from within the migrant imaginary" (197–98).

5. The fundamental question about Rodriguez's views on affirmative action is whether Rodriguez is dubious about opportunity programs for the disadvantaged in general, or whether he would favor such a program if class were also considered. Rodriguez frames his critique of affirmative action as skepticism, primarily about the ways in which the policy has been historically implemented, specifically "for not defining carefully who, in their eyes, was disadvantaged or not" (interview with Torres 178). But though stressing the difficulties in deciding who should benefit from such programs and for how long—when does one "*stop being disadvantaged*"—Rodriguez clearly believes that disadvantage is discernible (*Hunger* 150, emphasis in the original). Within *Hunger of Memory*, one finds the basis for a radically class-based, one might even say Marxist, approach to disadvantage and inequality. "It became easy to underestimate, even to ignore altogether, the importance of *class*. Easy to forget that those whose lives are shaped by poverty and poor education (cultural minorities) are least able to defend themselves against social oppression, whatever its form" (*Hunger* 149–50, emphasis in the original). This passage makes clear that Rodriguez emphasizes social class in considering socioeconomic status and does not consider economic class in strictly financial terms.

Rodriguez's arguments against bilingual education are tied to his arguments about the importance of recognition through a shared public language and culture by others as a person. See, for example, chapters 1 and 4—"Aria" and "Complexion"—of *Hunger of Memory*.

6. Though his lament of the replacement of the Latin Mass with the vernacular following Vatican II might suggest a certain nostalgia for tradition (*Hunger* 101), Rodriguez's religious liberalism—"I was a liberal Catholic" (105)—is abundantly evident. Rodriguez belongs to a progressive parish, the Most Holy Redeemer in San Francisco, "where my partner and I are acknowledged by the other people in the parish as a couple" (interview with Carstensen). What's more, the supposedly conservative or neoconservative Rodriguez offered vigorous, activist-style criticism of the role of conservative churches in the passage of California's Proposition 8

ban on gay marriage, which he described as "a deliberate civic intrusion by the churches" (interview with Carstensen). Religion is also the topic of Rodriguez's current cultural and philosophical musings as evident in his most recent book, *Darling*, which reflects on the big three monotheistic "desert religions" of Christianity, Judaism, and Islam.

In his penetrating analysis, "The Art of Being Richard Rodriguez," J. A. Marzán argues that "to advance his career he [Rodriguez] used conservatives, with whose sexual views he disagreed" (58).

7. The more inclusive identity term Latino is reflected in the title of *The Norton Anthology of Latino Literature* (Stavans et al. 2011).

8. See, for example, Henry Staten, who writes, "I believe, however, that Rodriguez's critics have not sufficiently noted the irony in his view of himself.... This irony belies the absoluteness of the cultural either-or (either Chicano or American) that he proclaims; his cultural situation lies, rather, at the complex intersection of a both-and and a neither-nor. He does not map this intersection accurately, but neither do those who would define the authenticity of his selfhood strictly in relation to an 'organic human collective' called 'la raza' (Saldívar 169)" (104).

9. Antonio Marquez gently reminds us that "to read *Hunger of Memory* is not to read sociology or history, but rather a literary construction of a person's memories." Rodriguez's writing, Marquez stresses, is "highly stylized" (133).

10. Herrnstein and Murray argue that class inequality between the races may in part be due to heritable differences in intellect. For a devastating critique of *The Bell Curve*, see the 1996 revised and expanded edition of Stephen Jay Gould's *The Mismeasure of Man*. For a much earlier critique of popular racial myths about intelligence and heritability, see Paul Ehrlich and Shirley Feldman.

11. Su also argues that the invocation of racial memory, particularly in fictional works, is useful for "positing alternative narratives of the past" and "to encourage imaginative explorations of existing portrayals of minority populations from alternative points of view" (380–81).

12. See *Beyond Ethnicity*, in which Sollors pragmatically notes the hermeneutic consequences of the fact that ethnic literature is "often read against an elusive concept of authenticity" (11). See also *The Invention of Ethnicity*.

See also Siemerling and Schwenk. Particularly salient to the current discussion are Katrin Schwenk's introduction (1–9); Monika Kaup's "Crossing Borders" (100–111); and Ernst Rudin's "New Mestizos" (112–29).

See, for example, Walter Benn Michaels's "Race into Culture." Michaels also takes up a critique of nonbiological essentialism in *The Shape of the Signifier*: "The race that antiessentialists believe in is a historical entity, not a biological one. In racial antiessentialism, the effort to imagine an identity that will connect people through history is replaced by the effort to imagine a history that will give people an identity" (137). Additionally, Michaels interrogates the conflation of history and personal memory implicit in the notion of racial memory: "[T]he obvious objection to thinking of history as a kind of memory is that things we are said to remember are things that we did or experienced, whereas things that are said to belong to our history tend to be things that were neither done nor experienced by us" (135).

13. In their introduction to the seminal anthology *Criticism in the Borderlands*, Héctor Calderón and José David Saldívar note the importance of seeing Latino/Chicano literature as part of, rather than separate from, American literature, citing "the need for a new history of American literature, one that would include the contributions of women and cultural groups ignored by the academy" (1). This is not to ignore differences, but rather to be more inclusive of diverse voices and experiences. Lyn Di Iorio Sandín captures this spirit in describing her "ultimate aim" in *Killing Spanish* as an attempt "to garner a wider audience for a compelling body of literary works" (15).

14. Sonia Saldívar-Hull incisively critiques the extent to which similar assumptions excluded the experiences of minority women by relying on "a type of essentialism that assumes the universality of Women's experience" (205).

15. Along with his arguments about "the epistemic status of cultural identity," Mohanty's postpositivist realist approach in *Literary Theory and the Claims of History* also gives prominence to the vital role of interpretation in identity politics and identity formation (203–4).

16. On mestizaje—the mixing of races and cultures—see Gloria Anzaldúa, *Borderlands/La Frontera*.

17. For a thoroughgoing spatial theorization of Latino (in this case, Chicana) literature and identity, see Mary Pat Brady, *Extinct Lands, Temporal Geographies*.

18. The *Oxford English Dictionary* defines *brown study* as "a state of mental abstraction or musing: 'gloomy meditations.'"

19. It is the visibility of ethnicity that Werner Sollors seems to be stressing in using the phrase "and being perceived by others" in the definition of ethnicity offered in *The Invention of Ethnicity*: "By calling ethnicity—that is, belonging and being perceived by others as belonging to an ethnic group—an 'invention,' one signals an interpretation in a modern and postmodern context. There is a certain, previously unrecognized, semantic legitimacy in insisting on this context" (xiii). I underscore the importance of Sollors's emphasis on interpretation and context. Calling ethnicity an invention highlights the cultural aspects of ethnicity. Finally, the use of the word *belonging* could be taken to indicate the role of self-identification in ethnic identities.

20. Defining culture is a notoriously fraught enterprise. For the purposes of this discussion, culture has three key traits: it is not static; it is humanly created; and no individual's biological makeup and cultural inheritance are directly linked.

21. De Castro also notes that "[w]hile his celebration of intercultural connections and of hybridity echoes that of Chicano theorists of the border—and is a sign that Rodriguez participates in contemporary critical paradigms—his analysis reaches

conclusions that contradict those of other Chicano critics" (118). Because Rodriguez confounds easy political categorization—"he hold[s] positions associated with both the political right and left"—"his writings offer a possible starting point for a re-evaluation of Chicano identity and discourse" (118-19).

22. In her review of *Brown*, Margo Jefferson cites at least one reader (a writer) whose opinion of the trajectory of Rodriguez's writing cuts in a direction counter to that of academic responses to his books: as someone admiring of *Hunger of Memory*, but critical of *Brown* as a "regression . . . to identity politics" (27).

23. In addition to noting Rodriguez's vexed relationship with the Chicana/o movement, Limón also notes the widespread rejection of Rodriguez in academic circles: "[W]e are confronted with a perplexing issue, namely that the only public intellectual [Rodriguez] from Mexican America has been rejected by most, if not all, of a leading [institutional] intelligentsia that would also claim some substantial intellectual and political representation of Mexicans in the United States" (393).

24. Invoking queer theory, Randy Rodríguez cites an added element of heteronormativity in the rejection of Richard Rodriguez's writing by the Chicano intelligentsia: "Mexican American and Chicano homosexuals, though, were in many ways the greatest threat to Chicano/a nationalism because of the symbolic potential of cultural emasculation Chicano men feared. To allow Rodriguez's soft assimilationist narrative to represent 'the' Mexican experience in the United States would symbolize the potential loss of Chicano masculine vigor and nerve. He served as an-'other' sign designating what Chicana/o literature and culture could not tolerate and therefore had to exclude and repress" (411).

See Yaakov Perry for a more recent queer reading of Rodriguez—one that focuses on Rodriguez's key trope of desire: "a reading of desire's exposition and the figuration of sexual (dis)orientation in the text" (156).

25. See, for example, Gustavo Pérez Firmat: "Rodriguez demurs, asserting that his 'most real life' lies in his controversial views on such issues as bilingualism and affirmative action" (*Tongue Ties* 147).

26. In chapter 3, "The Prince and I," Rodriguez complicates notions of "authenticity . . . the Puritan dilemma" (*Brown* 52) through the story of Timm Williams, a "full-blooded" Yurok who transformed himself into the Stanford University mascot, Prince Lightfoot. The Yurok headdress that Williams donned on game days was not that of his native tribe, but a feathered headdress apparently borrowed from the "Plains Indian[s]" (57). His "authentic" ethnic costume was largely imagined as authentic; much of it—he made the headdress himself—was a "theatrical invention of himself" (57). His ostensibly authentic portrayal was impure, though seen by those hungry for authenticity as authentic.

27. For another trenchant deconstruction of racial and ethnic authenticity, see Rey Chow's "Where Have All the Natives Gone?" (*Writing Diaspora* 27-54).

28. Fachinger cites from Jennifer Browdy de Hernandez's "The Plural Self" (57).

Note that other critics have observed just the opposite: that a double-voice of some sort is clearly present in Rodriguez's work. Gustavo Pérez Firmat—building on the work of preeminent scholar of autobiography studies, Paul John Eakin—writes that "Eakin has called attention to the presence of two voices in this book [*Hunger of Memory*], one narrative and the other expository.... What I would add to Eakin's insight is that the two voices are not just distinct but, to some extent, dissonant" ("Art of Abstraction" 259). See also Eakin's illuminating book, *Touching the World*, especially pages 117–37.

29. Browdy de Hernandez's work on ethnic autobiography is insightful and inspirational, making all the more poignant the point that even when scrupulously avoided—see, for example, Browdy de Hernandez's "The Plural Self"—essentialist notions can work themselves back into the academic discourse about ethnicity in unexpected ways (58n4).

Epilogue

1. Nor could *Native Son* have been a book about the psychological effects of racism had the main characters all been white. The social context in which the book was written, and that Wright wanted to critique, determined that the race of the protagonist would be the same as that of the author. Wright's racial experiences led him to want to write such a book, and the extratextual experiences of his readers lead them to imagine Bigger's blackness along the same lines that they imagine the author's. As with ethnic nonfiction, the race and ethnicity of the author are informing the ways in which the text is meaningful to readers.

2. See, for example, the dichotomy that Walter Benn Michaels sets up between reader subject position and authorial intent: "[I]f you think the intention of the author is what counts, then you don't think the subject position of the reader matters, but if you don't think the intention of the author is what counts, then the subject position of the reader will be the only thing that matters" (11).

    I reject, as a logical fallacy, the either-or framing of Michaels's claim. To the extent that the author's intentions play a role, they still do not fix the meaning of the text in a deterministic way. To be meaningful, those intentions have to first be understood. And to be understood, as with most utterances, texts have to be situated in context. It is context that makes language meaningful, and consequently that makes texts meaningful. Nor can the role of the reader be ignored, because readers are situated in the same context in which texts are made meaningful. As members of social reality readers not only constitute part of the text's meaning, they constitute part of the context in which the text can be meaningful at all.

Works Cited

Acosta, Oscar "Zeta." *The Autobiography of a Brown Buffalo*. New York: Vintage, 1989. [San Francisco: Straight Arrow Books, 1972]. Print.
Adams, Timothy Dow. *Telling Lies in Modern American Autobiography*. Chapel Hill: U of North Carolina P, 1990. Print.
Alarcón, Norma. "Tropology of Hunger: The 'Miseducation' of Richard Rodriguez." Palumbo-Liu. 140–52. Print.
Alcoff, Linda Martin. *Visible Identities: Race, Gender, and the Self*. New York: Oxford UP, 2005. Print.
Aldama, Frederick Luis, ed. *Analyzing World Fiction: New Horizons in Narrative Theory*. Austin: U of Texas P, 2011. Print.
———. *Brown on Brown: Chicano/a Representations of Gender, Sexuality, and Ethnicity*. Austin: U of Texas P, 2005. Print.
———. *Postethnic Narrative Criticism: Magicorealism in Oscar "Zeta" Acosta, Ana Castillo, Julie Dash, Hanif Kureishi, and Salman Rushdie*. Austin: U of Texas P, 2003. Print.
———. *A User's Guide to Postcolonial and Latino Literature*. Austin: U of Texas P, 2009. Print.
Anderson, Benedict Richard O'Gorman. *Imagined Communities*. London: Verso, 1991. Print.
Andrews, William L. Introduction. *African American Autobiography: A Collection of Critical Essays*. Ed. Andrews. Englewood Cliffs: Prentice-Hall, 1993. 1–7. Print.
Anzaldúa, Gloria. *Borderlands/La Frontera: The New Mestiza*. 2nd ed. San Francisco, CA: Aunt Lute Books, 1999. Print.

Appiah, Kwame Anthony. *The Ethics of Identity*. Princeton, NJ: Princeton UP, 2005. Print.
Ashley, Kathleen, Leigh Gilmore, and Gerald Peters, eds. *Autobiography and Postmodernism*. Amherst: U of Massachusetts P, 1994. Print.
Baldwin, James. *Nobody Knows My Name*. 1954. New York: Vintage, 1961. Print.
———. *Notes of a Native Son*. 1955. Boston, MA: Beacon, 1984. Print.
Barthes, Roland. "The Death of the Author." *Image, Music, Text*. Trans. Stephen Heath. New York: Hill and Wang, 1977. 142–48. Print.
Beltrán, Cristina. "Racial Shame and the Pleasure of Transformation: Richard Rodriguez's Queer Aesthetics of Assimilation." *Aztlán: A Journal of Chicano Studies* 37.1 (Spring 2012): 37–64. Print.
Benstock, Shari. Introduction. *The Private Self: Theory and Practice of Women's Autobiographical Writings*. Ed. Benstock. Chapel Hill: U of North Carolina P, 1988. 1–6. Print.
Bogel, Fredric V. *The Difference Satire Makes: Rhetoric and Reading from Jonson to Byron*. Ithaca: Cornell UP, 2001. Print.
Boyd, Brian. *On the Origin of Stories: Evolution, Cognition, and Fiction*. Cambridge, MA: Belknap Press of Harvard UP, 2009. Print.
Brady, Mary Pat. *Extinct Lands, Temporal Geographies: Chicana Literature and the Urgency of Space*. Durham: Duke UP, 2002. Print.
Brah, Avtar. *Cartographies of Diaspora: Contesting Identities*. New York: Routledge, 1996. Print.
Browdy de Hernandez, Jennifer. "The Plural Self: The Politicization of Memory and Form in Three American Ethnic Autobiographies." *Memory and Cultural Politics: New Approaches to American Ethnic Literatures*. Ed. Amritjit Singh, Joseph T. Skerrett Jr., and Robert E. Hogan. Boston, MA: Northeastern UP, 1996. 41–59. Print.
———. "Postcolonial Blues: Ambivalence and Alienation in the Autobiographies of Richard Rodriguez and V.S. Naipaul." *a/b: Auto/Biography Studies* 12.2 (1997): 151–65. Print.
"Brown Study." *Oxford English Dictionary*. OED.com, 2009. Web. 20 Aug. 2012.
Butler, Judith. *Gender Trouble: Feminism and the Subversion of Identity*. 1990. New York: Routledge, 2006. Print.
Butler, Robert. *Native Son: Black Hero*. New York: Twayne, 1991. Print.
———. "Seeking Salvation in a Naturalistic Universe: Richard Wright's Use of His Southern Religious Background in *Black Boy (American Hunger)*." *Southern Quarterly* 46.2 (Winter 2009): 46–60. Print.
Calderón, Héctor, and José David Saldívar. *Criticism in the Borderlands: Studies in Chicano Literature, Culture, and Ideology*. Durham, NC: Duke UP, 1991. Print.
Camacho, Alicia Schmidt. *Migrant Imaginaries: Latino Cultural Politics in the U.S.-Mexico Borderlands*. New York: New York UP, 2008. Print.

Cappetti, Carla. "Black Orpheus: Richard Wright's 'The Man Who Lived Underground.'" *Melus* 26.4 (Winter 2001): 41–68. Print.

Castillo, Debra A., and María Socorro Tabuenca Córdoba. *Border Women: Writing from La Frontera*. Minneapolis: U of Minnesota P, 2002. Print.

Cayton, Horace. "Frightened Children of Frightened Parents." *Twice-a-Year* 12–13 (Spring-Summer/Fall-Winter 1945): 262–69. Rpt. in Reilly 184–88. Print.

Cheah, Pheng, and Jonathan D. Culler, eds. *Grounds of Comparison: Around the Work of Benedict Anderson*. New York: Routledge, 2003. Print.

Chow, Rey. *Writing Diaspora: Tactics of Intervention in Contemporary Cultural Studies*. Bloomington: Indiana UP, 1993. Print.

Cohn, David L. Untitled. *Atlantic Monthly* 165 (May 1940): 659–61. Rpt. in Reilly 91–93. Print.

Collingwood, R. G. "The Poetic Expression of Emotion." *Aesthetics: A Reader in Philosophy of The Arts*. Ed. David Goldblatt and Lee B. Brown. Upper Saddle River, NJ: Prentice-Hall, 1997. 314–19. Print.

Cooley, Thomas. *Educated Lives: The Rise of Modern Autobiography in America*. Columbus: Ohio State UP, 1976. Print.

Couser, G. Thomas. *Altered Egos: Authority in American Autobiography*. New York: Oxford UP, 1989. Print.

Culler, Jonathan. "Anderson and the Novel." Cheah and Culler 29–52. Print.

———. *Literary Theory: A Very Short Introduction*. New York: Oxford UP, 2000. Print.

———. *Structuralist Poetics: Structuralism, Linguistics, and the Study of Literature*. Ithaca, NY: Cornell UP, 1975. Print.

Cutler, John Alba. "Disappeared Men: Chicana/o Authenticity and the American War in Viet Nam." *American Literature* 81.3 (Sept. 2009): 583–611. Print.

Cutter, Martha J. *Lost and Found in Translation: Contemporary Ethnic American Writing and the Politics of Language Diversity*. Chapel Hill: U of North Carolina P, 2005. Print.

Davis, Ben, Jr. Untitled. *Sunday Worker* [New York] 14 Apr. 1940, sect. 2: 4, 6. Rpt. in Reilly 68–76. Print.

Davis, Charles T. "From Experience to Eloquence: Richard Wright's *Black Boy* as Art." Andrews 138–50. Print.

de Castro, Juan E. "Richard Rodriguez in 'Borderland': The Ambiguity of Hybridity." *Aztlán* 26 (2001): 101–26. Print.

de la Campa, Roman. "Latin, Latino, American: Split States and Global Imaginaries." *Comparative Literature* 53.4 (2001): 373–88. Print.

Denissova, Tamara. "Richard Wright: The Problem of Self-Identification." *Mississippi Quarterly* 50 (Spring 1997): 239–53. Print.

Dennett, Daniel Clement. *Consciousness Explained*. Boston, MA: Little Brown, 1991. Print.

DeSoto, Aureliano Maria. "On the Trail of the Chicana/o Subject: Literary Texts and

Contexts in the Formation of Chicana/o Studies." *Multiethnic Literature and Canon Debates*. Ed. Mary Jo Bona and Irma Maini. Albany: SUNY P, 2006. 41-60. Print.

Du Bois, W. E. B. "Richard Wright Looks Back." *New York Herald Tribune Weekly Book Review*. 4 Mar. 1945: 2. Rpt. in Reilly 132–33. Print.

———. *The Souls of Black Folk*. 1903. New York: Modern Library, 1996. Print.

Duffus, R. L. "Deep-South Memoir." *New York Times Book Review*. 4 Mar. 1945: 3. Rpt. in Reilly 133–35. Print.

Durczak, Jerzy. *Selves Between Cultures: Contemporary American Bicultural Autobiography*. 1999. San Francisco, CA: International Scholars Publications; Lublin, Poland: Rozprawy Wydzialu Humanitycznego, 1994. Print.

Eakin, Paul John. Foreword. Lejeune vii–xxviii. Print.

———. *How Our Lives Become Stories: Making Selves*. Ithaca, NY: Cornell UP, 1999. Print.

———. Introduction. *The Ethics of Life Writing*. Ed. Eakin. Ithaca, NY: Cornell UP, 2004. 1–16. Print.

———. *Living Autobiographically: How We Create Identity in Narrative*. Ithaca, NY: Cornell UP, 2008. Print.

———. *Touching the World: Reference in Autobiography*. Princeton, NJ: Princeton UP, 1992. Print.

Ehrlich, Paul R., and S. Shirley Feldman. *The Race Bomb: Skin Color, Prejudice, and Intelligence*. New York: Quadrangle/New York Times Books, 1977. Print.

Ellison, Ralph. *The Collected Essays of Ralph Ellison*. New York: Modern Library, 1995. Print.

———. Introduction. 1981. *Invisible Man* vii–xxiii. Print.

———. *Invisible Man*. 1952. New York: Vintage, 1995. Print.

Fabre, Michel. *The Unfinished Quest of Richard Wright*. Trans. Isabel Burn. 2nd ed. Urbana: Illinois UP, 1993. Print.

Fachinger, Petra. "Lost in Nostalgia: The Autobiographies of Eva Hoffman and Richard Rodriguez." *MELUS* 26.2 (Summer 2001): 111–27. Print.

Fine, Laura. "Claiming Persona and Rejecting Other-Imposed Identities: Self-Writing in the Autobiographies of Richard Rodriguez." *Biography* 19.2 (1996): 119–36. Print.

Foucault, Michel. "What Is an Author?" Trans. Josué V. Harari. *The Foucault Reader*. Ed. Paul Rabinow. New York: Pantheon, 1984: 101–20. Print.

Gaines, Ernest J. *The Autobiography of Miss Jane Pittman*. New York: Dial, 1971. Print.

Gayle, Addison. *Richard Wright: Ordeal of a Native Son*. Garden City, NY: Anchor Press/Doubleday, 1980. Print.

Gilmore, Leigh. "The Mark of Autobiography: Postmodernism, Autobiography, and Genre." Ashley, Gilmore, and Peters 3–18. Print.

Gonzales, Manuel G. *Mexicanos: A History of Mexicans in the United States*. 2nd ed. Bloomington: Indiana UP, 2009. Print.

González, Marcial. *Chicano Novels and the Politics of Form: Race, Class, and Reification.* Ann Arbor: U of Michigan P, 2009. Print.

Gould, Stephen Jay. *The Mismeasure of Man.* 1981. New York: Norton, 1996. Print.

Guajardo, Paul. *Chicano Controversy: Oscar Acosta and Richard Rodriguez.* New York: Peter Lang, 2002. Print.

Hakutani, Yoshinobu. *Richard Wright and Racial Discourse.* Columbia: U of Missouri P, 1996. Print.

Hames-García, Michael. "Dr. Gonzo's Carnival: The Testimonial Satires of Oscar Zeta Acosta." *American Literature* 72.3 (2000): 463–93. Print.

Hamilton, Patrick L. *Of Space and Mind: Cognitive Mappings of Contemporary Chicano/a Fiction.* Austin: U of Texas P, 2011. Print.

Herrnstein, Richard J., and Charles Murray. *The Bell Curve: Intelligence and Class Structure in American Life.* 1994. New York: Free Press, 1996. Print.

Higashida, Cheryl. "Aunt Sue's Children: Re-viewing the Gender(ed) Politics of Richard Wright's Radicalism." *American Literature* 75.2 (June 2003): 395–425. Print.

Hofstadter, Douglas R. "Analogy as the Core of Cognition." *Best American Science Writing 2000.* Ed. James Gleick. New York: HarperCollins, 2000: 116–43. Print.

———. "Prelude... Ant Fugue." *The Mind's I: Fantasies and Reflections on Self and Soul.* Ed. Douglas Hofstadter and Daniel Dennett. New York: Basic Books, 1981. 149–91. Print.

Jefferson, Margo. "The Color Brown." *New York Times Book Review* (16 Feb. 2003): 27. Print.

Kim, Daniel Y. *Writing Manhood in Black and Yellow: Ralph Ellison, Frank Chin, and the Literary Politics of Identity.* Stanford: Stanford UP, 2005. Print.

Kim, Sue J. "Anger, Temporality, and the Politics of Reading *The Woman Warrior.*" Aldama, *Analyzing World Fiction* 93–108. Print.

Laclau, Ernesto. "On Imagined Communities." Cheah and Culler 21–28. Print.

Lareau, Annette. *Unequal Childhoods: Class, Race, and Family Life.* Berkeley: U of California P, 2003. Print.

Latour, Bruno. *We Have Never Been Modern.* Trans. Catherine Porter. Cambridge: Harvard UP, 1993 [Paris: La Découverte, 1991]. Print.

Lawtoo, Nidesh. "Dissonant Voices in Richard Rodriguez's *Hunger of Memory* and Luce Irigaray's *This Sex Which Is Not One.*" *Texas Studies in Language and Literature* 48.3 (Fall 2006): 220–49. Print.

Lee, A. Robert. *Multicultural American Literature: Comparative Black, Native, Latino/a, and Asian American Fiction.* Jackson: UP of Mississippi, 2003. Print.

Lee, Sue-Im. "'It's Badly Done': Redefining Craft in *America Is in the Heart.*" Aldama, *Analyzing World Fiction* 199–225. Print.

Lejeune, Philippe. *On Autobiography.* Ed. Paul John Eakin. Trans. Katherine Leary. Theory and History of Literature 52. Minneapolis: U of Minnesota P, 1989. Print.

Lim, Jeehyun. "'I Was Never at War with my Tongue': The Third Language and the Performance of Bilingualism in Richard Rodriguez." *Biography* 33.3 (Summer 2010): 518–42. Print.

Limón, José E. "Editor's Note on Richard Rodriguez." *Texas Studies in Language and Literature* 40.4 (Winter 1998): 389–95. Print.

Loesberg, Jonathan. "Autobiography as Genre, Act of Consciousness, Text." *Prose Studies* 4 (1981): 169–85. Print.

Loya, Joe. *The Man Who Outgrew His Prison Cell: Confessions of a Bank Robber.* New York: Rayo, 2004. Print.

Luis-Brown, David. *Waves of Decolonization: Discourses of Race and Hemispheric Citizenship in Cuba, Mexico, and the United States.* Durham: Duke UP, 2008. Print.

Marquez, Antonio C. "Richard Rodriguez's *Hunger of Memory* and the Poetics of Experience." *Arizona Quarterly* 40.2 (1984): 130–41. Print.

Martin, Raymond, and John Barresi. *The Rise and Fall of Soul and Self: An Intellectual History of Personal Identity.* New York: Columbia UP, 2006. Print.

Martínez, Ernesto Javier. *On Making Sense: Queer Race Narratives of Intelligibility.* Stanford, CA: Stanford UP, 2013. Print.

Martínez, Rubén. "My Argument with Richard Rodriguez: Or, a Defense of the Mexican-American Chicanos Love to Hate." *LA Weekly* (2–8 Oct. 1992): 18–21. Print.

Martín-Rodríguez, Manuel. *Life in Search of Readers: Reading (in) Chicano/a Literature.* Albuquerque: U of New Mexico P, 2003.

Marzán, J. A. "The Art of Being Richard Rodriguez." *Bilingual Review* 27.1 (Jan.–Apr. 2003): 45–64. Print.

McCall, Dan. *The Example of Richard Wright.* New York: Harcourt, Brace and World, 1969. Print.

McCracken, Ellen. *New Latina Narrative: The Feminine Space of Postmodern Ethnicity.* Tucson: U of Arizona P, 1999. Print.

———. "The Postmodern Continuum of Canon and Kitsch: Narrative and Semiotic Strategies of Chicana High Culture and Chica Lit." Aldama, *Analyzing World Fiction* 165–81. Print.

McNamara, Kevin R. "A Finer Grain: Richard Rodriguez's *Days of Obligations*." *Arizona Quarterly* 53.1 (Spring 1997): 103–22. Print.

Michaels, Walter Benn. "Race into Culture: A Critical Genealogy of Cultural Identity." *Critical Inquiry* 18.4 (Summer 1992): 655–85. Print.

———. *The Shape of the Signifier.* Princeton, NJ: Princeton UP, 2004. Print.

Milian Arias, Claudia M. "Brown Is the Color of Philosophy: An Interview with Richard Rodriguez." *Nepantla: Views from South* 4.2 (2003): 269–82. Print.

Miller, Nancy K. "The Entangled Self: Genre Bondage in the Age of Memoir." *PMLA* 122.2 (Mar. 2007): 537–48. Print.

Mohanty, Satya. *Literary Theory and the Claims of History: Postmodernism, Objectivity, Multicultural Politics.* Ithaca, NY: Cornell UP, 1997. Print.

Moya, Paula M. L. *Learning from Experience: Minority Identities, Multicultural Struggles.* Berkeley: U of California P, 2002. Print.

Nehamas, Alexander. "Writer, Text, Work, Author." *The Death and Resurrection of the Author?* Ed. William Irwin. Westport: Greenwood Press, 2002. 95–116. Print.

O'Brien, Tim. *The Things They Carried*. 1990. Boston, MA: Mariner Books, 2009. Print.

Olney, James, ed. *Autobiography: Essays Theoretical and Critical*. Princeton, NJ: Princeton UP, 1980. Print.

———. "Some Versions of Memory / Some Versions of Bios." *Autobiography*. 236–67. Print.

Ong, Walter J. *Orality and Literacy: The Technologizing of the Word*. London: Routledge, 1982. Print.

Palmer, Alan. *Fictional Minds*. Lincoln: U of Nebraska P, 2004. Print.

———. *Social Minds in the Novel*. Columbus: Ohio State UP, 2010. Print.

Palumbo-Liu, David, ed. *The Ethnic Canon: Histories, Institutions, and Interventions*. Minneapolis: U of Minnesota P, 1995. Print.

———. Introduction. *The Ethnic Canon*. 1–27. Print.

Paredes, Raymund A. "Autobiography and Ethnic Politics: Richard Rodriguez's *Hunger of Memory*." Payne, *Multicultural Autobiography* 280–96. Print.

Parikh, Crystal. *An Ethics of Betrayal: The Politics of Otherness in Emergent U.S. Literatures and Culture*. New York: Fordham UP, 2009. Print.

Parini, Jay. Introduction. *The Norton Book of American Autobiography*. Ed. Parini. New York: W. W. Norton, 1999. 11–20. Print.

Patell, Cyrus R. K. *Negative Liberties: Morrison, Pynchon, and the Problem of Liberal Ideology*. Durham, NC: Duke UP, 2001. Print.

Payne, James Robert. Introduction. *Multicultural Autobiography*. Ed. Payne. xi–xxxiii. Print.

———, ed. *Multicultural Autobiography: American Lives*. Knoxville: U of Tennessee P, 1992. Print.

Pérez Firmat, Gustavo. "Richard Rodríguez [sic] and the Art of Abstraction." *Colby Quarterly* 32.4 (1996): 255–66. Print.

———. *Tongue Ties: Logo-Eroticism in Anglo-Hispanic Literature*. New York: Palgrave MacMillan, 2003. Print.

Perry, Yaakov. "Metaphors We Write By: (Dis)Orientation and the Border in Richard Rodriguez's *Hunger of Memory*." *MELUS* 34.3 (Fall 2009): 155–82. Print.

Porte, Joel. *In Respect to Egotism: Studies in American Romantic Writing*. New York: Cambridge UP, 2009. Print.

Pratt, Mary Louise. *Imperial Eyes: Travel Writing and Transculturation*. New York: Routledge, 1992. Print.

Putnam, Hilary. "Reference and Understanding." *Meaning and Use: Papers Presented at the Second Jerusalem Philosophical Encounter*. Ed. Avishai Margalit. Dordrecht: D. Reidel, 1979. 199–217. Print.

Quine, W. V. O. *Ontological Relativity and Other Essays*. New York: Columbia UP, 1969. Print.

———. *Word and Object*. Cambridge: Technology Press of the Massachusetts Institute of Technology, 1960. Print.

Rafferty, Terrence. "My Wife Is Mad." *New York Times Book Review* 15 Apr. 2007: 9. Print.

Reilly, John M., ed. *Richard Wright: The Critical Reception*. New York: Burt Franklin, 1978. Print.

Relyea, Sarah. "The Vanguard of Modernity: Richard Wright's *The Outsider*." *Texas Studies in Literature and Language* 48.3 (Fall 2006): 187–219. Print.

Restrepo, Laura. *Delirium*. [Delirio.] Trans. Natasha Wimmer. New York: Nan A. Talese/Doubleday, 2007 [2004]. Print.

———. Untitled panel discussion. Cornell University, Uris Hall. Ithaca. 19 Apr. 2007. Print.

Rodriguez, Ralph E. *Brown Gumshoes: Detective Fiction and the Search for Chicana/o Identity*. Austin: U of Texas P, 2005. Print.

Rodríguez, Randy A. "Richard Rodriguez Reconsidered: Queering the Sissy (Ethnic) Subject." *Texas Studies in Language and Literature* 40.4 (1998): 396–423. Print.

Rodriguez, Richard. *Brown: The Last Discovery of America*. New York: Penguin, 2002. Print.

———. *Darling: A Spiritual Autobiography*. New York: Viking, 2013. Print.

———. *Days of Obligation: An Argument with My Mexican Father*. New York: Penguin, 1992. Print.

———. *Hunger of Memory: The Education of Richard Rodriguez*. New York: Bantam, 1983. [New York: Godine, 1982]. Print.

———. Interview by Jeanne Cartensen. "Why Churches Fear Gay Marriage." *Salon* (25 Nov. 2008): <http://www.salon.com/news/features/2008/11/25/proposition_8_religion/print.html>. Web. 21 Aug. 2009.

———. Interview by David D. Cooper. "Interview with Richard Rodriguez." *Fourth Genre: Explorations in Nonfiction* 5.2 (Fall 2003): 104–32. Print.

———. Interview by Nick Gillespie and Virginia Postrel. "The New, New World: Richard Rodriguez on Culture and Assimilation." *Reason Magazine* (Aug./Sept. 1994): <http://reason.com/archives/1994/08/0/the-new-new-world>. Web. 25 May 2011.

———. Interview by Claudia M. Milian Arias. "Brown Is the Color of Philosophy: An Interview with Richard Rodriguez." *Nepantla: Views from South* 4.2 (2003): 269–82. Print.

———. Interview by Timothy S. Sedore. "'American Opera': An Interview with Richard Rodriguez." *South Carolina Review* 35.1 (2002): 5–16. Print.

———. Interview by Timothy S. Sedore. "'Born at the Destination': An Interview with Richard Rodriguez." *New England Review* 22.3 (2001): 26–37. Print.

———. Interview by Timothy S. Sedore. "Violating the Boundaries: An Interview with Richard Rodriguez." *Michigan Quarterly Review* 38.3 (1999): 424–46. Print.

———. Interview by Hector A. Torres. "'I Don't Think I Exist': Interview with Richard Rodriguez." *Melus* 28.2 (2003): 165–202. Print.

———. Interview by Gregory Wolfe. "A Conversation with Richard Rodriguez." *Image* 24 (2002): 53–75. Print.
———. Introduction. Loya xi–xiv. Print.
———. "The Invention of Hispanics and the Reinvention of America." *AEI Online* (14 April 2003): <http://www.aei.org/include/pub_print.asp?pubID=16962>. Web. 30 July 2005.
———. "Remarks of Richard Rodriguez." Convocation on Providing Public Library Service to California's 21st Century Population. 23 May 1997. <http://www.library.ca.gove/LDS/convo/convoc21.html>. Web. 30 July 2005.
Rodríguez, Richard T. *Next of Kin: The Family in Chicano/a Cultural Politics*. Durham, NC: Duke UP, 2009. Print.
Rorty, Richard. *Philosophy and the Mirror of Nature*. Princeton, NJ: Princeton UP, 1979. Print.
Rowley, Hazel. *Richard Wright: The Life and Times*. New York: Henry Holt, 2001. Print.
Saldívar, José David. *Border Matters: Remapping American Cultural Studies*. Berkeley: U of California P, 1997. Print.
Saldívar, Ramón. *Chicano Narrative: The Dialectics of Difference*. Madison: U of Wisconsin P, 1990. Print.
Saldívar-Hull, Sonia. "Feminism on the Border: From Gender Politics to Geopolitics." *Criticism in the Borderlands: Studies in Chicano Literature, Culture, and Ideology*. Ed. Héctor Calderón and José David Saldívar. Durham, NC: Duke UP, 1991. 203–20. Print.
Samuels, Shirley. *Facing America: Iconography and the Civil War*. New York: Oxford UP, 2004. Print.
Sánchez, Rosaura. "Calculated Musings: Richard Rodríguez's Metaphysics of Difference." Palumbo-Liu 153–73. Print.
Sandín, Lyn Di Iorio. *Killing Spanish: Literary Essays on Ambivalent U.S. Latino/a Identity*. New York: Palgrave MacMillan, 2004. Print.
Sayre, Robert F. *The Examined Self: Benjamin Franklin, Henry Adams, Henry James*. 1964. Madison: U of Wisconsin P, 1988. Print.
Searle, John R. *The Construction of Social Reality*. Berkeley, CA: Free Press, 1995. Print.
Siemerling, Winfried, and Katrin Schwenk, eds. *Cultural Difference and the Literary Text: Pluralism and the Limits of Authenticity in North American Literatures*. Iowa City: U of Iowa P, 1996. Print.
Sokal, Alan. "Transgressing the Boundaries: Towards a Transformative Hermeneutics of Quantum Gravity." *Social Text* 46.7 (1996): 217–52. Print.
Sollors, Werner. *Beyond Ethnicity: Consent and Descent in American Culture*. New York: Oxford UP, 1986. Print.
———. *The Invention of Ethnicity*. New York: Oxford UP, 1989. Print.
Smith, Sidonie. "Identity's Body." Ashley, Gilmore, and Peters 266–92. Print.
Smith, Sidonie, and Julia Watson, eds. Introduction. *Women, Autobiography, Theory: A Reader*. Madison, U of Wisconsin P, 1998. 3–52. Print.

Staten, Henry. "Ethnic Authenticity, Class, and Autobiography: The Case of *Hunger of Memory*." *PMLA* 113.1 (Jan. 1998): 103–16. Print.

Stavans, Ilan. *Bandido: Oscar "Zeta" Acosta and the Chicano Experience*. New York: IconEditions, 1995. Print.

Stavans, Ilan, Edna Acosta-Belén, Harold Augenbraum, María Herrera-Sobek, Rolando Hinojosa, and Gustavo Pérez Firmat, eds. *The Norton Anthology of Latino Literature*. New York: Norton, 2011. Print.

Stone, Albert E. "After *Black Boy* and *Dusk of Dawn*: Patterns in Recent Black Autobiography." Andrews 171–95. Print.

———. *Autobiographical Occasions and Original Acts: Versions of American Identity from Henry Adams to Nate Shaw*. Philadelphia: U of Pennsylvania P, 1982. Print.

Su, John J. "Ghosts of Essentialism: Racial Memory as Epistemological Claim." *American Literature* 81.2 (June 2009): 361–86. Print.

Thaddeus, Janice. "The Metamorphosis of Richard Wright's *Black Boy*." *American Literature* 57.2 (1985): 199–214. Print.

Tompkins, Jane P. *Sensational Designs: The Cultural Work of American Fiction, 1790–1860*. New York: Oxford UP, 1985. Print.

Trilling, Lionel. "A Tragic Situation." *Nation* 160.7 (Apr. 1945): 391–92. Rpt. in Reilly 151–53. Print.

van Delden, Maarten. "Crossing the Great Divide: Rewritings of the U.S.-Mexican Encounter in Walter Abish and Richard Rodriguez." *Studies in Twentieth-Century Literature* 25.1 (Winter 2001): 118–39. Print.

Viramontes, Helena María. *Under the Feet of Jesus*. 1995. New York: Plume, 1996. Print.

Walker, Margaret. *Richard Wright, Daemonic Genius: A Portrait of the Man, a Critical Look at His Work*. New York: Amistad, 1988. Print.

Wallach, Jennifer Jensen. "Building a Bridge of Words: The Literary Autobiography as Historical Source Material." *Biography* 29.3 (Summer 2006): 446–61. Print.

Ward, Jerry W., Jr. Introduction. 1998. Wright, *Black Boy* xi–xix. Print.

Warren, Kenneth W. *What Was African American Literature?* Cambridge, MA: Harvard UP, 2011. Print.

Webb, Constance. *Richard Wright: A Biography*. New York: G. P. Putnam's Sons, 1968. Print.

Whitman, Walt. *Whitman: Poetry and Prose*. College edition. Ed. Justin Kaplan. New York: Library of America, 1996. Print.

Wright, Richard. *Black Boy (American Hunger): A Record of Childhood and Youth*. 1945. New York: Perennial Classics, 1998. Print.

———. *Eight Men*. 1961. New York: Thunder's Mouth Press, 1987. Print.

———. "The Ethics of Living Jim Crow: An Autobiographical Sketch." *American Stuff: An Anthology of Prose and Verse by Members of the Works Progress Administration*. New York: Viking, 1937: 39–52. Rpt. in Wright, *Uncle Tom's Children* 1–15. Print.

———. "How 'Bigger' Was Born." *Native Son* vii–xxxiv. Print.

———. *Lawd Today*. 1963. Boston, MA: Northeastern UP, 1986. Print.
———. "The Man Who Lived Underground." 1945. *Eight Men* 27–92. Print.
———. *Native Son*. Original 1940 ed. New York: HarperPerennial, 1989. Print.
———. *The Outsider*. 1953. New York: Harper & Row, 1993. Print.
———. *12 Million Black Voices: A Folk History of the Negro in the United States*. 1941. Foreword by Noel Ignatiev. Introd. David Bradley. New York: Thunder's Mouth Press, 2002. Print.
———. *Uncle Tom's Children*. 1938. The Restored Text Established by the Library of America. Introd. Richard Yarborough. Notes by Arnold Rampersad. New York: Perennial, 2004. Print.

Index

academic literature. *See* scholarship and academic literature
Acosta, Oscar "Zeta," 135–37, 180n9
activism, 149–50
Adams, Timothy Dow, 40, 48–49, 55, 122–23, 174n9, 176n8
aesthetics, literary, 37, 58–65, 146, 177n1
affirmative action, 99–101, 148–49, 178n3, 183n5, 186n25
African American literature, x–xi, 52–55, 168, 175n4
agency, 6–7, 14, 27, 38, 96, 167
Alarcón, Norma, 94, 98–99, 101–2, 148–49
Alcoff, Linda Martín, 7, 156
Aldama, Frederick Luis, xv–xvi, 8, 158
alienation, isolation, loneliness, or solitude, 68, 74, 85–86, 93
alter ego, 169–71
ambition, 27–28
American Hunger (Wright), 70–71
American literature: African, x–xi, 52–55, 168, 175n4; autobiography in, 18; *Black Boy* in tradition of, 19; Chicana/o literature within, 185n13; ethnic literature in relation to, xi, xii, 19, 173n1; ethnic self in contemporary, 33; identity search in, 32–33; religious narrative in, xiii
Anderson, Benedict, 27, 178n8, 180n10
Andrews, William, 19
antirealism, 10–14
Anzaldúa, Gloria, 4, 158, 185n16
Appiah, Kwame, 174n5
assimilation and integration: class mobility in, 99, 107–10, 150; in ethnic autobiographies, 37–38, 93–99, 102, 103–12, 117, 119, 150, 161, 179n2, 181n1; of ethnic identity, 89–90, 93–95, 110–11, 148; identity politics in, 148, 150, 181n2; individualism connected to, 93–100, 102–12, 117; inequality maintained by arguments for, 94–95, 99; linguistic, 103, 106–8, 110–11, 140–42; loss in, 102, 110–11, 140–42; to mainstream culture, 29–30, 37–38, 89–90, 95, 103–4, 107–11, 119, 150, 161, 179n2; national, 180n10; scholarship and, 109–10, 148
Augustine, Saint, 19, 118

authenticity: of autobiographies for readers, 46–47, 50, 55, 64, 123–25, 176n8, 180n7; *Brown* resisting narrative of ethnic, 4; of ethnic autobiographies, 2–3, 41, 42, 46–50, 54–56, 64, 125–26, 176n8; in ethnic identity, 136–37, 146, 150–53, 160–64, 186n26; in ethnic literature, 184n12. *See also* essentialism

author: death of, 8–9, 12, 131, 169; ethnic autobiography and readers' assumptions of, 10, 18–19, 129–31; ethnic identity and impact on, xi, xiv–xv, xvi–xvii, 128–31, 139, 154, 161–64, 166–69; fiction and ethnicity of, 166–68; implied author as reader construction of, xv–xvi, 131–32; intentionality of, 124, 187n2; ontological, 114–15; referentiality of, 124, 126–27, 130, 133, 138; in textual meaning to readers, 18–19, 57, 129–30, 165–66, 168–70, 187nn1–2

authority, 80–81

autobiography: in all writing, 45; in American literature, 18; false memoir, 180n7; imagination and truth in, 122–23; memory as root of, 123; mirror of, xvii–xviii, 7–9; oral tradition and, 123; pact in, 47, 123, 175n7; postmodern self and, 9–10; reader expectations of, 46–47, 50, 55, 64, 123–25, 176n8, 180n7; reading conventions of, 121, 123–25; referentiality in, 9–10, 123–27, 166, 179n4; self in, 1, 9–10, 18; social relations impacting, 18. *See also* ethnic autobiography

The Autobiography of a Brown Buffalo (Acosta), 135

Bakhtinian theory, 162–63
Baldwin, James, 19, 29, 35, 36, 46, 53, 65, 177n1

Barresi, John, 9
Barthes, Roland, 169
Beltrán, Cristina, 94–95
Benstock, Shari, 9
bilingual education, 148–49, 183n5, 186n25
binary oppositions, 38
Black Boy (Wright), 175n1; alienation, fear, and hunger in, 68, 74, 83, 84; in American literary tradition, 19; authenticity of, 2–3, 41, 42, 46–50, 54, 55, 56, 176n8; blues and artistic depiction of, 81–82; consciousness repressed in, 89; as conversion and religious narrative, xiii; emotional truth over realism in, 61–63; as ethnic autobiography of collective identity, 41–42, 48, 50, 54, 82–83; ethnic self as distinct yet representative in, 2–3, 22, 39–43, 48, 49–50, 53–55, 57–58, 63–64, 71–72, 88, 174n9; existentialism in, 3, 26–27, 65–81, 83, 177n2; falsehood and dissembling in, 40–41, 56, 59; family violence in, 79–80; freedom through literacy in, 86–87; as hybrid text, 2, 72, 177n2; individualism in, 67–68, 73, 74, 80–81, 84–85; insight as epiphany in, 5; literary ethnic self in, x; moral exceptionalism from racism in, 84–86; narrative transcendence in, 65–66; performance of racial self in, 39–40; power of unquestioned authority in, 80; protagonists of *Native Son* and, 166–67; as protest literature, 54–58; race and reader expectations in, xiv–xv, 43, 51–52, 64; race treatment in, x, 52–54, 58–59, 62–64; racism combated through writing in, 5–6, 43–44, 47, 48, 54, 57–58, 72–73, 87–88; racism transcended in, 75; romantic hero's social rebellion in, 71–77, 80, 83–84; sexuality in, 54, 176n12;

as slave narrative, 19, 86–87; as sociological document, 52–53, 58, 177n2; as testimony, 2, 41–42; triumphalist version of, 70–71; Übermensch protagonist in, 67, 69–70; universality of particular in, xiii

blues, 81–82

body, embodied self, and corporeality: abduction of, 12–14; corpus of print culture and, 6, 142; discursive and, 10, 12–13, 17; in ethnic autobiography, xvii, 6–7, 10, 11, 17, 124–25, 126; ethnicity inscribed on, 96–97; literary ethnic self and, 114; literary theory on, 12–13; as means of resistance, 14; narrative self and, xvii, 6–7, 10, 11, 17, 126, 173n1; ontological, 6, 114–15, 131–32; in society, 9, 17–18; subject and subjectivity in, 9–10, 17, 21, 174n6; visibility of ethnic, 7, 10, 14, 114–15

Bogel, Frederic, 135–36

border culture and theory, 4, 158, 162–63, 181n12, 185n21

Borderlands/La Frontera: The New Mestiza (Anzaldúa), 158

The Brief Wondrous Life of Oscar Wao (Díaz), 5

Browdy de Hernandez, Jennifer, 102, 163, 187n29

Brown (Rodriguez): assimilation to mainstream culture in, 37–38, 104, 150; black suit in, 153–54; community and individual in, 104; cultural miscegenation and freedom in, 158–59; ethnic authenticity narrative resisted in, 4; ethnic identity and print culture in, 142–43; miscegenation in, 150, 157–59, 160–61; performance and theatricality in, 147–48; race impacting thought in, 155; satire in, 134

Butler, Judith, 13, 22, 96, 178n2

Butler, Robert, xiii, 75–76

Camacho, Alicia Schmidt, 179n2, 182n4
Castillo, Debra, 162–63
Cayton, Horace, 58–59, 60–61, 177n15
character representativeness, 169–70, 174n9
Chicana/o or Latino: literature, x–xi, 20, 152, 180n8, 185n13; Rodriguez in studies and scholarship of, 3, 158–59, 185n21, 186nn23–24
Chicana/o or Latino identity, 184n7; assimilation of, 148; collective, 136–37, 152–53; community desire and, 99; cultural indeterminacy of, 146; cultural nationalism and, 25–26, 137, 159; ethnic authenticity in, 152; ethnic genre and satirizing, 134–37; queer exodus from, 25–26
class: affirmative action based on, 100, 178n3, 183n5; assimilation and mobility of, 99, 107–8, 109–10, 150; collective identity through, 23–24; consciousness, 150; culture and relation to, 23–24, 107–10, 150; difference of language and relation to, 108; in ethnic disadvantage, 27; race and, 26–30, 100, 105, 106, 155, 178n3, 184n10; in social justice, 27, 34
cognition, x–xi, 10, 148–49
collective identity, action, or experience: Chicana/o or Latino, 136–37, 152–53; through class, 23–24; consciousness or memory of, 151–52, 163–64; ethnic, 26, 77–78, 82–83, 106–7, 151–53, 162–64; ethnic autobiography on, 41–42, 48, 50–51, 71–72, 82–83, 106–7, 116–17; of mainstream society, 26; masculinity of romantic hero through, 77–81; in politics, 31; power of, 80–81; of racism, 3, 41, 42, 48, 50–52, 75, 77–78, 82–83,

collective identity, action, or experience (*continued*)
106–7, 151, 178n8; rebellion against or rejection of, 24, 26, 82–83; satire and, 136–37; self and, 18, 22, 82–83; society imposing, 67, 82–83

Collingwood, R. G., 60

Communism, 26, 44, 175n6

community: ethnic authenticity and hegemony of, 152–53; ethnic self and, 3, 38, 83, 89, 97–101, 104–12, 148, 153, 182n3; expanding kinship and, 24–25; individual and tension with, 6, 31, 32, 38, 80–83, 104–5, 120; individualism and desire for, 95–96, 99, 111–12; print culture for imagined, 26–27

comparative literature and studies, xi, xiv, xviii, 1, 88–91, 171

Confessions (Augustine), 19, 118

consciousness: *Black Boy* and repression of, 89; class, 150; collective memory or, 151–52, 163–64; culture shaping, 155; of embodied self, 96–97; of miscegenated ethnic identity, 89–90, 142–43, 160, 178n7; nature of, 179n3; ontology of, 8; print culture and ethnic, 138, 142–43, 178n6; racial, 106, 178n7; reading, writing, and, 1–2, 76–77, 86–87, 126, 144, 173n1; Rodriguez's political, 94–95

conservatism: fundamental attribution error in politics of, 98–99; *Hunger of Memory* and politics of, 95, 97–103; neo-, 98–99, 103–4, 148–49, 182n4, 183n6; of self and relation to individual, 97–99

constructivism, 11, 13–14

context, textual, 121–22, 165–66

conversion narrative, xiii, 94

Cooley, Thomas, xiii, 118

corporeality. *See* body, embodied self, and corporeality

corpus, 6, 142

Culler, Jonathan, 20, 121, 126–27, 180n10

culture, 10–11, 174n3; African American literature on black, 52–55, 168, 175n4; agency gained through, 96; assimilation to mainstream, 29–30, 37–38, 89–90, 95, 103–4, 107–11, 119, 150, 161, 179n2; autobiography as activity of, 18; border, 162–63; class and relation to, 23–24, 107–10, 150; common language and shared, 144; consciousness shaped by, 155; definition and nature of, 111, 156–57, 178n5, 185n20; ethnic identity as separate from mainstream, 29, 52–53, 89, 101–2; ethnicity as, 153–59, 160; ethnic self and tension with ethnic, 116–18; gender and feminization of, 171–72; hegemonic mainstream, 103–4; indeterminacy of Latino, 146; loss of, 160; miscegenation of, 4, 24–25, 30, 32, 89, 103–4, 110–11, 119, 150, 157–59, 160–63, 185n21; narratives of, 31, 156; nationalism in, 8, 25–26, 137, 159; oral tradition or, 120–21, 123, 144; race as, 156; race trumped by, 145, 155–56; in Spanish language, 160; visibility of, 156–57. *See also* print culture

Cutler, John Alba, 164

Cutter, Martha, 103, 159

Darling: A Spiritual Autobiography (Rodriguez), 171–72, 184n6

Days of Obligation: An Argument with My Mexican Father (Rodriguez), 4, 102, 103; assimilation to mainstream culture in, 119, 150, 179n2; common language and shared culture in, 144; crossover aesthetics in, 146; as dialectical, 118–19, 144; ethnic culture's tension with ethnic self in, 116–18; ethnic self and print culture in, 119–25, 138,

142–44; miscegenation in, 119, 158; nostalgia in, 117–18; plural ethnic identity in, 143–44; on print culture language, 139, 142–43; religious narrative in, 117, 118–19, 150, 178n4
de la Campa, Román, 144–45, 146
democracy, 28–29
Dennett, Daniel, 173n1, 179n3
desire, 93, 95–96, 99, 111–12
determinism, 65–66
dialectic and dialectical, 118–19, 144
Díaz, Junot, 5, 33
difference or otherness, 102, 108, 163
The Difference Satire Makes: Rhetoric and Reading from Johnson to Byron (Bogel), 135–36
disadvantage, 100–101
discursive: class mobility, 108; environment and visibility, 66–67; indeterminacy, 17; interpretation of race, 154–55; oral framing, 120–21; readerly conventions, 121–22; self and embodied self, 10, 12–13, 17
dissembling. *See* falsehood or dissembling
Dostoyevsky, Fyodor, 69
Douglass, Frederick, 5, 87
Du Bois, W. E. B., 2, 40–42, 48, 54, 56, 178n7

Eakin, Paul John, 9, 123–24, 125, 186n28
Ellison, Ralph, 32–33, 35–36, 56, 58, 81–83, 178n5
embodied self. *See* body, embodied self, and corporeality
Emerson, Ralph Waldo, 17, 32–33, 180n6
emotion and emotional truth: as aesthetic principle, 58–64; in contemporary literary tradition, 60; historical truth compared to, 59; morality and link to, 59–60; of racial trauma, 2–3, 51, 61–62; realism subverted for, 61–63; Wright's prose style emphasizing, 35–36, 58, 59–64
engaged literature, xii–xiii, 37, 62, 65, 106, 177n1
epistemic privilege, xvi, 25–26, 153
epistemology and epistemic value, 9–14, 16–17, 114–15, 130
equality, 81, 85
erasures, textual, 141–42, 181n11
essentialism: in ethnic studies, 14, 151, 164; in identity, 151–52, 163–64; racial, 97, 105–6, 136, 154–55, 160–61, 184n12, 185n14
"The Ethics of Living Jim Crow, an Autobiographical Sketch" (Wright), 42, 69, 175n3, 177n4
ethnic autobiography: ambition in, 27–28; assimilation in, 37–38, 93–99, 102, 103–12, 117, 119, 150, 161, 179n2, 181n1; authenticity of, 2–3, 41, 42, 46–48, 49–50, 54–56, 64, 125–26, 176n8; body or corporeal self in, 17, 124–25, 126; on collective identity, 41–42, 48, 50–51, 71–72, 82–83, 106–7, 116–17; consistent ideology in Rodriguez, 102–3; embodied and narrative self in, xvii, 6–7, 10, 11, 17, 124–25, 126; epistemology and epistemic value of, 9–11, 114–15; as ethnically representative, 2–3, 17–19, 22–23, 33, 39–43, 46, 48, 52–58, 63–64, 71–72, 88, 120–21, 161–64, 170–71, 174n9; ethnic identity's complexity in, xvii–xviii, 3, 4, 67, 104–5, 143–44, 164, 184n8; fiction or non-autobiographical text as, 4–5, 44–46, 49, 170; identity and ethnicity understood through, 1; narrative arc of, 179n1; nostalgia in, 29–30, 96–97, 102, 110–11, 117–18, 161, 162, 184n9; predominant themes in, 11; readers' assumptions of ethnicity in, xvii–xviii, 10, 18–19, 41, 43, 46, 48, 55, 88,

ethnic autobiography (*continued*)
114–16, 119, 120–21, 125–27, 129–31, 134, 143, 187n1; referentiality in, 11, 125–27; revisability in, 11; skeptical realist approach to, 17–18; as sociological document, 52–54, 58, 176n10, 177n2. See also *Black Boy*; *Brown*; *Hunger of Memory*

ethnicity, ethnic identity, or ethnic self: agency for subjects of, 38, 96, 167; alter ego of, 169–71; assimilation of, 89–90, 93–95, 110–11, 148; authenticity in, 136–37, 146, 150–53, 160–64, 186n26; author impacted by, xi, xiv–xv, xvi–xvii, 128–31, 139, 154, 161–64, 166–69; body and inscription of, 96–97; class in disadvantage of, 27; collective, 26, 77–78, 82–83, 106–7, 151–53, 162–64; community and, 3, 38, 83, 89, 97–101, 104–12, 148, 153, 182n3; consciousness of miscegenated, 89–90, 142–43, 160, 178n7; in contemporary American literature, 33; as culture, 153–59, 160; definition and nature of, 21–22, 156–57; difference or otherness of, 163; ethnic autobiography and complexity of, xvii–xviii, 3, 4, 67, 104–5, 143–44, 164, 184n8; ethnic autobiography and readers' assumptions of, xvii–xviii, 10, 18–19, 41, 43, 46, 48, 55, 88, 114–15, 116, 119, 120–21, 125–27, 129–31, 134, 143, 187n1; ethnic autobiography for understanding, 1; ethnic culture and tension with, 116–18; in ethnic studies and literary theory, 12; existentialism in, 31, 66–67, 71–72; in fiction, 166–69, 171–72; framing of, x–xviii, 4–5; genres of, 127–30; identity politics and conforming, 161–62; individualism and neoconservatism, 148–49; literary, x, xvi, xviii, 33, 88, 113–16, 120–25, 138; mainstream culture and separation from, 29, 52–53, 89, 101–2; masculinity of, 105, 107; through narrative, 5–6, 8, 37; nostalgia or memory in racial or ethnic identity, 117–18, 151, 161–64, 184nn11–12; oral culture and, 144; pluralism in, 143–45, 149, 158–59; print culture and, 3, 4, 6, 34–35, 76–77, 83–89, 114, 116, 119–25, 137–44, 178n6; prose style for reader experience of, 36, 61; race compared to, 90–91, 156, 157, 174n2; reading, writing, and consciousness of, 1–2, 76–77, 86–87, 126, 144, 173n1; referentiality and revisability of, 2, 7–8, 23, 33–34, 66–67, 126–27, 142; representativeness of, 2–3, 17–19, 22–23, 33, 39–43, 46, 48, 52–58, 63–64, 71–72, 88, 120–21, 129, 161–64, 167–71, 174n9; similar personal experience and, xii; society and relation to, 1, 7, 21–22, 67–68, 69, 74, 77, 88–90, 105–6, 116, 126, 136–37, 146, 155–56, 168; studies of, 12, 14, 138, 151, 164; theory on, 90, 171; time and changes in, 89–90; visibility of, xv–xvi, 2, 4–5, 6, 7, 10–11, 14, 90, 96–97, 114–16, 119, 143, 154, 156–57, 185n19. See also Chicana/o or Latino identity

ethnic literature: American literature in relation to, xi, xii, 19, 173n1; authenticity in, 184n12; classification of, 127–29; determination of, 20–21; as genre, xi–xii, 127–30, 134–37; hybrid or crossover, 146; national literature in relation to, 19; reader expectations of, x–xi, xii, xiii–xviii, 4–5, 119, 127–28, 167–71, 187n1; representative truth in, 56–57;

resistance to conventions of, xii–xiii; revisability of ethnic identity in, 142; segregation of, xi, xii, 127–28; shared literary tradition and, xiii–xiv; social relations reflected in, xiv; universality of particular and, xii–xiii
exceptionalism, moral, 69, 84–86
existentialism: alienation, fear, and hunger, 68, 74, 83, 84, 85–86; ethnic, 31, 66–67, 71–72; free will and social context in, 71; French, 68–69; influences, 69; meaning, 68, 76, 85; racial, 3, 66–67, 69; self, 76; social rebellion, 75–76; violence, 76, 167; in Wright's work, 3, 26, 27, 65–81, 83, 167, 177n2, 177n4
experience, personal, xii
extratextual demands or features, xvi–xvii, 165–66

Fachinger, Petra, 161–64, 186n28
falsehood or dissembling, 40–41, 55–58, 59
family, 24, 72, 74–75, 79–80
fear, 68, 84, 85–86
feminist approaches, 7, 10, 14, 78–79. *See also* gender
feminization of culture and religion, 171–72
fiction or non-autobiographical text, 4–5, 44–46, 49, 166–71
Foucault, Michel, 37, 169, 173n1
freedom and free will, 5, 71, 86–87, 158–59
French existentialism, 68–69
fundamental attribution error, 98–99

gender, 22, 26, 34, 78–79, 96, 171–72, 178n2
genre, 173n2; constraints of, 122–23; definition and nature of, 121; ethnic literature as, xi–xii, 127–30, 134–37; greater particularization of, 128; reading conventions and, 120, 135, 179n5; satire as, 134–36; text and reader expectations shaped by, 4, 121, 128–29, 134, 135
"Ghosts of Essentialism" (Su), 151
Gilmore, Leigh, 17
Gould, Stephen Jay, 184n10

Hakutani, Yoshinobu, 75
Hames-García, Michael, 136
hegemony, 103–4, 138–39, 152–53
hermeneutics. *See* interpretation
Higashida, Cheryl, 78–79
Hofstadter, Douglas, 179n3
homosexuality. *See* queer
human and humanity: individuality for claiming, 84; racial role as lacking, 40, 46, 68, 73, 76–77, 84; reading for gaining, 86–87
hunger, 27–28, 68, 83
Hunger of Memory (Rodriguez): affirmative action treatment in, 99–101; ambition in, 27–28; assimilation and individualism in, 93–99, 102–12, 117, 161, 181n1; community desired by individual in, 95–96, 99, 111–12; conservative politics and, 95, 97–103; as conversion narrative, 94; cultural miscegenation in, 158–59; culture and relation to class mobility, 107–10, 150; disadvantage treatment in, 100–101; ethnic identity and masculinity in, 105, 107; ethnicity as embodied in, 96–97; ethnic self and community in, 3, 97–101, 104–12; ethnic self as distinct yet representative in, 22–23, 161–64; on identity dimensions, 25–26; literary ethnic self in, x; nostalgia in, 29–30, 96–97, 102, 110–11, 184n9; on private and public

Hunger of Memory (Rodriguez) (*continued*)
　identity, 95–96, 101–2, 104–12, 139; race treatment in, x, 105–6, 155; as religious narrative, xiii

hybrid and hybridity, 4, 102, 136–37, 146, 151, 153, 158, 161–63, 185n21. *See also* miscegenation

identity: American literature and search for, 32–33; through assimilation and integration, 29–30; complexity and contradiction of, 38, 164; cultural nationalism and, 8, 159; essentialist notions of, 151–52, 163–64; ethnic autobiography for understanding, 1; gender, 78–79, 96, 178n2; *Hunger of Memory* on dimensions of, 25–26; interdependence of aspects of, 104–5; mirror of autobiography and, 7–9; narrative self or, xvii, 6–11, 17, 124–25, 126, 173n1; performative aspect of, 23, 96, 147–48; politics, 148–50, 152, 161–62, 181n2; postnationalist, 25; from realist account, 8; referentiality and revisability as poles of, 7, 10; theory on, 7, 102, 145–46, 151–52, 158; visibility of, 7, 143. *See also* collective identity, action, or experience; ethnicity, ethnic identity, or ethnic self; private and private identity; public and public identity; race, racism, and racial identity or self; self and selfhood

ideology, consistent, 102–3
imagination, 90, 122–23, 178n8
implied author, xv–xvi, 131–32
indeterminacy, 17, 146
individual and individualism: assimilation connected to, 93–100, 102–12, 117; in *Black Boy*, 67–68, 73, 74, 80–81, 84–85; community and tension with, 6, 31, 32, 38, 80–83, 104–5, 120; community desire of, 95–96, 99, 111–12; humanity claimed through, 84; language in, 31, 106–7; neoconservative ethnic, 148–49; racism and suppression of, 73; self and relation to conservative, 97–99. *See also* self and selfhood

inequality, 94–95, 99, 108–9, 111
innocence, 74
insight, 5
integration. *See* assimilation and integration
intentionality, 124, 130–33, 187n2
interdependence, 10, 31–32, 104–5
interpretation: author ethnicity and impact on, xi, xiv–xv, 154; ethnic framing impact on, xvi; ethnic visibility and consequences for, 4–5, 154; literary and supernatural, 20–21; race and discursive, 154–55; theory of, 125
intimacy, 113–14, 127
Invisible Man (Ellison), 56, 176, 177
isolation. *See* alienation, isolation, loneliness, or solitude

journalism, 174n7

kinship, 24–25
knowledge, xvi

language and linguistics: agency through, 96; assimilation through, 103, 106–8, 110–11, 140–42; culture composed of, 111, 178n5; culture in Spanish, 160; difference of class and relation to, 108; in ethnic studies, 138; individualism through, 31, 106–7; literary, 20; in literary ethnic self, 115–16, 138; meaning and conventions of, 107, 112, 121, 132–33, 179n5; miscegenation of, 103, 110–11, 145–46, 159, 162;

ontology of, 9–10, 13, 115; of print culture, 138–40, 142–43, 144; private, 116–17, 138, 140, 179n5; public identity through public, 29, 106–8, 109, 139, 140, 144, 180n10; racism through, 73; referents in, 132–33; self as construct of, 12–13, 115–16; shared culture and common, 144; shared referents in, 132; Spanish imprint on English, 145–46, 159; subaltern mastering, 29–30; theory of, 122, 124. *See also* print culture

Latino identity. *See* Chicana/o or Latino identity

Latino literature. *See* Chicana/o or Latino

Lee, A. Robert, 102

Lejeune, Phillipe, 123–24

liberalism, classical, 97–98

Lim, Jeehyun, 138, 182n4

Limón, José, 159, 186n23

literacy, 5, 86–87, 109, 111. *See also* reading and reading conventions; writing

Literary Theory and the Claims of History (Mohanty), 14–15, 133, 152, 185n15

literature, literary, and literary tradition: aesthetics, 37, 58–65, 146, 177n1; African American, x–xi, 52–55, 168, 175n4; comparative studies and, xi, xiv, xviii, 1, 88–91; determination of, 20–21; emotional truth in contemporary, 60; engaged, xii–xiii, 37, 62, 65, 106, 177n1; ethnic literature and shared, xiii–xiv; ethnic self, x, xvi, xviii, 33, 88, 113–16, 120–25, 138; genre shaping text and reader expectation, 4, 121, 128–29, 134, 135; intimacy of, 113–14, 127; Latino, x–xi, 152; morality in, 59–60; national, 19; postmodern, 12–14, 37, 174n4; readers defining, 20; self's referentiality and revisability, xviii, 133;

supernatural interpretations of, 20–21; theory, 9–10, 12–17, 60, 132, 133, 173n1, 174n4; writing and protest literature, 35. *See also* ethnic literature; genre; protest literature

loneliness. *See* alienation, isolation, loneliness, or solitude

loss, 102, 110–11, 140–42, 160

Loya, Joe, 113–16, 130–31

ludic, 56, 134, 147–48, 174n4, 176n14

lying. *See* falsehood or dissembling

Martin, Raymond, 9

Martínez, Ernesto, 25

Marzán, J. A., 23, 96

masculinity, 24–38, 77–81, 105, 107

McCracken, Ellen, xv, 170

meaning: existential, 68, 76, 85; through gender, 171–72; linguistic conventions constituting, 107, 112, 121, 132–33, 179n5; of race, 105–6; social, 2, 14–15, 30–31, 74, 76, 89, 154–55, 165–66, 179n5, 181n12; textual, xv–xviii, 18–19, 57, 115, 121–22, 124–25, 129–30, 133, 135, 139, 142–43, 165–66, 168–70, 180n6, 180n8, 187nn1–2

memory. *See* nostalgia or memory

Mencken, H. L., xvi, 5, 87

mestizaje, 4, 116, 143–44, 153, 158. *See also* miscegenation

Michaels, Walter Benn, 151–52, 169, 184n12, 187n2

Miller, Nancy, 18, 182n3

mirror of autobiography, xvii–xviii, 7–9

miscegenation: in *Brown*, 150, 157–59, 160–61; cultural, 4, 24–25, 30, 32, 89, 103–4, 110–11, 119, 150, 157–59, 160–63, 185n21; of ethnic identity, 89–90, 142–43, 160, 178n7; freedom through, 158–59, 160–61; linguistic, 103, 110–11, 145–46, 159, 162; racial, 4, 24–25, 89, 103, 110, 150, 160–61

mobility, class and social, 99, 107–8, 109–10, 150, 176n14
modern psyche, 34–35
Mohanty, Satya, 14–15, 133, 185n15
morals and morality, 59–60, 69, 84–86
Moya, Paula, 14, 103, 148–49, 178n1, 179n2, 181n1
multiethnic literature, xiv

Nabokov, Vladimir, xvi, 123, 140, 162
narrative: arc of ethnic autobiography, 179n1; *Brown* resisting ethnic authenticity, 4; conversion, xiii, 94; cultural, 31, 156; ethnic identity through, 5–6, 8, 37; falsehood in racial, 40–41, 55–56; formal shaping devices of, xv–xvi; *Hunger of Memory* as conversion, 94; identity or self, xvii, 6–11, 17, 124–25, 126, 173n1; religious, xiii, 117–19, 149–50, 171–72, 178n4, 183n6; slave, xiii, 5, 19, 86–87; transcendence, 65–66
national and nationalism, 8, 19, 24–26, 137, 159, 180n10
Native Son (Wright), 2, 35; agency of ethnic subject in, 167; Communism in, 44; determinism of, 65–66; emotional truth over realism in, 63; as ethnic autobiography, 5, 44–45, 46, 49; ethnicity and reader assumptions in, 46, 187n1; existential violence in, 76, 167; fame from, 42; protagonists of *Black Boy* and, 166–67; as protest literature, 65, 177n1; racial role as subhuman in, 46; representativeness of, 46, 167–68; romantic hero's social rebellion in, 75–76
neoconservatism, 98–99, 103–4, 148–49, 182n4, 183n6
Nietzsche, Friedrich, 69–70
non-autobiographical text. *See* fiction or non-autobiographical text

nostalgia or memory: autobiography rooted in, 123; collective consciousness or, 151–52, 163–64; in ethnic autobiographies, 29–30, 96–97, 102, 110–11, 117–18, 161, 162, 184n9; ethnic or racial, 117–18, 151, 161, 162, 163–64, 184nn11–12. *See also Hunger of Memory*

O'Brien, Tim, 59
Olney, James, 33, 48, 174n9, 176n9
Ong, Walter, 34
ontology, 113, 129; of author, 114–15; of body, 6, 114–15, 131–32; of consciousness, 8; linguistic, 9–10, 13, 115; of literary self, 133; of pluralism, 144–45; textual, 131–32
oral tradition or culture, 120–21, 123, 144
otherness. *See* difference or otherness

Palumbo-Liu, David, 19
Paredes, Raymund, xiii, 94, 181n1
Park, Robert, 88
particular and particularization, 128, 140
past, 102
Patell, Cyrus, 174n5
Payne, James Robert, 19
Pérez Firmat, Gustavo, 159, 186n25, 186n28
performance, performative aspect, and theatricality, 23, 39–40, 96, 147–48
pluralism, 143–45, 149, 158–59. *See also* miscegenation
politics: collective identity through, 31; fundamental attribution error in conservative, 98–99; *Hunger of Memory* and conservative, 95, 97, 98, 99–102, 103; identity, 148–50, 152, 161–62, 181n2; queer, 183n6; Rodriguez's consciousness of, 94–95; Wright's, 78–79, 176n10

postmodernism, 12–14, 37, 174n4
postnationalism and postnationalist citizenship, 25
postpositivism, 14–15, 133, 185n15
poststructuralism, 12, 13, 17, 174n4
power, 80–81, 111
Pratt, Mary Louise, 22, 111
present, 102
print culture: classification and approaches to, 120; corpus of body and, 6, 142; embodied and narrative self in, 6; ethnic or racial self and, 3, 4, 6, 34–35, 76–77, 83–89, 114, 116, 119–25, 137–43, 178n6; for imagined community, 26–27; language of, 138–40, 142–43, 144; loss in assimilation of, 140–42; modern psyche's formation through, 34–35; rebellion inspired by, 83–84; Spanish imprint on English, 145–46; subaltern mastering, 29–30; universality of, 140–41
private and private identity: *Hunger of Memory* on public and, 95–96, 101–2, 104–12, 139; language, 116–17, 138, 140, 179n5; past and association with, 102
prose style, 35–36, 58, 59–64
protest literature: *Black Boy* as, 54–58; emotional truth over realism in, 63; literary writing and, 35; *Native Son* as, 65, 177n1; race and racism treatment in, 5–6, 43–45, 47–55, 57–59, 62–64, 72–77, 87–88, 175n5; truth through falsehood in, 56
provocation and provocative, 148
public and public identity: *Hunger of Memory* on private and, 95–96, 101–2, 104–12, 139; present and association with, 102; through public language, 29, 106–9, 139, 140, 144, 180n10; recognition of self in, 104–12

Putnam, Hilary, 132–33
queer: exodus from Chicano nationalist identity, 25–26; politics, 183n6; reading, 186n24; sexuality, 164; theory, 125–26, 186n24
Quine, W. V. O., 132–33

race, racism, and racial identity or self: American democracy undermined by, 28–29; class and, 26–30, 100, 105, 106, 155, 178n3, 184n10; collective experience or identity of, 3, 41, 42, 48, 50–52, 75, 77–78, 82–83, 106–7, 151, 178n8; Communism and treatment of, 26, 175n6; consciousness, 106, 178n7; as culture, 156; culture trumping, 145, 155–56; discursive interpretation of, 154–55; emotional truth in trauma of, 2–3, 51, 61–62; equality qualified for, 81, 85; essentialism of, 97, 105–6, 136, 154–55, 160–61, 184n12, 185n14; ethnicity compared to, 90–91, 156, 157, 174n2; existentialism in, 3, 66–67, 69; falsehood regarding, 40–41, 55–58; gender in, 78–79; humanity lacking in role of, 40, 46, 68, 73, 76–77, 84; individualism suppressed in, 73; through language, 73; literary self through, 33, 88; meaning of, 105–6; miscegenation of, 4, 24–25, 89, 103, 110, 150, 160–61; morality in face of, 69, 84–86; nostalgia or memory in ethnic or, 117–18, 151, 161–64, 184nn11–12; performance of, 39–40; print culture and, 3, 76–77, 83–89; in protest literature, 5–6, 43–45, 47–55, 57–59, 62–64, 72–77, 87–88, 175n5; readers' expectations of, xiv–xv, xvi, 43, 46, 48, 51–52, 64, 88; rebellion against, 72–75, 83–84; recognition of self and, 32; in

race, racism, and racial identity or self (*continued*)
Rodriguez and Wright's work, ix, x; as social construct, 105–6, 154–55; social justice for, 43–45, 47, 48, 63–64; subject and subjectivity, 90; thought and thinking impacted by, 155; time and changes in, x; transcendence of, 75–77; violence in, 51–52. *See also* ethnicity, ethnic identity, or ethnic self; ethnic literature

readers and reader expectations: author and implied author or alter ego formed by, xv–xvi, 131–32, 169–71; of autobiography, 46–47, 50, 55, 64, 123–25, 176n8, 180n7; discursive conventions of, 121–22; emotional truth over realism for, 62–63; ethnic autobiographies and ethnicity conceived by, xvii–xviii, 10, 18–19, 41, 43, 46, 48, 55, 88, 114–15, 116, 119, 120–21, 125–27, 129–31, 134, 143, 187n1; ethnic experience through prose style for, 36, 61; ethnic literature and, x–xi, xii, xiii–xviii, 4–5, 119, 127–28, 167–71, 187n1; genre in shaping, 4, 121, 128–29, 134, 135; *Hunger of Memory* and politics impacting, 101–2; Latino literature and impact on Latino, 152; literature defined by, 20; mirror of autobiography and ethnic identity shaped by, xvii–xviii; of race and racism, xiv–xv, xvi, 43, 46, 48, 51–52, 64, 88; romantic hero and identification of, 74; in textual meaning, 18–19, 57, 125, 129–30, 133, 165–66, 168–70, 180n6, 180n8, 187nn1–2

reading and reading conventions: of autobiography, 121, 123–25; conscious self and, 1–2, 76–77, 86–87, 126, 144, 173n1; constraints from, 120–21, 122–23; genre and, 120, 135, 179n5; humanity gained through, 86–87; literary ethnic self and, 120–25; queer, 186n24; for Rodriguez and Wright, 34–35, 142, 143, 144; sexuality through, 143; textual context in, 121–22; theory of, 125. *See also* print culture

realism and reality: anti-, 10–14; emotional truth over, 61–63; epistemological model of biocultural, 10–11; identity from account of, 8; in non-autobiographical text, 44–45; postmodern literary theory and treatment of, 12–13; postpositivist or philosophical, 14–15; reductionism resisted for, 15; skeptical, 1, 14–18, 130; social, 15–16, 170–71; Wright's text and lack of, 61. *See also* ontology; society, social relations, and social reality

rebellion: against authority, 80–81; against collective identity, 24, 26, 82–83; against family, 72, 74–75, 80; print culture inspiring, 83–84; against racism and racial self, 72–75, 83–84; of romantic hero against society, 71–77, 80, 83–84

recognition, of self, 32, 104–12

reductionism, 15

referentiality and referent: of author, 124, 126–27, 130, 133, 139; in autobiography, 9–10, 123–27, 166, 179n4; correspondence of words and their, 132–33; of ethnic self, 2, 7–8, 33–34, 66–67, 126–27; in fiction, 166; as identity pole, 7, 10; of literary self, xviii, 133; revisability interacting with, 11, 66–67; time frame in ethnic, 33–34

relativism, absolute, 13–14

religion and religious narrative, xiii, 117–19, 149–50, 171–72, 178n4, 183n6 representativeness: author alter ego and character, 169–70; of ethnic identity, 2–3, 17–19, 22–23, 33, 39–43, 46, 48, 52–58, 63–64, 71–72, 88, 120–21, 129, 161–64, 167–71, 174n9; impossibility of absolute, 26; for reader as racial critique, 48; social impact from, 23; of truth in ethnic literature, 56–57. *See also* collective identity, action, or experience

Restrepo, Laura, 129

revisability: of ethnic identity, 2, 7–8, 23, 66–67, 142; as identity pole, 7, 10; of literary self, xviii; referentiality interacting with, 11, 66–67

Reynolds, Paul, 42, 175n2

Rodriguez, Ralph, 20

Rodríguez, Richard T., 24

romantic hero, 71–81, 83–84

Rorty, Richard, 8

Saldívar, José David, 158, 185

Saldívar, Ramón, 94–95, 101, 158

Samuels, Shirley, 178n5

satire, 134–37

scholarship and academic literature: assimilation and, 109–10, 148; Chicana/o, 3, 158–59, 185n21, 186nn23–24; on cultural miscegenation, 158–59; on ethnic authenticity, 151–52, 161; on realism, 14–15; Rodriguez and Wright in, 3, 30–31, 158–59, 185n21, 186nn22–24

Searle, John, 132, 154, 179n3

segregation, xi, xii, 127–28, 176n14

self and selfhood: in autobiographies, 1, 9–10, 18; classical liberalism and conservative individualism in relation to, 97–99; collective identity and, 18, 22, 82–83; definition and nature of, 21; embodied and discursive, 10, 12–13, 17; epistemological model for biocultural reality of, 10–11; existential, 76; gender and, 22; as linguistic or social construct, 12–13, 18, 21–22, 30–34, 74, 77, 115–16, 119, 174n5; narrative identity or, xvii, 6–11, 17, 124–25, 126, 173n1; postmodern epistemological model of, 12–14; reading, writing, and consciousness of, 1–2, 76–77, 86–87, 126, 144, 173n1; recognition of, 32; referentiality and literary, xviii, 133; triangulation of ethnicity, society, and, 1, 7, 89–90, 116. *See also* body, embodied self, and corporeality; ethnicity, ethnic identity, or ethnic self; race, racism, and racial identity or self

sexuality, 24–38, 54, 143, 164, 176n12

Shakespeare, William, 6, 29, 34, 131, 142, 147

skeptical realism, 1, 14–18, 130

slave narratives, xiii, 5, 19, 86–87

Smith, Sidonie, 10, 17

social justice: class in, 27, 34; in ethnic studies, 14; postmodernism in application of, 13–14; racial, 43–45, 47, 48, 63–64; through Wright's prose style, 35. *See also* protest literature

society, social relations, and social reality: autobiography impacted by, 18; body and embodied self in, 9, 17–18; collective identity imposed by, 67, 82–83; collective identity of mainstream, 26; as community of individuals, 32; constructivism in, 11; context in, x, 1–3, 18, 20, 71, 74–75, 77, 130–31, 135, 154, 165–66, 170, 180n9, 187n1; engaged literature on, xii–xiii, 37, 62, 65, 106, 177n1; ethnic identity and, 1, 7, 21–22, 67–68, 69, 74, 77, 88–90, 105–6, 116, 126, 136–37, 146, 155–56, 168; ethnic literature and, xiv; existentialism, free will,

society, social relations, and social reality *(continued)*
and context of, 71; location in, xi, xiv, 9–10, 21–22, 24, 72; meaning in, 2, 14–15, 30–31, 74, 76, 89, 154–55, 165–66, 179n5, 181n12; race as construct of, 105–6, 154–55; realism and, 15–16, 170–71; representativeness and impact on, 23; romantic hero and rebellion against, 71–77, 80, 83–84; segregation restricting mobility in, 176n14; self as construct of, 12–13, 18, 21–22, 30–34, 74, 77, 119, 174n5; theory on, 22, 177n1; writing for connection to, 36–37. *See also* community
sociology, 52–54, 58, 176n10, 177n2
Sokal, Alan, 181n11
solitude. *See* alienation, isolation, loneliness, or solitude
Sollors, Werner, 151, 184n12, 185n19
split-state predicament, 144–45
Staten, Henry, 184n8
Stone, Albert, 18, 70
Su, John, 151, 184n11
subaltern, 29–30
subject and subjectivity: agency for ethnic, 38, 96, 167; body and, 9–10, 17, 21, 174n6; ethnic and racial, 90

Tabuenca Córdoba, María, 162–63
testimony or testimonio, 2, 18, 41–42, 125, 136
text: context in, 121–22, 165–66; erasures in, 141–42, 181n11; extratextual features of, 165–66; genre framing, 4, 121, 128–29, 134, 135; imagination and truth in, 122–23; meaning of, xv–xviii, 18–19, 57, 115, 121–22, 124–25, 129–30, 133, 135, 139, 142–43, 165–66, 168–70, 180n6, 180n8, 187nn1–2;

ontology of, 131–32; realism lacking in Wright's, 61
Thaddeus, Janice, 70
theatricality. *See* performance, performative aspect, and theatricality
theory: Bakhtinian, 162–63; border, 4, 158, 162–63, 185n21; of ethnic self, 90, 171; of identity, 7, 102, 145–46, 151–52, 158; of interpretation and reading, 125; linguistic, 122, 124; literary, 9–10, 12–17, 60, 132, 133, 173n1, 174n4; postmodern, 12–14, 37; queer, 125–26, 186n24; of satire, 135–36; social, 22, 177n1
third language, 138, 182n4
thought and thinking, 155. *See also* consciousness
time and time frame, ix–x, 33–34, 89–90
transcendence, 65–66, 75, 76–77
triangulation: of author, reader, and text, 130, 165–66, 168–69; of self, ethnicity, and society, 1, 7, 89–90, 116
tribalism, 174n8
Trilling, Lionel, 52, 63
triumphalism, 70–71
truth, 8, 15–16, 55–59, 122–23. *See also* authenticity; emotion and emotional truth
12 Million Black Voices: A Folk History of the Negro in the United States (Wright), 41, 49

Übermensch protagonist, 67, 69–70
Uncle Tom's Children (Wright), 78–79
Under the Feet of Jesus (Viramontes), 5, 169–70
universality, xii–xiii, 6, 140–41
A User's Guide to Postcolonial and Latino Borderland Fiction (Aldama), xv

violence, 51–52, 76, 79–80, 167

Viramontes, Helena María, 5, 169–70
visibility and visible: of culture, 156–57; discursive environment and, 66–67; of ethnicity, xv–xvi, 2, 4–7, 10–11, 14, 90, 96–97, 114–15, 116, 119, 143, 154, 156–57, 185n19; identity, 7, 143; interpretation and consequences of, 4–5, 154

Walker, Margaret, 49–50, 54, 176n11
Ward, Jerry, 67, 69–70
Watson, Julia, 10
weapons, words as, 5–6, 57–58, 87–88
Webb, Constance, 68
Whitman, Walt, 18, 20, 32, 122, 147, 152
Williams, William Carlos, 141–42
words, 5–6, 57–58, 87–88, 132–33
writing: autobiographical form in all, 45; blues informing Wright's, 81–82; conscious self and, 1–2, 126; ethnic identity and language in, 138; protest literature and literary, 35; racism combated through, 5–6, 43–45, 47–49, 50–51, 57–58; social connection through, 36–37; truth through falsehood in, 56. *See also* print culture

www.ingramcontent.com/pod-product-compliance
Lightning Source LLC
Chambersburg PA
CBHW020651230426
43665CB00008B/387